AWAKENINGS
Stories of Recovery and Emergence from Schizophrenia

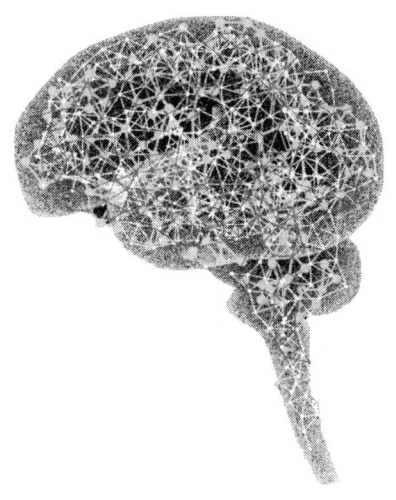

Bethany Yeiser, BS
Henry A. Nasrallah, MD

Awakenings. Copyright @ 2024 Bethany Yeiser, BS and Henry A. Nasrallah, MD

All rights reserved. No part of this book may be used or reproduced in any way without written permission from Bethany Yeiser, BS or Henry A. Nasrallah, MD.

See www.curesz.org for contact information.

Printed in the United States of America.

Published by Amazon Kindle Direct Publishing.

Amazon Kindle edition ISBN 978-0-9903452-4-4.

Cover design by Matcheri Keshavan, MD.

Book and cover formatting by Eric Oehler, BS.

FIRST EDITION

CONTENTS

Foreword by Henry A. Nasrallah, MD XI

PART ONE
Preface to Awakenings and Part One by Bethany Yeiser, BS 3

1. **Introduction**
   Schizophrenia is an Invisible Illness 5
   The Stigma of Schizophrenia 7
   Global Mental Health 9

2. **Developing Schizophrenia**
   Schizophrenia and What Happens Before 13
   A Choice to Be Homeless 15
   Marijuana and Schizophrenia 17
   Exercise and Diet 18
   About Tardive Dyskinesia 20
   Mourning Lost Time 22

3. **Legislation and Treatment Programs**
   Wish List for Schizophrenia 25
   Mental Health Courts 27

4. **Louisiana Mental Health Law Act** 31

5. **911 and 988** 35

6. **A New Name For Schizophrenia, A Brain Disorder**
   Schizophrenia is a Brain Disorder 37
   Renaming Schizophrenia 38

7. **Debunking Myths of Schizophrenia** 41

8. **Looking Back and Moving Forward**
   Pieces of Love 43
   Stories of Hope 45

PART TWO
Preface to Part Two by Bethany Yeiser, BS 49

1. **Carlos Larrauri:** *Thriving in Law School* 51
2. **Leif Gregersen:** *From Hospital Patient to Hospital Faculty* 57

3. Liz Rapp: *Managing a Nonprofit and Family of Five* 61
4. Brandon Staglin: *President, One Mind* 65
5. Christina Bruni: *Thriving as a Librarian and Advocate* 73
6. Laurie Russell:* *When a Patient Becomes an Academic* 75
7. Matthew Racher: *Musician and Peer Specialist* 77
8. J. Peters:* *Author and Social Worker* 81
9. Lesley McCuaig: *Athlete and Mental Health Counselor* 89
10. Darrell Herrmann: *Computer Programmer and Volunteer* 93
11. Meghan Caughey: *Artist, Professor and Author* 99
12. Robert Ross:* *IT Expert and Poet* 103
13. Ashley Smith: *Author, Advocate and Mom* 107
14. Rebecca Chamaa: *Writer and Wife* 111
15. Zach Feld: *Finishing College and Seeking a Career* 113
16. Liz Grace:* *Conquering Deafness and Schizophrenia* 117

Recovered on Clozapine 123

17. Bethany Yeiser: *President of the CURESZ Foundation* 125
18. Daniel Laitman: *Working as a Stand-Up Comic* 133
19. Chelsea Kowal: *Back to School* 137
20. Rhea: *Researcher on OCD and Early Psychosis* 143
21. Kirk Reitelbach: *Celebrating Fifteen Years as a Paralegal* 147
22. Millie Vine:* *Successful Chef* 151
23. Emeka Chima: *Expert in Information Systems and Peer Support Specialist* 155
24. Alexandra Johann:* *Peer Support Specialist, Career Coach and Volunteer* 157
25. Robert Francis:* *Fifteen Years as a Social Worker* 161
26. Lucas Peluffo: *Spanish-English Translator and Secretary* 165
27. Eric Smith: *Social Worker and Advocate* 167
28. Michael B: *Managing Full-Time College* 171

*The name has been changed to protect the privacy of those involved in the story.

PART THREE
Preface to Part Three 175

1. Schizophrenia and its Many Impacts 177
2. Treatment Checklist 181

Cutting-Edge and Underutilized Medications 185

   3. **Schizophrenia and Clozapine** 187
      Removing Barriers to Clozapine Use by Jonathan Meyer, MD 187
      Clozapine Question and Answer by Erik Messamore, MD, PhD 189
      Clozapine Side Effects: Worth the Risks by Henry Nasrallah, MD
      and Richard Sanders, MD 193

   4. **Long-Acting Injectables Introduction** 195
      Hope in a Needle by Craig Chepke, MD 196
      Empower Yourself by Craig Chepke, MD 198

   5. **Tardive Dyskinesia Introduction** 201
      Be Your Own Advocate by Craig Chepke, MD 202
      More than a Side Effect by Craig Chepke, MD 203
      Dawn of Hope by Craig Chepke, MD 204
      More than Skin Deep by Craig Chepke, MD 205
      Impact on Patients' Lives by Craig Chepke, MD 206

Essays on Schizophrenia 209

   6. *On Renaming Schizophrenia* by Carol North, MD 211
   7. *Negative Symptoms of Schizophrenia* by Henry Nasrallah, MD 215
   8. *A Decade of Drug Discovery for Schizophrenia: TAAR1 and Muscarinic Agonists* by Elizabeth Beam, MD, PhD and Jacob Ballon, MD 217
   9. *The Seven Catastrophic Consequences of Psychotic Recurrences* by Henry Nasrallah, MD 221
  10. *Telemedicine and Schizophrenia: A Brave New World* by Craig Chepke, MD 225
  11. *Suicide and Schizophrenia* by Stephen Rush, MD 227
  12. *Comorbidities in Schizophrenia: A Hidden Medical Emergency* by Craig Chepke, MD 229
  13. *Secondary Psychosis* by Stephen Rush, MD 233
  14. *Enough is Enough: The Case for Assisted Outpatient Treatment* by Ashoke Rampuria, MS, Vinita Rampuria, MSW, and Ann Corcoran, RN, MSN.. 237

CURESZ Programs and Resources 239

  15. *Introduction to CURESZ FriendSZ Caregiver's Mentoring: The Family Burden of Schizophrenia* by Mary Beth De Bord, JD 241
  16. *CURESZ on Campus: Education in the Age of Risk* by Bethany Yeiser, BS ... 243
  17. *CURESZ Programs* by Catherine Engle, LPCC-S 245
  18. *The Cognition Self-Assessment Rating Scale for Patients with Schizophrenia* by Henry Nasrallah, MD 249

Acknowledgements 255

FOREWORD
by Henry A. Nasrallah, MD

"Schizophrenia is the worst disease affecting mankind." This was the first sentence in an editorial about psychiatric disorders, published in one of the most prestigious journals in medicine.[1] A year after that editorial was published, clozapine was approved by the FDA for treatment-resistant and refractory schizophrenia, comprised of patients whose delusions and hallucinations failed to respond to multiple antipsychotic drugs, and had to be locked up in a state hospital for the rest of their lives.

Clozapine promptly shattered the widely prevailing hopelessness surrounding chronic schizophrenia by eliminating the persistent and disabling psychotic symptoms of many patients suffering from schizophrenia and restoring their healthy mind to them. The phenomenon of completely unexpected recovery from a chronic disabling and stigmatizing psychosis was regarded as miraculous and referred to as a mental "awakening" after it was administered to many patients with severe and untreatable schizophrenia after its launch in 1989.[2] *Time Magazine* highlighted those "awakenings" in an article describing extremely sick patients with schizophrenia who recovered completely, discharged from the institutions, and resumed their lives with their families and friends.[3]

Since the introduction of clozapine, dramatic advances and breakthroughs have been achieved in understanding the scientific underpinnings of schizophrenia over the past 4 decades including neurochemistry, neurophysiology, neuropathology, neurobiology, neurogenetics and neuroimaging. The receptor profile of clozapine (stronger serotonin 5-HT2A receptor antagonism than dopamine D2 receptor antagonism, the reverse of the receptor binding profile of the older antipsychotics like chlorpromazine and haloperidol) prompted the pharmaceutical industry to develop entirely new "second-generation" antipsychotics (also referred to as "atypical").

The 11 members of the second-generation antipsychotics, modeled after clozapine's receptor profile, were sequentially introduced by 10 pharmaceutical

---

[1] Editorial: Where next with psychiatric illness? *Nature* 1988; 336:95-96.
[2] Stahl SM: "'Awakening' from schizophrenia: Intra-molecular polypharmacy and atypical antipsychotics." *Journal of Clinical Psychiatry* 1997; 58:381-382.
[3] Wallis C and Willwerth J: "Awakenings: schizophrenia A new drug brings patients back to life." *Time*, Monday July 6, 1992.

companies between 1993 and 2020, but none of them is as efficacious as clozapine for treatment-resistant or refractory schizophrenia. Amazingly, after several decades of use, the exact mechanism by which clozapine eliminates ongoing and persistent hallucinations and delusions remains a scientific mystery. Once that mystery is solved, it may lead to unprecedented understanding of how a "healthy brain" can become a "psychotic brain" that results in progressive brain tissue loss (both gray and white matter), destroying young peoples' lives and costing society over $150 billion every year (direct and indirect costs).

Many myths still shroud schizophrenia, and the harmful stigma of severe mental illness is still prevalent around the world despite momentous discoveries proving that schizophrenia is a neurologic illness, like Parkinson's' disease, multiple sclerosis, and Alzheimer's disease, which are associated with compassion, not hurtful prejudice and stigma. Unfortunately, many mental health professionals, including some psychiatrists, still have no expectations that persons with schizophrenia can ever recover (and many of them have never used clozapine). The movie industry has contributed to portraying psychosis as "dangerous" and patients with schizophrenia are depicted in movies like Psycho, as potential murderers when, in reality, the vast majority of persons with schizophrenia are victims rather than perpetrators of crime. Most of the crimes are committed by individuals with antisocial personality psychopathic traits, not persons suffering from schizophrenia.

This book is produced by the CURESZ Charitable Foundation, established by Bethany Yeiser and me in 2016. Bethany's story of complete recovery from schizophrenia is remarkable and astonishing. She developed psychosis during college and became homeless for several years with ongoing delusions and hallucinations before she was finally hospitalized. Her auditory hallucinations could not be controlled by several atypical antipsychotic drugs, following which she was referred to me. I diagnosed her with treatment-refractory schizophrenia and started her on clozapine. She tolerated the side effects very well and her continuous loud auditory hallucinations disappeared within a few months. After her recovery, she enrolled at the University of Cincinnati and graduated with honors in molecular biology. With my encouragement, she then published a memoir of her journey of recovery, and became a motivational speaker, advocating for a wider use of clozapine in individuals with unremitting psychotic symptoms of schizophrenia. It is tragic that a small proportion of patients with refractory schizophrenia in the U.S. have ever received a trial of clozapine (4.5% out of 30% of schizophrenia patients identified as non-responsive to standard antipsychotics).

One of the first initiatives that Bethany and I embarked on after establishing the CURESZ Foundation was to assemble a "Clozapine Experts Panel" (over 100 psychiatric clinicians nationally) to whom families can take their sons or daughters with treatment-resistant schizophrenia, to receive a trial of clozapine. A map of the USA showing the locations of the clozapine experts is found on the CURESZ Foundation website (curesz.org).

This book is designed to inform, advocate, and inspire. Among the many CURESZ initiatives, we assembled a group of "Survivors" whose stories of recovery are heart-warming and inspiring. Contrary to the notion that people with schizophrenia are permanently and completely disabled, the Survivors are thriving and highly functioning, including a law student, a librarian, a musician, a computer programmer, an athlete, a university faculty, artists, authors, poets, and homemakers. They are a living testimonial of the "awakenings" experienced by persons who returned to their normal selves and triumphed over schizophrenia, either with clozapine or with other antipsychotic medications. We hope that the readers of this book will recognize that persons diagnosed with schizophrenia should not be "written off" as forever disabled, but that with appropriate treatment, they can recover and pursue their life goals.

Untreated or inadequately treated schizophrenia can experience recurrent episodes of psychosis, which are associated with several grave consequences.[4] These include brain atrophy (both gray and white matter), the need for higher antipsychotic doses (treatment-resistance), inability to return to college or their job (functional disability), estrangement from their families and friends, an extremely high rate of suicide, imprisonment, and homelessness. Psychotic relapses and their tragic consequences can be significantly prevented by long-acting injectable formulations of antipsychotics (administered intramuscularly every 1, 2, 3 or 6 months), eliminating the need for pills to which most patients do not adhere. It is perplexing that 85% of patients with schizophrenia do not receive long-acting injectable antipsychotics to protect them from relapse, and 99% of U.S. patients with schizophrenia never received the long-acting injectable antipsychotic at the time of discharge from the first hospitalization to prevent any further brain damage. The outcome of schizophrenia can be dramatically improved with very early use of long-acting intra-muscular antipsychotic medications[5] and preventing a second episode.[6]

Although there is no cure yet for schizophrenia (much more federal funding is needed to achieve that), judicious use of existing medications can significantly stabilize a considerable proportion of patients, but 30% of the schizophrenia syndrome patients who are deemed treatment-resistant, or refractory must receive clozapine as early as possible. But only 45-50% of this treatment-refractory group

---

[4] Nasrallah HA: "10 devasting consequences of psychotic relapses." *Current Psychiatry* 2021; 20:9-12.
[5] Nasrallah HA: "3 steps to bend the curve of schizophrenia." *Current Psychiatry* 2022; 21:6-9.
[6] Nasrallah HA: "Is preventing the second episode a disease-modifying strategy for schizophrenia?" *Schizophrenia Research* 2023:252:326-328.

improve with clozapine. Those who do not may recover with electro-convulsive therapy (ECT) according to several studies.[7] ECT has been shown to regrow several brain regions in patients with schizophrenia.

I hope that you, the readers of this book, will glean many key details about schizophrenia from the various resources provided. I am sure that you will be moved and exhilarated by the twenty-eight stories of recovery in Part Two of this book, and will be deeply inspired by how those young people with lived experience in schizophrenia have been leading fulfilling and productive lives. Recovery from schizophrenia is a reality, not a myth. This book provides living proof of how a comprehensive biopsychosocial approach to managing schizophrenia, including early use of clozapine for the most severe patients, can pave the way to remarkable, even stunning, awakenings.

---

[7] Alisa, Mathur N, Malhotra AK, Braga RJ: Electroconvulsive therapy and schizophrenia: a systematic review. *Molecular Neuropsychiatry* 2019; 5:75-83.

PART ONE

PREFACE TO AWAKENINGS AND PART ONE
by Bethany Yeiser, BS

Schizophrenia drastically changed the course of my life. The illness forced me to drop out of college, made me paranoid towards family and friends, and left me homeless on the streets of Los Angeles for several years. However, thanks to treatment with a powerful yet underutilized antipsychotic medication called clozapine, and with the support of family and friends, my symptoms gradually disappeared. As the fullness of my normal self-re-emerged, I experienced a stunning "awakening." Through rekindling relationships, and eventually returning to college, I reclaimed my life. During the past 15 years, the hallucinations and delusions that crowded my thoughts, altered my behavior, and plunged me deeper and deeper into illness have remained completely absent.

To me, the key to recovery is having a healthy, functioning mind. The signs of recovery include a meaningful social life balanced with purposeful activity such as school, work, or volunteering. My life today is filled with wonderful relationships. My main work involves conducting the multifaceted business of the CURESZ Foundation where I serve as President. (CURESZ is an acronym for Comprehensive Understanding via Research and Education into SchiZophrenia.) I co-founded the CURESZ Foundation in 2016 with the internationally renowned psychiatrist who helped me recover, Professor Henry Nasrallah, MD, who serves as the Scientific Director of the Foundation. Our main mission is to help others achieve recovery through education and research.

In 2014, I published my memoir, *Mind Estranged: My Journey from Schizophrenia and Homelessness to Recovery*. Publishing the book opened an exciting new chapter of life for me, both personally and professionally. Keeping my schizophrenia recovery and life story a secret from 2007-2014 was an existence of living in the shadows. My diagnosis of schizophrenia held me back from developing deep relationships for fear of being misunderstood and rejected. When my memoir was published, it felt as though I had come out into broad daylight. I finally felt free and liberated to openly share my life.

At the same time *Mind Estranged* was published, my mother Karen, a retired nurse, also published a companion book called *Flight from Reason: A Mother's Story of Schizophrenia, Recovery and Hope*. It parallels the same time frame as *Mind Estranged* and describes the family burden of schizophrenia and the joy of witnessing my recovery, from my mother's perspective as a former healthcare professional.

Part One of this book includes my compiled writings about schizophrenia and related disorders from over the past few years, following the publication of my memoir. Topics range widely from schizophrenia as an invisible illness to the experience of individuals with psychosis in the mental health courts and related legislation, to diet and exercise, and the need for creating a new name for schizophrenia, due to the unfortunate stigma attached to it. As you read Part One of *Awakenings*, I invite you to join me on a journey deep into the mind of an individual living with schizophrenia.

During my lived experience through schizophrenia, I have recognized that I am not alone in my complete recovery. I have actively sought out others who are thriving despite developing schizophrenia. Many of these people have become friends and colleagues.

The CURESZ Foundation highlights diverse stories of "Survivors" who have experienced their own "awakenings." Twenty-eight of these remarkable individuals are featured in Part Two of this book. I am proud of and grateful for the many Survivors who have generously agreed to share their inspiring stories in order to help others.

Education empowers people to recover. In Part Three of *Awakenings*, the CURESZ Foundation offers education about schizophrenia as a brain disorder, highlights cutting-edge and underutilized medications, and features many programs, including our caregiver's mentoring program and support group.

Through the essays, stories and resources offered in this book, I hope to enable many more people struggling with schizophrenia to achieve complete recovery like I did. I look forward to seeing many more "awakenings!"

1
INTRODUCTION

SCHIZOPHRENIA IS AN INVISIBLE ILLNESS

On a day-to-day basis, countless people walk by. We see all sorts of faces — happy, sad, concerned, and joyful. There are people in a hurry and people walking slowly. With a quick glance, we cannot know what their lives are like, what they are experiencing, what medical conditions they have, or what family problems they may face, including schizophrenia.

Schizophrenia is classified as a psychotic disorder. Psychosis refers to a disconnection from reality, characterized by hallucinations (unreal sensory experiences such as hearing voices) and delusions (fixed false beliefs). When effectively treated, schizophrenia is an invisible illness. One in 100 people throughout the world will develop it, and people with schizophrenia who are living in recovery (commonly taking antipsychotic medication) do not stand out in the crowd any more than people with arthritis or those with high blood pressure. People with schizophrenia are everywhere and blended into every strata of society.

Over the years, one of the things that has most surprised me is the number of people living with schizophrenia I meet who are thriving with healthy, balanced lives. Their symptoms are in remission or near remission, thanks to faithful medication compliance. Over the years, I've met a librarian, a nonprofit executive, a chef, a counselor, an artist, social workers, full-time college students, and many others who live with fulfillment and joy despite a diagnosis of schizophrenia. They are a part of the normal flow of life we describe as a community.

Unfortunately, the long-standing stigma of the word "schizophrenia" continues to negatively frame and define public perception of all people with the diagnosis. The stigma against schizophrenia may lead some to believe that people with schizophrenia do stand out and could never blend into normal society. And the negative and basically hopeless stereotype continues despite very significant advances in schizophrenia treatment. In reality, there is an important difference between persons with schizophrenia who are untreated and treated. This is the case for most illnesses in society.

When I was entering the earliest phase of schizophrenia (referred to as the "prodrome," see article on page 13) my parents, professors, and friends did not recognize that schizophrenia was the underlying problem. My mom, who had attended nursing school in the 1970s, had only seen the sickest and most disabled people with schizophrenia. Many lived in a world of hallucinations, looking blankly into the distance or having conversations with the voices in their minds. Back then, medications were often not as effective as some of the medications today, and recovery was not as common. The older drugs had a high chance of causing involuntary movement disorders, including tardive dyskinesia and severe Parkinsonian movements.

The people my mother saw living with schizophrenia in the 1970s did not typically blend into a crowd. In 1999 when I was developing schizophrenia, at first, I did still blend in, though my life was out of balance. I developed an obsession with studying and working in the research laboratory that was so strong, I could not take even a short break. I also preferred being alone and cut off friends and family. Later, I discovered that my parents believed I was going through some sort of a latent adolescent phase, actively seeking to become a much more independent adult. A more serious problem was dismissed.

Years later, when I rigidly chose to be fully estranged from family and was living outside in a churchyard, undiagnosed, I stood out from society very distinctly. I wandered around the university campus community, spending hours in parks and looking for discarded food from the garbage. I still wonder how many people noticed me.

I was so young. I had once been a student in good standing and was still college-age. I'm sure some questioned why I didn't simply get a job. The reality was that my mind was shattered, too broken to work any job at all or seek help. Due to the loud and distracting voices in my mind, I could not focus and spent many hours at a time every day staring into space.

After I fully recovered in 2008, and did blend into society again, I tried disclosing my schizophrenia to a few people, but received a very poor response with a lack of understanding. Then, I decided to keep the illness mostly to myself. I was a face in the crowd, attending college again and scoring high grades. During the time when I chose not to disclose my illness, I believe that no one knew about it or ever suspected that I might have a brain disorder.

Today, through my work with the CURESZ Foundation, many people I have encountered over the years are also in full remission or nearly so, but many have no interest in telling their story. They want to leave schizophrenia behind and move on, which I understand. But each person who has conquered severe mental illness and decides to disclose their medical condition under their real name, or a pen name, makes a difference.

When I interact with people beginning their journey through schizophrenia, following their initial diagnosis, I share with them the truth: People who have recovered from schizophrenia are everywhere. There is hope. Many enjoy their lives, just like you and me. They work, volunteer, manage households, and enjoy family and friends. Today, thanks to modern treatments and with faithful medication compliance, most people will recover to some extent, and many will recover fully.

I am proud of the remarkable people I know with schizophrenia who make a contribution to society every day and live with purpose and joy, thanks to effective modern treatment.

THE STIGMA OF SCHIZOPHRENIA

In 2008, when fully recovered from schizophrenia, I was ready to disclose to family, friends, and acquaintances about the particulars of my journey through schizophrenia into full and sustained recovery. It was important to me to explain all I had gone through and share that recovery from schizophrenia is indeed possible, thanks to antipsychotic medication. In my case, what brought me into high-level sustained recovery and a new life was the only FDA-approved medication for treatment-resistant psychosis, clozapine.

However, when sharing my journey with new friends at the university, as well as old friends from various periods of my life, people who heard my diagnosis distanced themselves and seemed to act as though I must be dangerous, or erratic, or perhaps no longer trustworthy.

It is my impression that the stigma of brain disorders in general — such as anxiety, bipolar disorder, and depression — is improving. When celebrities such as Olympian swimmer Michael Phelps come out publicly with their stories of recovery, they normalize mental illness and provide insight. Today, bipolar disorder, described as a serious mental illness by prominent professionals, is also recognized as sometimes being associated with creativity, productivity, and artistry.

For every story in the media of schizophrenia recovery, however, there seems to be many others about violence and erratic behavior resulting from psychosis. Notably, these instances of dangerous behavior are generally associated with lack of treatment, medication noncompliance, or illicit substance use. Statistics confirm that people in treatment for schizophrenia are no more violent than the general community, yet many in the general public are unaware of this.[1] In fact, people with schizophrenia are more likely to be victimized than to be perpetrators of violence.

Because of the stigma associated with schizophrenia, I eventually refrained

---

[1] Treatment Advocacy Center. (2016, June). "Risk factors for violence in serious mental illness." Treatment Advocacy Center. https://www.treatmentadvocacycenter.org/evidence-and-research/learn-more-about/3633-risk-factors-for-violence-in-serious-mental-illness.

from disclosing my diagnosis to most other people. This left me feeling alone — like I was living under a shadow. I felt isolated and reluctant to pursue deep and meaningful relationships.

But in 2011, following my college graduation, my doctor encouraged me to write my memoir. When I published *Mind Estranged* in 2014, I disclosed everything.

Today, as I share my experience publicly, I still see stigma and a lack of understanding, and have encountered it at three levels.

Stigma in General Community

First, there is a strong tendency to negatively sensationalize and distort schizophrenia in the general public. For example, on Halloween in the past, I have found "Gone Mental" holiday costumes in various stores. Some of my friends who advocate for people affected by brain disorders faithfully create petitions every year to either rename these costumes or get them out of stores. It always amazes me, as you would never see a diabetes costume or a cancer costume. Yet mental illness is particularly associated with fear, lack of understanding, and sensationalism, which is cruel. Stigma in the general public can also lead to a personal stigma experienced in the lives of patients who have the diagnosis.

Stigma Among Doctors

Second, I have experienced schizophrenia stigma in the general medical community, including clinicians in fields other than psychiatry. In 2008, prior to my recovery, I saw a family doctor for a routine checkup. When she saw antipsychotic medication in my chart, she told me "You would not need this medication if you hadn't used drugs!" I told her I had never used drugs. Drugs, including marijuana, can cause an onset of psychotic symptoms and sometimes schizophrenia (see article on page 17), but many people with schizophrenia have never abused substances. Looking back, this doctor's comment was judgmental and inappropriate, not to mention ill-informed. Many use substances to self-medicate, and substance abuse is in fact known to be a disability.

Stigma About Psychiatrists

Finally, I have experienced stigma among psychiatrists. When I was diagnosed in 2007, my parents were told after about 36 hours in the hospital that I was "permanently and totally disabled." The doctor did not offer hope for recovery. It seemed that leaving the hospital and being stable enough to even live in the community was the highest goal I could hope for. Unfortunately, subsequent psychiatrists also offered little hope and limited options to recover and rebuild my life.

Fortunately, in 2008, I met Dr. Henry Nasrallah, who would challenge the stigma, and his thinking was quite the opposite of other psychiatrists. Dr. Nasrallah carefully studied my life history and accomplishments, including my research publications, violin accomplishments, and high grades prior to the onset of my schizophrenia. Subsisting in the community was not good enough for him — he was determined to do anything in his power to get me back to college, back to work, and back to meaningful relationships. I owe a debt of gratitude to him for his dedicated care and forward thinking. He helped me achieve full recovery with clozapine and social support.

The Choice to Disclose
One of my mentors over the years has been a successful Texas psychiatrist who recovered from schizophrenia and has practiced for decades. She once told me that the people in her life who knew her when she was sick could not imagine her well. At the same time, the people in her life who know her today, healthy and thriving, cannot imagine her sick. I have found the same to be true in my own life. When I share my story today, I think it is hard for many to imagine me being overcome by the devastating symptoms of schizophrenia.

Often, I am asked by other people with schizophrenia whether or not they should disclose their illness in relationships. I have no single answer for this question, as it is a personal choice. I have found it best to connect with others through common interests such as professional aspirations and hobbies in order to build trust first. Once a relationship of trust and friendship is established, it is more natural to share medical issues. Certainly, having schizophrenia should not have to be the most important thing about a person's life.

When I consider the stigma of schizophrenia, I feel we still have a long way to go. However, stories of full recovery (which I hope include my own) prove that today recovery is truly possible.

I am honored to have the opportunity to speak and write about my recovery with hopes that this stigma will greatly diminish over time. As I encounter so many others in full recovery, I am optimistic.

GLOBAL MENTAL HEALTH
On May 24, World Schizophrenia Day, I reflected on my own recovery from schizophrenia, which has lasted 15 years, thanks to excellent medical care in the United States. I also reflected on the experience and treatment of schizophrenia throughout the world. Schizophrenia treatment can be impacted by the misunderstanding associated with the diagnosis as well as the shortage of mental health workers.

The incidence of schizophrenia is about 1% worldwide,[1] with males at higher risk of developing the disease.[2] It affects every country, culture, ethnicity, and people of any socioeconomic status, just like most other medical illnesses.

The stigma of schizophrenia strongly lives on (and it can be worse in developing nations). Members of the general public, both globally and in the United States, may not understand that schizophrenia is a treatable brain disorder and that many patients recover and resume their lives.

Throughout the world, there is also a shortage of mental health workers. The World Health Organization's Mental Health Atlas 2017 reported that in low-income countries, the rate of mental health workers could be as low as 2 per 100,000 population, compared with more than 70 in high-income countries.[3]

I am honored to be friends with an American couple, both psychiatrists trained in Ohio, who spent months working in West Africa as psychiatric physicians and are currently training in Kenya to study the East African culture and learn to practice medicine most effectively in Africa.

While in West Africa, this couple encountered desperately psychotic people who were tied or roped like dogs. These individuals were suffering without any form of mental health treatment. Unfortunately, when medications are offered in this part of the world, often, the only ones available are older antipsychotics with harsh side effects. Some are totally ineffective because they are outdated or corrupted with various substances.

In addition to challenges with obtaining effective medication, psychiatrists practicing in developing parts of the world may be more likely to encounter primitive beliefs, such as believing that psychotic behavior results from demon possession.

Families living in impoverished parts of the world often cannot afford food, or the most basic medical treatment, let alone pay for psychiatric care and/or medication. Lack of psychiatric medication is tragic for depression and anxiety but can be even worse when the patient is experiencing psychosis.

Helping Your Own People

In 2002, while living in Kenya, I met a Rwandan man and his family who were on an extended visit to Kenya. He had completed a master's degree in counseling, and his dream was to return to his home country to counsel people who had suffered through the genocide in 1994. What better experience could a struggling

---

[1] Treatment Advocacy Center. (2018). *Schizophrenia – fact sheet. Treatment Advocacy Center.* https://www.treatmentadvocacycenter.org/evidence-and-research/learn-more-about/25-schizophrenia-fact-sheet.

[2] Javitt, D. C. (2014). "Balancing therapeutic safety and efficacy to improve clinical and economic outcomes in schizophrenia: a clinical overview." *The American Journal of Managed Care, 20* (8 Suppl), S160-165. https://pubmed.ncbi.nlm.nih.gov/25180705/.

[3] WHO's Mental Health Atlas 2017 highlights global shortage of health workers trained in mental health. https://www.who.int/hrh/news/2018/WHO-MentalHealthAtlas2017-highlights-HW-shortage/en/ Accessed May 21, 2021.

Rwandan have than to work with a highly educated man from his own country, speaking his own language, who had fled the genocide himself? Through the passion and drive of individuals like this man, there is hope.

When my psychiatrist friends were living in West Africa, they spent much of their time training nurses to deal with psychiatric emergencies and psychosis. But I look forward to a time when more of the best psychiatrists, nurses, and other professionals, many of whom train in the United States or other parts of the developed world, decide to return to their home countries to serve and train their own people.

In addition to training clinicians and counselors, a steady supply of antipsychotic medication needs to be available. When I was living in Kenya, an American doctor brought in a supply of antibiotics and administered them to the needy. Bringing antipsychotics into the developing world is much more complicated because these medications, unlike antibiotics, need to be taken regularly, indefinitely.

It is always important to open our eyes to the needs of people living far away. Mine were opened wide when living in Africa.

I hope to one day live in a world where even the poorest individuals can obtain badly needed and high-quality treatment for brain disorders, wherever they may reside.

2

DEVELOPING SCHIZOPHRENIA

SCHIZOPHRENIA AND WHAT HAPPENS BEFORE

Occasionally, I hear people with schizophrenia say that they have had the condition their entire lives. However, that is most likely not true.

Like many other biological illnesses, schizophrenia has a typical age of onset. Very few people in their 30s develop Alzheimer's disease. It can happen, but it is very rare. Schizophrenia typically does not present until later in a person's teen years or into their early-to-mid 20s, though a change in behavior prior to the formal onset of the illness may precede it by months or even years. Some people develop schizophrenia in their 30s, but this is less common. Generally speaking, when a person develops schizophrenia later in life, they have a better prognosis.

With schizophrenia, the first psychotic symptoms are referred to as a "first psychotic break" or "first episode." Prior to this first break, they may lose interest in things they used to love such as playing a musical instrument, participating in sports, working, or spending time with friends and family. Eventually, they may even lose the motivation to get up in the morning and go to school or to work, or lose interest in self-care, forgetting to eat or shower.

This phase immediately prior to a first psychotic episode is called the "prodrome phase." The prodrome phase is usually identified only in hindsight. While it is going on, there is no way of knowing if normal personality changes and experiences that come with adolescence are occurring or if a brain disease is the influencer.

My first psychotic break happened upon returning from a trip to Africa. I was 20 years old and a college student living far away from my family. After having lived in Africa for three months serving those living in poverty, I returned to the United States. Suddenly I could not even pass my exams. It was my senior year, and I was supposed to graduate in May. Instead, I dropped out and became homeless.

Looking back, it is hard to tell exactly when my prodrome began. However, I believe that schizophrenia was emerging during my freshman year of college.

The University of Southern California in Los Angeles was my dream school, and I had begun classes there in the fall of 1999. When I arrived, I was extremely busy with difficult classes, research, and serving as concertmaster of the school's community orchestra. My parents were concerned that I was overextended and had no real social life, but they were also proud of my research achievements and grades. And looking back, all my friends were busy and highly competitive.

The difference with me was that I could never stand to take a short break without focusing all my thoughts on my research or upcoming exams. I never went to parties or social activities, even when I had time.

Following the first semester of my freshman year, my grades began to plummet. Confused, I was obsessed with doing "something more." I was convinced that my research work could lead to awards which I could not win by getting A's in my classes, and I was frequently at the laboratory, even when there was nothing to do. I seriously considered that a project going on in the laboratory where I worked might win a Nobel Prize, which was unrealistic. And I never considered the reality of how lower grades would impact my future.

I took another turn for the worse during the beginning of my junior year, when the September 11, 2001 terrorist attacks happened. Again, I began to look for "something bigger" to do with my life other than to build a traditional career. I became obsessed with traveling. From that point on, my grades were consistently low. The second semester of my junior year, I took easy classes and scored C's. I spent all my time planning an extended humanitarian trip to Africa.

It is common for college students to go through a "junior slump" and score lower grades for a time. Also, sometimes, students are encouraged to travel overseas and learn about new cultures and languages, which I was doing. I blended in. I had no idea that schizophrenia was about to emerge.

Common prodromal symptoms of schizophrenia may include social withdrawal, suspiciousness, grandiosity, distractibility, decreased school function, and hostility. Parents and educators should be aware that schizophrenia can develop during a student's high school or college years. When students have an alarming change in personality or loss of interest in things they used to love, which cannot be explained, it is important to look at their family history. Does mental illness run in the family? If it does, these students should be carefully assessed by a mental health professional to see if there are further warning signs. Even if there is no known history of mental illness in a person's family, it is still important to pay attention.

High school and college students would greatly benefit from education regarding the warning signs of emerging schizophrenia. There is no shame in asking for help, and early intervention is vital to achieve the best possible outcome. Schizophrenia, bipolar disorder, and depression are brain diseases which are treatable today. Despite having a psychiatric diagnosis, most people who commit to long-term treatment can live happy and meaningful lives.

A CHOICE TO BE HOMELESS

I was homeless from March 3, 2003, until March 3, 2007.

But today, 15 years later, I live a very different life. Since 2009, I have lived in the University of Cincinnati community. I graduated magna cum laude from the University of Cincinnati in molecular biology 12 years ago.

In 2017, I moved from an apartment I shared with a college student into my own one-bedroom apartment. I have a spacious living room, a large bedroom, and my own full kitchen. One of my favorite things to do is serve waffles, eggs, and coffee to friends who drop by.

The living room of my apartment serves as my office. I work as an author and mental health advocate from home. As a speaker, I travel extensively.

Being homeless was a terrible experience. To say I never would want to go back in time and be homeless again is an understatement. I suffered every day. But while I was homeless, several people — including my parents — offered me a free place to stay with no strings attached. I rejected everyone, choosing to spend rainy nights sleeping outside under an overhang in the front of a Los Angeles church. I considered the churchyard to be my home.

Through my work today, I respond regularly to families who have loved ones with schizophrenia and other brain disorders. One of the biggest surprises I have found over the past few years is the enormous number of moms and dads who contact me about their loved one behaving as I did 2003-2007, totally refusing family and friends for help and preferring the homeless life.

A mom recently contacted me about her son who was in a physics PhD program at a major Oregon university. Months before his anticipated graduation, he took off and began living out of his car in a community far away from the university. This mother contacted me at a loss, not knowing how to proceed.

I encouraged the mom of the physics graduate student to try to get her son a diagnosis and, if appropriate, treatment. My hope was that, if he began treatment, he would be able to resume his studies at the university as I did.

Looking back, I always thought that my choice to be homeless was rational and truly my own choice. However, when I began my first antipsychotic medication, I began asking myself questions. Why did I live outside when so many families would have had me, including my own family? Why was I not in touch with my own mom and dad? We never fought, and they had given me and my brother wonderful opportunities and memories. I also wondered why I had dropped out of college. As the medication cleared my mind, my desire to be homeless was replaced by a new and clearer outlook on life.

I also spoke with a mom whose son spent six years sleeping in a library at a Wisconsin university where he had completed bachelor's degrees in physics and computer science.

Years after he began abusing his privileges on campus, his mother contacted campus security at his university and discovered that they knew her son. She helped him move into stable housing. But soon after, he left again, preferring to be homeless. A doctor determined he was not a danger to himself or others or gravely disabled. Because he did not fit those criteria, it was impossible to mandate that he begin treatment. Soon after, he disappeared. His mother later spent tens of thousands of dollars hiring a private detective to find him, all to no avail.

I also recently interacted with a woman who had been given a psychiatric diagnosis in her 20s. She was considering selling her house, giving away her possessions and becoming homeless. She said her goal was to benefit others who were homeless. I tried to explain to her that if she began antipsychotic medication, she might view things differently and change her mind. I encouraged her to find other, more effective ways to help the homeless without losing or giving away everything she owned or doing something else she might regret.

But what surprised me most was her reasoning — that she would help the homeless the most by becoming homeless herself. I recall thinking the same way as I moved out of my apartment in 2003 with nowhere to go.

We live in an amazing era for the advanced treatment of brain disorders. If no medications were available to me, I believe I would still be sleeping outside. Or I may have been picked up by police for loitering or trespassing and taken to jail for months or years. Decades ago, my schizophrenia would have been a life sentence, as I may have spent my entire adult lifetime in an institution. But with today's medical advancement, I was able to begin a medication that enabled me to graduate from college, and today I encourage others to reclaim their lives and dreams.

There is hope for the chronically homeless with schizophrenia who spend months or years living outside. The keys usually include dedicated mental health treatment, often with medication. I never used substances or alcohol while sleeping outside, but many do. Offering the homeless rehabilitation programs to deal with substance abuse is also vital.

When I see homeless people living outside in Cincinnati, I pray that those who need it will have access to decent healthcare like I found. I hope each of them will someday find health and a new chance at life.

MARIJUANA AND SCHIZOPHRENIA

I was diagnosed with schizophrenia in 2007. My first psychiatrist said I was permanently and totally disabled. My second psychiatrist decided my case was too complicated and immediately dropped me as a patient before I could even find another doctor. My third psychiatrist wanted me to spend my days in an institutional day program because he believed I would never again work, attend school, live independently, or enjoy normal society or meaningful relationships.

My doctors were wrong. I beat the odds. Twelve years ago, I graduated from college in molecular biology with a 3.8 GPA. Today, I work 30 hours a week, which includes time spent in education and advocacy as I run the CURESZ Foundation. Looking back, I am grateful that I was never pressured at any time to use marijuana.

Marijuana use has been found to be linked to psychosis, sometimes including long-term schizophrenia. Regular users are four-fold more likely to develop schizophrenia than their peers,[1] and adolescents who use cannabis are more likely to develop psychosis in a dose-dependent fashion.[2]

It is no surprise that cannabis use can lead to psychosis. In the brain of a person with schizophrenia, a dopamine surge can happen naturally, leading to hallucinations, delusions, paranoia, and other symptoms. Cannabis use triggers a similar dopamine release, producing schizophrenia-like symptoms. Marijuana use also affects other neurotransmitters in the brain including glutamate, anandamide, and serotonin.[3] These chemical changes mimic the changes in the brain of a person with schizophrenia.

Smoking cigarettes can also have detrimental effects on developing brains. Minors who smoke cigarettes are twice as likely as their peers who do not smoke to develop psychosis.[4]

I interact often with families who have loved ones diagnosed with schizophrenia and are seeking education and guidance. Many express frustration with their loved ones because they are not thriving in recovery due to continued marijuana use, which complicates their recovery.

They often explain that their son or daughter uses marijuana to help manage their symptoms of paranoia or hallucinations. However, families and patients must

---

[1] Messamore, E. (2019). "The cannabis-psychosis-schizophrenia connection." CURESZ Foundation. https://curesz.org/wp-content/uploads/2019/10/SPECIAL-HIGHLIGHT-OF-CANNABIS-AND-PSYCHOSIS.pdf.

[2] Bagot, K., Milin, R., & Kaminer, Y. (2015). "Adolescent initiation of cannabis use and early onset psychosis." *Substance Abuse*, 36(4), 524-533.

[3] Hayward, E. (2002, February 1). "Mental health toll of cannabis soared after Scots went soft on the drug six years ago, data suggests." *Dailymail.com*. https://www.dailymail.co.uk/news/article-10461599/Mental-health-toll-cannabis-soars-Scots-went-soft-drug-six-years-ago-data-suggests.html.

[4] Scott, J, Matuschka, L., Niemelä, S., Miettunen, J., Emmerson, B., & Mustonen. (2018). "Evidence of a casual relationship between smoking tobacco and schizophrenia spectrum disorders." *Frontiers in Psychiatry, 20*. https://doi.org/10.3389/fpsyt.2018.00607.

understand that, though marijuana use may provide temporary symptom relief, marijuana use can also cause long-term brain damage to the brain's white matter,[5] which can lead to impulsivity and other problems. Cannabis use also leads to nonadherence to antipsychotics[6] and has been found to reduce the effectiveness of antipsychotic medication.[7]

Additionally, if a young person is taking an antipsychotic, smoking cigarettes may make it up to 50 percent less effective, though their cognition may improve while smoking.[8]

Because I once experienced hallucinations, paranoia, and delusions myself (16 years ago), I have deep empathy for people wanting the symptom relief marijuana can bring. However, substances such as marijuana can make the psychosis permanently worse. My unexpected and full recovery may have been hindered if I had used drugs, which could have led to brain damage. I will never know for sure.

My goal is to help patients catch a vision for the new life they can have if they stop using marijuana, smoking cigarettes, and/or taking other substances, which all increase the fragility of the brain and vulnerability to psychiatric illness. The hope is that when they are off these drugs, there will be a greater chance that they will stay in remission from psychosis, enabling them to pursue education or purposeful work, and enjoy a thriving, higher quality of life.

It is imperative that we educate young people about the risks of marijuana and other substances to help reduce risk of developing lifelong psychiatric illness.

EXERCISE AND DIET

Research indicates that there is a link between how we eat and how we feel, and our diet affects our brains. Many neurotransmitters are shared between the gut and the brain. In fact, if we are stressed, digestion in the gut can speed up or slow down.[11] Eating meals regularly with others also has psychological benefits

---

[5] Weir, K. (2015 November). "Marijuana and the developing brain." American Psychological Association, 46(10). https://www.apa.org/monitor/2015/11/marijuana-brain#:~:text=Some%20of%20those%20brain%20abnormalities,helps%20enable%20communication%20among%20neurons.

[6] Treatment Foglia, E, Schoeler, T., Klamerus, E., Morgan, K., & Bhattacharyya, S. (2017). "Cannabis use and adherence to antipsychotic medication: a systematic review and meta-analysis." *Psychological Medicine, 47*(10), 1691-1705.

[7] Arnold, J. (2018, July 27). "Study suggests cannabis compound can make schizophrenia medication less effective." Brain and Behavioral Research Foundation. https://www.bbrfoundation.org/content/study-suggests-cannabis-compound-can-make-schizophrenia-medication-less-effective.

[8] Lyon, E. (1999 October 1). "A review of the effects of nicotine on schizophrenia and antipsychotic medications." Psychiatric Services. https://ps.psychiatryonline.org/doi/full/10.1176/ps.50.10.1346.

[9] Pharmacy Times. (2016, May 16). How smoking affects medications. Pharmacy Times. https://www.pharmacytimes.com/view/how-smoking-affects-medications.

[10] Upham, B. (2019 November 6). Smoking increases risk for depression and schizophrenia, study suggests. Everyday Health. https://www.everydayhealth.com/schizophrenia/new-research-suggests-that-smoking-increases-risk-for-depression-and-schizophrenia/.

[11] Diet and Mental Health. https://www.mentalhealth.org.uk/a-to-z/d/diet-and-mental-health. Retrieved September 28, 2021.

because it provides an opportunity to feel connected to other people.

As I celebrate my full recovery from schizophrenia since 2008, I attribute my success in part to my commitment to healthy eating, regular exercise, and avoiding alcohol, cigarettes, and street drugs.

People with schizophrenia often have a more difficult time maintaining a healthy diet, as antipsychotic medications may cause patients to crave unhealthy foods including carbohydrates and sugar.[12] Antipsychotic-induced weight gain can be mitigated by a commitment to healthy eating and regular exercise. From the beginning of a patient's journey to recovery, he or she should discuss diet options with a doctor, dietician, or other professional.

As with persons in the general population, it is important for those with brain disorders to eat green leafy vegetables every day, get enough protein, consume whole-grain foods, and drink milk (dairy or soy or oat or nut milk made of cashews or almonds) for a healthy intake of calcium.[13]

Many studies suggest that schizophrenia symptoms can be lessened to some extent by certain supplements or diets. I believe that taking the supplements recommended by my doctor (and choosing healthy foods) over the years may have helped improve my ability to focus as well as my overall functioning. Various diets also have been shown to help with some symptoms of schizophrenia in some patients. However, there is still limited data on the effectiveness of these diets and why they work more or less in various patients.

Sometimes, I interact with persons with schizophrenia who plan to discontinue medication in favor of a new diet and/or supplements. Though diet and supplements can make a big difference in a person's recovery, stopping prescribed medication is dangerous and may lead to relapse. Diet and supplements alone are usually not enough.

In addition to eating a healthy diet, I swim at least once a week and take long walks every other day. There is no substitute for exercise. Not only does it keep my weight in check, but it also boosts my cognition, refreshes me, and helps produce endorphins that actually make me feel happy.[14]

To achieve the highest level of recovery, it is advisable for patients, especially those on antipsychotic medications, to avoid alcohol. Alcohol may reduce the effectiveness of antipsychotic medications and may raise the risk of medication side effects.[15]

When dealing with schizophrenia, the fundamental interventions are gener-

---

[12] Living with Schizophrenia. (2021 September 28). Healthy Living: Schizophrenia and Diet. Living with Schizophrenia. https://livingwithschizophreniauk.org/information-sheets/healthy-living-schizophrenia-and-diet/.

[13] Centers for Disease Control and Prevention. (2023, March). Healthy eating for a healthy weight. Centers for Disease Control and Prevention. https://www.cdc.gov/healthyweight/healthy_eating/index.html.

[14] Healthline. (2021 October 8). How to hack your hormones for a better mood. Healthline. https://www.healthline.com/health/happy-hormone.

[15] Cooper, C.M. (2021 July 15). Can I drink alcohol while taking antipsychotics like Abilify and Seroquel? GoodRX Health. https://www.goodrx.com/blog/alcohol-with-seroquel-abilify-antipsychotics/.

ally antipsychotic medication, the opportunity to speak with someone about how schizophrenia affects you personally, setting goals, and building a support system. But diet and exercise also play a key role in the recovery process. Eating a healthy diet should be a high priority for new patients — from the very first day they are diagnosed and into the future.

ABOUT TARDIVE DYSKINESIA

In the first week of May, many mental health advocates, psychiatrists, and patients around the country observe Tardive Dyskinesia Awareness Week. Tardive dyskinesia (TD) is a condition impacting the nervous system that causes involuntary movements, and it may occur after the prolonged use of certain psychiatric medications. Risk factors for TD include long duration of antipsychotic treatment, older age, female gender, diagnosis of a mood disorder, postmenopausal status, abusing drugs and alcohol, and diabetes.

I spent the week reading articles to learn more about involuntary movement disorders and was inspired by stories of TD recovery.

Over the years, I heard of TD but was not very familiar with it. I had witnessed TD only once, in the face of an older man at a homeless shelter. The poor homeless man whom I encountered many years ago had severe TD. I couldn't help noticing how he continually stuck out his tongue and puckered his lips every several seconds. I was struck by his movement disorder and felt sorry for him.

Personally, I began taking antipsychotics in 2007, and after 10 years, I did not expect to ever develop tardive dyskinesia.

But in 2017, only a few months after the first medication for TD was approved by the FDA, I noticed that my mouth was unusually dry, and I felt as though I had developed a tic in my face.

I thought back to the homeless man with TD, which made me certain I did not have tardive dyskinesia because my symptoms seemed different and mild.

But my involuntary movements progressively became worse. I noticed movement in my mouth as though I were chewing gum, even though nothing was in my mouth. I started licking my front teeth. I tried drinking more water, as well as using lip gloss to moisten my mouth and lips, but to no avail.

When meeting with friends, I found myself looking away, trying to get their focus off my face. I had been recording motivational interviews about schizophrenia recovery for the CURESZ Foundation and began to wonder if I would need to stop appearing in videos, and even possibly change my career.

But what career would be possible with these disfiguring movements, especially in my face? I thought of lawyers, math teachers, or real estate agents struggling with TD. Most jobs would be very difficult due to face-to-face interaction with others.

About that time, after I had struggled with the movements for a few months, one of my doctors noticed my TD over a virtual conference call. He confirmed that the movements I was experiencing were indeed tardive dyskinesia. He also offered me hope. In 2017, after there had been no effective treatment available for TD for decades, two new medications for TD were approved by the FDA.

Thanks to this psychiatrist, I gained a greater understanding of TD as a serious and disfiguring neurological movement disorder and a potential side effect of medications that block dopamine receptors, which can affect the face, neck, arms, body, and legs. TD is a late-onset side effect that may occur after prolonged exposure to certain medications, including antipsychotic drugs which are approved by the FDA for the treatment of schizophrenia, bipolar disorder, and treatment-resistant depression.

However, today, there is hope for recovery from TD. The two FDA-approved medications for TD are called VMAT-2 inhibitors. These medications interfere with the packaging of dopamine into synapses (spaces between nerve cells) in the brain. In doing so, they reduce the hypersensitivity of dopamine receptors in the region of the brain that controls muscle movements and gradually eliminate the involuntary and embarrassing movements of TD.

The newer, "second-generation" antipsychotic medications (from the 1980s forward) are associated with lower rates of TD compared to the older, "first-generation" class of antipsychotics.

As I write this article, I have been on a VMAT-2 inhibitor for over six years. The medication has not eliminated my involuntary movements completely but has helped significantly. Thanks to this medication, I continue to appear in videos about schizophrenia recovery and still work as a mental health advocate.

Today, it is vital for psychiatrists to carefully watch their patients on antipsychotics for tardive dyskinesia. I know a doctor who explained to me that he was bald — and he hated being bald — but when he visited his doctor, he didn't mention it because he knew there was nothing to be done. TD used to be the same way. But today, psychiatrists and neurologists have treatment options, so it is absolutely necessary to identify and treat TD as soon as possible, ideally when it is still mild and before it progresses.

I know a nurse who said, "You are pregnant, or you are not pregnant. You have TD, or you don't!" Her message was to recognize and treat tardive dyskinesia as soon as possible for the best possible outcome.

During the last 10 years, I have been so encouraged by medication breakthroughs and enjoy learning about new drugs in the pipeline. The VMAT-2 inhibitors are one of the biggest advances we have seen for a long time, offering hope for TD.

MOURNING LOST TIME

Sometimes, I find myself mourning over how much time was lost while I was suffering from acute mental illness.

During the years I expected to be in school studying for a PhD, I was instead homeless, dirty, and eating out of garbage cans.

But even during my years homeless and dirty, I learned some valuable life lessons.

For one, I learned to relate to homeless people who are suffering.

In the past, when I saw homeless people living on the streets, I used to think it was their own fault. I thought they should stop bothering people in the community, get off the streets, and check into a homeless shelter. I never considered that many of these people struggle with severe untreated brain disorders, which is why they might refuse help.

When I was homeless myself, I never even considered going to a shelter, preferring to sleep outside under the stars and to eat trashed food every day, rather than to visit a food bank.

I know what it's like to wash up in public bathrooms, hoping every minute that no one else will come in. I know what it's like to feel dirty underneath my clothes because I badly need a shower. But, in my illness, I still refused all help from friends and family. I know what it's like to be paranoid of the people in my life who love me most, and I remember the experience of being cold, hungry, and confused for months on end, while living outside.

My schizophrenia diagnosis in 2007 was one of the biggest surprises in my life, because I believed nothing was wrong with me. It was also a slap in the face. I began to think about my four homeless years, and it seemed these years had been entirely wasted.

When diagnosed with schizophrenia, I had no college degree, was not married, did not have children, and did not have any marketable skills that could help me get a job above minimum wage. I mourned my lost years and could see no good coming from them.

Once diagnosed, it took an additional year to find the right medication. I wish my doctors had tried clozapine (for my treatment-resistance) sooner so that I had not wasted yet another 12 months.

Today, when I look back on these five years, beginning at my first episode up until my recovery, I think about what else I learned and find purpose in this time. When I present my story to audiences, I often share how I stopped wanting to sleep outside after becoming compliant with taking an antipsychotic medication that cleared my mind.

When patients and their families write to me about their experience on ineffective medications, I empathize. I can share how much I suffered during my own 12 months trying five different medications. When I tell patients to never give up, I also know what that means. I know what it's like to have a ravenous appetite because of medications, muscle rigidity, involuntary movements, and other side effects that lower a patient's quality of life. And I know trying new medications can be frustrating.

Over the years, sometimes, I still mourn the five years I lost and wish my life had turned out differently. I mourn the loss of many hopes and dreams. Fortunately, when I recovered, I was able to transfer to the University of Cincinnati and graduate with my bachelor's degree in 2011. But the reality is that I was supposed to graduate in 2003, and I always planned on pursuing a graduate degree.

Today, I'm thankful for my bachelor's degree in molecular biology, which enables me to understand how my medication works to restore the health of my brain.

I don't have children, but I highly value and enjoy spending time with my friends' kids, as well as my 12-year-old piano student.

I don't work full time as the scientist I used to dream of becoming, but I am happy with my work, encouraging schizophrenia patients and their families.

Even though I don't have a doctorate, I fully understand what it means to be partially recovered from severe mental illness and to be homeless, and I can encourage others by sharing the events of my life.

Life certainly didn't turn out as planned, but today I have made peace with the direction my life has gone. I do not consider my illness to be a life sentence. I find contentment in speaking publicly about my recovery from schizophrenia. My bachelor's degree has better qualified me to become editor-in-chief of our CURESZ Foundation's newsletter.

For my readers who have lost time due to a psychiatric illness, I encourage you to never give up. Keep moving forward and making new goals. Consider what you've learned during the hardest times of your life and use those lessons to enrich your future.

Life may never turn out as you expected it to, but that doesn't mean you can't live a meaningful life. Focus on today and make every day worthwhile.

3

LEGISLATION AND TREATMENT PROGRAMS

WISH LIST FOR SCHIZOPHRENIA

When I was homeless, I regularly entered an abandoned building and slept there during the night. I considered the building's unlocked side door to be a miraculous provision from God because my thinking was confused due to mental illness. Sneaking into an open side door made more sense to me than asking anyone for help. While I was mentally ill and homeless, I refused all contact with my family for four and a half years.

Eventually, when the building became occupied, my last resort (as I saw it) was to spend every night in a local churchyard. The voices inside of my head began to speak to me right before my first week in the churchyard. The voices insulted me, commended me, and never really followed a logical pattern that made sense. But still, in my illness, I believed what they said. They explained that the churchyard was a modern-day "Garden of Eden" similar to heaven. And they eventually convinced me that my homeless lifestyle was perfect and that I could never have a better life.

Because I believed that "angels" residing in the "Garden of Eden" left food for me in the garbage cans, I never obtained free food from food banks. When I found food that was unspoiled, like sandwiches and soda, I questioned whether the "angels" had slipped it into the garbage or if someone had been directed through a dream to leave food for me.

Schizophrenia prevented me from working the simplest job. Prior to becoming ill, I had been a successful college student and had enjoyed earning money from my research work in biochemistry. I also worked as a violinist. But when I developed schizophrenia and became homeless, I quickly ran out of money. Occasionally, when I found pocket change left on the streets, I visited a local bakery and purchased their cheapest pastry. Despite growing up in a middle-class family, even pennies had become valuable to me.

As I look back on the tragedy of my homelessness, which was the direct result of severe untreated mental illness, I would like to list the things I wish would have happened instead.

1. Evaluation by the Police

I wish police had been trained to recognize the symptoms of severe mental illness, such as an unkempt and dirty appearance accompanied by mannerisms that are commonly seen when people are experiencing hallucinations, like seeing things and hearing voices in the absence of corresponding stimuli.

After about eight months living outside and hearing voices, I was still not recognized by police as mentally ill. Instead, I was arrested and jailed briefly for trespassing and looking for food in the garbage cans on the university campus where I had formerly been a student. In my insanity, I remembered being a successful student and believed I was unconditionally welcome on campus, despite my dirty and homeless appearance. I was wrong.

I wish that police had identified me as mentally ill several months before I was ever arrested and jailed for trespassing at my former university campus. I was badly in need of treatment, including medication.

2. Evaluation by a Psychiatrist

I wish a well-trained police officer had taken me immediately to a mental health facility for psychiatric evaluation. If I had been given the benefit of being evaluated by a physician (even if I had to be taken against my will), I believe that my mental illness would have been quickly recognized. Living outside, eating garbage, and spending my days in parks was behavior stemming from schizophrenia. Locking me in jail in order to change my behavior was frightening, and a lost cause. Serving jail time does not cure schizophrenia.

In order for people to be held in a hospital against their will for psychiatric evaluation, they must be considered at risk of hurting themselves or others. At the time when I was hearing voices as well as homeless, in early 2006, I believe most doctors could have easily identified me as a risk to myself due to my deplorable condition.

3. Early Intervention

I wish I had been diagnosed and treated immediately. If I had been, the voices may not have become louder and more treatment-resistant. Had I begun medication earlier, I probably would have spent less time in the hospital (at over $1,000 a day). Instead, I suffered, and the taxpayers footed the bill.

If I had been recognized as ill, and not just a law-breaker, my two expensive incarcerations would probably have been avoided (at well over $100 a day) as well as court costs. Searching trash for food to eat should have been an unmistakable warning sign that I needed help rather than criminal correction.

4. Working with Treatment Teams

I wish that I had never been homeless and that I had never become sick in the first place.

But once I was diagnosed, I was treated by doctors who prescribed antipsychotic medications. I was ready to see my parents again, and they became my advocates. We lived through a hellish year where I tried many different medications with nothing working well until I found clozapine, which brought me to full recovery. My parents also convinced me to apply for the Social Security income I qualified for because I could not work, and this helped me rebuild my life and eventually afford to live in an apartment nearby the university where I would finish my college degree.

There will always be people who are mentally ill, suffering from delusions, badly needing help, and refusing it, like me. The key is to find these people as soon as possible. Once we find them, treatment teams must never give up and always strive for the highest level of recovery.

MENTAL HEALTH COURTS

Mental health courts are special courts that serve people who have committed crimes they may never have committed if they had not been mentally ill. Some of these courts specialize in adjudicating cases for people who are homeless due to serious mental illness. (There are other special courts in existence today including drug court and veteran's court. Some states, such as Florida and Hawaii, have created girl's court for teenage girls who were abused or otherwise at-risk prior to committing crimes.)

The purpose of mental health courts is to help the people they serve to rebuild their lives. Courts may require participants to attend doctor's appointments, try new medications, engage in counseling or group therapy, or stay in a home or in supported living (rather than choosing to sleep outside). Sometimes, mental health courts require participants to apply for Medicaid, Social Security income, or other benefits. Experts in the program offer help with the paperwork needed to apply for these benefits.

A few years ago, I spent two months auditing mental health courts in downtown Cincinnati. I met compassionate judges and healthcare providers who knew that serving jail time does not cure schizophrenia or other mental illnesses. The goal of the mental health court is to provide the treatment necessary to deal with the root of the problem. The phrase "treatment in lieu of incarceration" is used often to express this approach.

The following describes my experience observing these special courts:

Walking into the courtroom, I noticed the friendly atmosphere. There were 10 to 15 people on the docket for the day. Some attended court once a week. Others attended less frequently. Every week, chips, brownies, and other snacks were laid out on a table in the courtroom. Many of these people seemed comfortable or even to be enjoying themselves.

When the court was in session, participants interacted with the judge as though he were a teacher, a mentor, or a parent. For people sticking to their treatment plans and cooperating, the judge could even become a friend.

One week, I saw a female judge encouraging a young woman who was carefully following her treatment plan and making an effort to rebuild her life. The judge asked about her love of dance, playfully reminding her, "You never know who will become famous!" I also saw a judge reward members of the docket with gift certificates to McDonald's and Cincinnati's Skyline Chili.

Another week, after the court was over, I watched a judge remove her robe, walk into the middle of the courtroom, and hug a young veteran who was on the docket.

Court did not always run smoothly, however. The most difficult issue that a judge had to address was lying. When members of the docket honestly admitted they had used drugs, the judge suggested various interventions, including the use of medications such as methadone. The judges were quick to offer second chances. However, when members on the docket used drugs and lied about it, the judges considered sending them to jail. I watched one judge send a few people to jail over the months that I audited court.

Overall, I was impressed by how honest most members of the docket were. They discussed doctors' appointments, medications, living arrangements, and their goals for the future.

When participants reached a point of rehabilitation where they no longer needed the supervision of the judge, usually over the course of 18 months or more, they "graduated" from the program. Graduates were acknowledged with a ceremony and a reception with cake.

I attended two graduations, along with the family and friends of graduates. At one of the graduations, I watched a young man in tears, thanking the judge and his treatment team for essentially "saving my life." Watching his gratitude for the treatment he received made me wish these courts were available in communities everywhere.

Some people on the docket liked the mental health court so much that by the time they graduated, they were hesitant to leave. Judges welcomed them to come back to visit.

Any patient who qualifies may benefit from a mental health court. Sometimes mentally ill people who commit crimes do not have family or friends to become their advocates, or they refuse contact with them. For people in this situation, mental health courts can act as a compassionate and effective support system. And these courts are far less expensive than the cost of sending people to jail.

4

LOUISIANA MENTAL HEALTH LAW ACT

Louisiana's Act 382 was passed in 2022. It makes it easier to detain a person with severe mental illness, requiring, in many cases, that they be psychiatrically assessed and receive treatment.

BEFORE THE NEW LAW

In the past, people with severe mental illness could not be detained against their will unless they were in imminent danger of hurting themselves or others or were "gravely disabled." Act 382 is necessary to prevent the severely mentally ill from descending into a world of hallucinations, delusions, and other cruel symptoms they may not even know they have. Some persons become homeless due to severe mental illness and may remain so for months or years. (In my case, it was years.) In addition, many people who are not ill enough to be legally detained for evaluation and treatment are still in grave danger of drug overdose or committing suicide. It is hoped that Act 382 will reduce tragic deaths while providing a pathway to diagnosis, treatment, and recovery.

Louisiana's new law recognizes that a person with severe mental illness may need treatment based on the deteriorative nature of the illness itself, not just their behavior. It is noted that half of people with schizophrenia and bipolar disorder likely will not seek help. Today, many families in Louisiana will no longer have to wait for a loved one to become violent to have them evaluated by a doctor. Now the big question is: Will this new law be put into practice or will it be largely ignored?

DISCONTINUATION OF TREATMENT AFTER RELEASE

Many families struggle and feel helpless as they watch loved ones slowly spiral into delusions, hallucinations, and paranoia. Commonly, a patient becomes ill enough to be hospitalized, spends a few days or weeks in a hospital, and sees improvement. However, following his or her release, there is often a quick discontinuation of their medication and other treatment. Many patients think they have been cured and no longer need the medication. Others complain of side effects.

(These complaints should be taken seriously and addressed with changes in the treatment plan, changes in diet, adjusting the dosage, switching to a new medication, or adding a medication to help with side effects.) Sometimes, asking an individual to patiently wait for side effects to diminish or for a medication to work is asking too much, and the person refuses to cooperate.

Often a period of slow and gradual mental decline follows discontinuation of a medication as the blood level of medication inexorably declines and finally reaches zero after a few weeks.

This period following discontinuation of the drug is a crucial time. In rare cases, the patient will be capable of managing their mental health without medication or treatment, at least for a while. However, much more often, symptoms return, sometimes worse than they were originally. Some patients will exhibit an acute psychosis following discontinuation of the medication, as I did.

Persons cycling in and out of the hospital have the highest chances of becoming disabled. Every time they discontinue and then restart antipsychotic medications, the medication may be less effective or ineffective.

MY EXPERIENCE

In 2007, following release from my first hospitalization, I quickly discontinued my medication due to extremely severe side effects. My muscle stiffness, restlessness, weight gain, sedation, and anhedonia (inability to experience pleasure) were nearly unbearable. I felt my doctor had been dishonest with me about the medication, and I imagined that all antipsychotic medications would be the same or worse.

However, two weeks after I discontinued my antipsychotic medication, my parents, whom I lived with at that time, saw my symptoms coming back slowly. I became more paranoid, restless, confused, and childlike. But, because I was not yet technically in danger of hurting myself or others, they could do nothing.

Parents like mine, with loved ones who have discontinued treatment and are spiraling downward, often call the CURESZ Foundation to ask for me and others to share our own experience. I always tell them to watch their loved one closely and to not be afraid to call 988 (before the launch of the new national helpline in 2022 it would have been 911 – see 988 chapter on page 35). If and when their loved one's condition deteriorates enough to meet the standard for involuntary commitment, I encourage them to take the opportunity to try to convince that individual to stay in treatment to begin a new life, while at the same time looking into becoming their legal guardian, to help keep them in treatment.

Long-acting injectables are an option. A guardian can mandate that the patient receive injections to help keep them from experiencing psychosis again. A situation in which the patient willfully consents to an injection, seeing it as freeing because he or she will not have to remember to take the pills, may be ideal.

I'm grateful that my parents called 911 on that day in April 2007 when I had become acutely psychotic after going off my medication. That hospitalization convinced me to have patience through several medication trials until I found the right one. During that time, I did exactly what the doctor recommended. I see that hospitalization as one of the biggest milestones in my life.

After we see whether Louisiana will in fact implement the guidelines outlined in Act 382, we will wait to see if other states will follow.

There has been extensive criticism about the general inability to detain persons for psychiatric evaluation. While it is important to fight for personal independence, it is hoped that mandating that individuals receive treatment sooner will result in long-term future benefits. It is also hoped that once these individuals recover, they will be grateful for their treatment. Being captive to a world filled with hallucinations, delusions, paranoia, and homelessness is not freedom. It is imprisonment. Treatment can set people free.

5

911 AND 988

As of July 16, 2022, all telephone service and text providers in the United States were required to activate the new national 988 mental health hotline. The 988 hotline connects families with mental health professionals who are available at all hours and every day of the year. Similar to 911, this 988 hotline was created in an effort to address psychiatric emergencies all around the country, including the five major US territories. The 988 number also links directly to a veteran's crisis line.[1]

DIRECT CONTACT WITH SUICIDE PREVENTION AND MENTAL HEALTH CRISIS COUNSELORS

Because the 988 hotline will put the family in crisis directly in touch with suicide prevention and mental health crisis counselors, it is hoped that crises will be resolved over the phone. The hotline is supported by the Substance Abuse and Mental Health Services Administration (SAMHSA). Police officers are only dispatched in rare cases.

POLICE RESPONSES TO MENTAL HEALTH CRISES BEFORE 988

I remember a time 16 years ago when the 988 hotline did not exist, and my parents called 911 to deal with my mental health emergency. I had gone off my medication and was acutely psychotic. Fortunately, I was not handcuffed or treated roughly by the police. They respected my dignity, calmed me down, and tried to make light conversation with me, which I appreciated. The crisis was resolved with a hospitalization that was a turning point in my life. Since that time, I have always stayed on my medication and have achieved recovery, which allows me to live a fulfilling, healthy life.

In other cases, patients may not be so fortunate.

I recently interacted with a family whose son appeared to be suffering from psychiatric problems. He had always been friendly, smart, and enjoyed fixing

---

[1] Substance Abuse and Mental Health Services Administration.(2022, July 15). "U.S. transition to 988 suicide & crisis lifeline begins Saturday." Substance Abuse and Mental Health Services Administration. https://www.samhsa.gov/newsroom/press-announcements/20220715/us-transition-988-suicide-crisis-lifeline-begins-saturday.

things. In the 1990s, after the launch of the Internet, he taught himself how to create a personal website. He took his computer apart and put it back together. In addition, he independently learned the computer language Linux.

But what he really loved most was rollerblading, skateboarding, snow skiing, and spending time with many friends. His life was full, and he looked forward to a bright future.

His family never dreamed that one day, severely mentally ill, he would cut off all connections with friends and family members, and lose a job that had once made him financially successful and very happy. In times of good health, he enjoyed the sport of hunting and collecting guns, which he kept with him long into his illness.

Eventually, due to many significant and troubling changes in his life, his father called the police requesting a mental health evaluation. He believed his son was mentally ill and wanted to make law enforcement aware of his gun collection. Unfortunately, this father was largely ignored. The young man had not yet been diagnosed with a mental illness. He was not yet considered a danger to self or others, and he could not be forcibly committed to a mental health facility for evaluation.

A few months later, when he was in the middle of a mental health crisis, neighbors called 911. The young man was shot by police that day and died instantly.

It is my greatest hope that the 988 hotline will save the lives of many Americans struggling with psychiatric crises and help mentally ill persons look forward to a brighter future — a future that many can only achieve when consenting to life-saving treatment.

> **IF YOU OR SOMEONE YOU LOVE IS CONTEMPLATING SUICIDE, SEEK HELP IMMEDIATELY. FOR HELP 24/7, DIAL 988 FOR THE 988 SUICIDE & CRISIS LIFELINE, OR REACH OUT TO THE CRISIS TEXT LINE BY TEXTING TALK TO 741741. TO FIND A THERAPIST NEAR YOU, VISIT THE PSYCHOLOGY TODAY THERAPY DIRECTORY.**

6

A NEW NAME FOR SCHIZOPHRENIA, A BRAIN DISORDER

SCHIZOPHRENIA IS A BRAIN DISORDER

Several years ago, at a church, I met a former professor who had developed Alzheimer's disease. She had become incapable of working at the university but did not know it. When she continued visiting certain classrooms and returning to her old office, which was now occupied by another professor, the university contacted her spouse. He made sure she did not travel to the campus again. No legal action was taken.

When the professor with Alzheimer's disease obtained medical help, her former colleagues consoled the family, calling to mind her many productive and memorable years at the university.

People with Alzheimer's disease, Parkinson's disease, and stroke are generally not held responsible for illness-induced odd or menacing behavior, unlike similar manifestations of schizophrenia. This is simply because Alzheimer's disease, Parkinson's disease and stroke are considered physical diseases, while schizophrenia is classically considered a mental illness.

Had this professor been considered "mentally ill," rather than physically ill, things may have turned out very differently.

I began to behave like this professor in 2002, during my first psychotic episode. Unaware that I was totally disabled, I hid in university campus libraries and lounges, believing I was unconditionally welcome there. Eventually, even while dirty and hallucinating, I remembered who I used to be– the researcher, the violinist, and the honors student. Like the professor, I could not acknowledge or accept that anything had changed.

Finally, Los Angeles police officers picked me up on the university campus and threw me in jail. My crime: trespassing on the campus of a university where I had once been a student. I was behaving like the professor.

If I had been diagnosed with Alzheimer's disease, I would have been treated with compassion, and I would not have been taken to jail. Trained medical staff would have worked with my family and friends to discuss and implement the best treatment option for my highest potential level of recovery.

But legal regulations prevented me from being picked up, and I was not encouraged to begin seriously needed medical treatment for my schizophrenia. Unless I was a danger to myself or others, police left me on the street as per protocol. I had to become severely ill before I was finally forced to obtain help.

In Parkinson's disease, Alzheimer's disease, and other diseases of the brain, early intervention is considered important. Early intervention is also important in schizophrenia. However, many people with schizophrenia suffer for years while the disease progresses before they are ill enough to qualify for evaluation without consent.

When schizophrenia is referred to as a mental illness, it may lead people to believe that odd behaviors are a choice, and not necessarily a medical problem of the brain that requires treatment. This perpetuates the social stigma of schizophrenia.

Thankfully, antipsychotic medications greatly improved my quality of life and allowed me to work and study again. Like a patient with Parkinson's psychosis, I could not control my behavior until I began taking appropriate medication, but treatment offered healing and hope.

It is my dream that someday, people described as mentally ill will be shown the understanding and compassion that is offered to individuals with all other diseases of the brain. Schizophrenia is a brain disease. Individuals with schizophrenia should undergo medical treatment instead of incarceration. Early treatment for schizophrenia is key to achieving the highest level of recovery.

RENAMING SCHIZOPHRENIA

When I was first diagnosed with schizophrenia, I was certain that my diagnosis was incorrect. I thought schizophrenia was an emotional disease or an experience. I thought that people with schizophrenia were weak and eccentric.

But when it comes to having or not having schizophrenia, maybe I was partly right, at least as far as nomenclature is concerned.

The term "schizophrenia" comes from Greek roots. "Schizo" means "split" and "phrenia" means "mind." This name was coined by a physician named Eugene Bleuler in 1908. Prior to 1908, it was called "dementia praecox" (referring to a dementia of younger people).

Today, the medical community recognizes that schizophrenia is not associated with a split mind (formerly termed multiple personality disorder but now called dissociative identity disorder). Rather, it involves a decreased ability to know what is real, often called a "break from reality."

When I was growing up, I never heard of a tsunami, as tsunamis used to be called tidal waves. The name was changed in the 1990s, long after scientists realized that tsunamis were not always associated with the tides. Over the years, names for illnesses and medical conditions have also changed.

In 2007, the diagnosis "mentally retarded and developmentally disabled" (MRDD) became "intellectually and developmentally disabled" (IDD) or simply "developmentally disabled" in many states and in countries worldwide.[1] It is amazing how much this name change has improved the lives of people with developmental disabilities. It has reduced stigma and given developmentally disabled people more dignity.

Manic-depressive disorder is also now called bipolar disorder. Multiple personality disorder recently was renamed dissociative identity disorder. Epileptic seizures, which once were considered mental illness, are now classified as neurological diseases of the brain.

In Japan, the name for schizophrenia was changed to the English equivalent of "integration disorder" in 2002. Integration disorder refers to a person's inability to process information about their environment, which may cause confusion about what is imagined and what is real. Hallucinations come from the brain's inability to process information from the five senses and delusions from the brain's inability to reach logical conclusions about various ideas.

Since this name change, the number of Japanese people recognizing they have the disease has greatly increased. Today in Japan, patients with integration disorder are more likely to consent to or even seek out treatment. This has also led to a greater acceptance of people with integration disorder in the community and a reduction in stigma.[2]

I especially like the name "integration disorder" because it is representative of the symptoms I used to have. When I developed schizophrenia, it was as though my brain could no longer process stimuli in my environment normally. This resulted in hearing voices from inside of my mind.

I also had problems integrating socially. My desire to be alone wasn't bad enough to be considered a sign of illness until I was about 20, and I had lost nearly all of my friends. I always thought it was just me and not a disease. In hindsight, because of schizophrenia, my social integration was abnormal.

Sometimes I wonder: when I was 20, if doctors had told me I had "integration disorder," would I have listened? I don't know. But I do know I would have been much more likely to recognize I had "integration disorder" than to believe I had "schizophrenia."

During my second hospitalization, my doctor sat down with me and explained that schizophrenia was a treatable brain disease and there was no shame in having it. It

---

[1] Prabhala, A. (2007). Mental Retardation is no more: New name is intellectual and developmental disabilities. Society for Accessible Travel and Hospitality. http://sath.org/index.php?sec=741&id=10130.
[2] Sato, M. (2006). "Renaming schizophrenia: A Japanese perspective." *World Psychiatry*, 5(1), 53-55. http://www.ncbi.nlm.nih.gov/pmc/articles/PMC1472254/.

was at that time that I learned the name "schizophrenia" was scientifically unsuitable.

I wish I had had a conversation about what schizophrenia is on the day I was diagnosed, or at least before I discontinued my meds and suffered through a second psychotic break. When I accepted that I had schizophrenia, I complied with medication and treatment. On meds, I rebuilt my life.

I would like to see the diagnostic term "schizophrenia" changed to either "integration disorder" or another name. But regardless, the most important thing is understanding that schizophrenia is a medical disease of the brain. It is treatable today. There is no shame in having any medical illness.

7
DEBUNKING MYTHS OF SCHIZOPHRENIA

Though schizophrenia affects about 60 million people (1% of the world's adolescent and adult population), it remains poorly misunderstood by the public.

Schizophrenia manifests with paranoid delusions and other false beliefs; auditory, visual and other hallucinations or false perceptions; unusual or bizarre behavior; difficulties with thinking; lack of motivation; impaired memory; difficulty making decisions; and the inability to distinguish what is real from what is not. These symptoms usually start in the late teens or early 20s, and are often referred to as symptoms of psychosis.

There are many common misconceptions. Let's clarify the truths about schizophrenia.

- Having schizophrenia is NOT a sign of moral failing or weakness.
- Genetic and environmental factors can both cause changes in brain structure and neurochemistry during fetal life, leading to schizophrenia in early adulthood.
- A person with schizophrenia has ONE personality. Not multiple.
- Behind the forehead is the frontal lobe, which is the CEO of everybody's life. This is responsible for "executive functions" (i.e., the ability to organize thoughts, think clearly, make plans, control impulses, and understand consequences). In schizophrenia, the prefrontal cortex does not function properly, leading to symptoms of disorganization and confusion. Another part of the brain called the limbic system (often called the "seat of emotions") is chemically abnormal in schizophrenia. It can result in psychotic symptoms, including hallucinations (hearing and seeing things that aren't really there), or delusions, which are fixed false beliefs.
- Sometimes the symptoms of schizophrenia include disconnected thoughts and language, trouble putting together coherent sentences, and often neglecting self-care by not showering or eating.

- Schizophrenia can NOT be overcome by willpower.
- Through intervention with antipsychotic medications, the abnormal chemical balance in the brain can be restored. These medications can also strengthen connections among the billions and billions of brain cells and help regenerate growth in the gray and white matter of the brain in several regions.
- Schizophrenia is NOT a hopeless condition.
- Partial or full recovery is possible for many patients. A combination of early intervention, uninterrupted medication, psychosocial rehabilitation, and family and peer support, can help with overcoming symptoms, preventing relapses (which can cause brain tissue loss), and reclaiming lives. With comprehensive treatment, persons living with schizophrenia can achieve their life goals and regain functioning in the three major domains of life — work, play, and love.

Debunking the myths of schizophrenia is an important step to understanding it as a medical condition.

Acknowledgements

Authored by Henry A. Nasrallah, M.D., Professor of Psychiatry, Neurology, & Neuroscience, University of Cincinnati College of Medicine, Helen M. Farrell, M.D., Harvard faculty, Boston Psychiatrist, and Bethany Yeiser, BS.

8

LOOKING BACK AND MOVING FORWARD

PIECES OF LOVE

Sometimes I find it hard to reconcile my past with the present.

Schizophrenia can be a cruel interrupter of life in all it entails.

I found myself on a journey I did not choose and never expected to take. I never dreamed of not graduating from college in 2003, four years after I enrolled at the University of Southern California. I also never expected to become homeless, let alone for four years, and in the same city where I had once been a dedicated student. Before my psychotic break, life was filled with targeted accomplishments, friends, and hope for the future.

Schizophrenia often presents as a ticking time bomb. Until it explodes, there are often no distinct warning signs.

While in high school, I was safe, happy, and thriving. Everyone in my life anticipated that as an adult, I would be highly successful. Sadly, because of my schizophrenia, it later seemed that would never happen.

I found, stored away in a cardboard box, various treasures from my childhood before schizophrenia changed my life. I found little figures made of rocks glued together and painted. There was a green frog and a bright blue creature with big eyes. Both made me laugh and remember youthful joy. The figures reminded me of church summer camp when I was a child, where we made various fun crafts. Each day, when summer camp was over, my brother and I would return to our house and go swimming.

In transferring these long-forgotten friends from the box to a place near my dresser, I blended them into my present life. Daily, I am greeted by love and joy from my childhood.

I also found old notebooks, t-shirts, badges, and "Olympic medals" from a girls' club that three of my friends and I had "founded." The materials were all painted with our club logo. The "Olympic medals" were from a competition we put together with multiple events, including a biking course, a swimming competition, and an obstacle course, running through our five acres of property.

I remember the youngest girl, Annie, won gold. My medal was silver for second place. There was so much love in the friendships of my youth before schizophrenia interrupted my life. The tokens of days past fill out and complete the circle of my life from wellness into illness, and then back again through recovery.

I found a dried-out pen from Israel, a gift from my first-grade teacher who had recently visited the Middle East. It fascinated me. I remember holding it and dreaming of going to Israel. Unfortunately, I never would have guessed that I would one day be deluded to believe that I would help secure peace in the Middle East, as my mind was failing me.

Near the bottom of the box, I found coins I collected as a child from all over the world. One coin from Hong Kong had a hole in its center, surrounded by Chinese characters. I used to hold the coin and dream of visiting Hong Kong one day. I never expected that I would indeed visit Hong Kong, but only while suffering from psychosis associated with schizophrenia. Now the coin is joined with my passport, which contains stamps from all the places around the world where I have traveled.

As I looked through these old treasures, I reflected on my years symptomatic with schizophrenia and isolated from love. The treasures reminded me of the love I experienced prior to the illness. While I was mentally ill, homeless, and isolating myself from family and friends, I suffered from financial poverty as well as a poverty of love. Years later, I would once again allow their love to flow into my life.

As painful as it may be, I realize that my life is a composite of all its different chapters together. Every chapter matters and finds greater significance in a cohesive, ongoing story. When people are affected by a serious illness, a pause or gap occurs. For me, difficult things and good things have joined to make me a more complete and more compassionate person.

My porcelain doll, given to me by a friend, is now in my bedroom on display and brings me joy. She has been freed from the storage box.

Reclaiming the pieces of love from the past and bringing them forward has enriched the healthy life I now live. Today, I am thankful for my antipsychotic medication, which has enabled me to return to a thriving and purposeful life, even though my life took unexpected turns that were more difficult than I would have ever imagined.

But the greatest surprise has been the little pills I take every day that brought me to recovery and enable me to work, volunteer, study, and revive meaningful relationships. I am thankful every day for the chance at a restored life I have been given on medication. When I look at the pen from the Middle East, I no longer believe that I alone can create world peace, but I have greatly enjoyed spending time with friends from Israel.

Schizophrenia can indeed be a cruel interruption of life. But today, there is hope for a return to the things we care about most and help us define who we are. I hope that my current advocacy work will play a small part in bringing peace and comfort to struggling families.

I am a survivor of a brain disorder. I hope that others affected by severe brain disorders can also bring pieces of love from their past into their present to nourish and complete the story of their lives.

STORIES OF HOPE

When schizophrenia left me disabled, I needed proof that others with this illness had reclaimed their lives and that I could too. Reading stories of hope from others with schizophrenia played a vital role in my recovery.

Before I was diagnosed with schizophrenia, I used to think that developing it was one of the worst things that could happen to a person. I did not know that it is a brain disease having some commonalities with stroke and Parkinson's disease, or that it is treatable.

My journey from treatment-resistant schizophrenia to full recovery was not easy, but today, I would like to have it serve as a beacon of hope to others.

Initially, I suffered from symptoms that became severe and eventually left me unable to work or experience the fullness of life. I tried five different medications over 12 months, all of which had severe side effects and little benefit. But, after a year, I finally found an effective medication, and my symptoms began to abate. My symptoms had included hearing voices and seeing things that were not real. Thanks to medication, these were almost entirely eliminated after six months.

With effective treatment, I was finally able to resume a meaningful professional and social life. I regained my ability to play the violin, returned to college, and graduated.

Years ago, I began to use the term "Schizophrenia Survivor" because this is how I feel about myself. Like individuals with other permanent conditions including diabetes, high blood pressure, and arthritis, I will always have schizophrenia. But with effective treatment, I have reclaimed my life.

In an effort to broaden my understanding of what other people with schizophrenia experience, to better understand myself, and to contradict misunderstanding and stigma, I established an online group of "Schizophrenia Survivors" in 2017. These are people from around the country and the world with schizophrenia who live productive and meaningful lives. Every Survivor who shares their story is in treatment, and probably always will be, to remain in recovery.

Like me, they have experienced an "awakening" of recovery in their lives.

With treatment, their symptoms have disappeared, or nearly so. We work, volunteer, and explore hobbies. We enjoy vibrant relationships with friends and family. Our hope has been realized.

It has been suggested to me that success stories like mine are exceptionally rare, and should be ignored, to avoid sparking false hope in struggling individuals. But when I stand in solidarity with other Schizophrenia Survivors, it is clear that we cannot all be the exception to the rule. Each of our stories is different, but they are all stories of hope.

Like me, a few of our Survivors completed bachelor's degrees during their recovery, in economics, information systems, engineering and other fields. Three people went on to graduate with a master's degree in social work, and another is currently in law school. A woman thrives in her work teaching others with severe mental illness to share their stories. Another woman works at a university teaching art.

Some of the Survivors, including myself, experienced thrilling delusions (fixed false beliefs) in the past during the illness. I remember believing I was about to become one of the top 10 most influential people in the world, and that I would soon marry a billionaire, and it is interesting to connect with others who once had similar thoughts.

And yet, with treatment, we have been restored to wellness and full recovery.

Unfortunately, many of us acutely feel the stigma of schizophrenia. Because of this, a few of our Survivors have written memoirs and inspirational blogs under a pen name. Survivors should have no shame in sharing their diagnoses, but the reality of the stigma that is pervasive today can be unforgiving.

When I initially shared my diagnosis, I lost many friends. But today, I stand tall with others who have recovered. There is no shame in having any disease or medical condition, including schizophrenia.

I am honored to be a part of this brave group of "Schizophrenia Survivors." We have beaten this disease and are proud of surviving it.

Our journey continues together.

PART TWO

PREFACE TO PART TWO
by Bethany Yeiser, BS

Over the last 15 years, I have been told many times that my full recovery from schizophrenia is the exception to the rule, or that I must have never actually had schizophrenia because I recovered, even though my symptoms were consistent with the DSM-5 criteria. In 2017, following the establishment and IRS approval of the charitable CURESZ Foundation, I sought out other people like me who were thriving despite a schizophrenia spectrum disorder (usually schizophrenia or schizoaffective disorder diagnosis) to prove that my recovery was not an exception. I wanted to find others who had also experienced their own "awakening."

The 28 brave people featured in this section of *Awakenings* have consented to let the CURESZ Foundation publish their life stories. You can also find them online at CURESZ.org under "Survivors," as well as several other stories.

Survivors have written their stories in first or third person. They vary widely in age, from their early 20s up to their 60s. While some have achieved a full recovery which has lasted over a year, others are celebrating over thirty years of symptom remission.

The medications and treatments Survivors have received to treat schizophrenia also vary widely. All Survivors continue to be engaged in treatment. Although their schizophrenia symptoms are in remission or nearly so, they understand that their neuropsychiatric illness has not been cured and will always need to be managed as a part of their life journeys.

Recovery from schizophrenia is indeed possible. There is always hope to return to a state of mental health.

1

CARLOS LARRAURI
Thriving in Law School

Carlos A. Larrauri, MSN, ARNP, enjoyed a happy childhood with a loving, middle-class family in Miami, Florida. His mother was a Cuban-American and his father immigrated to the United States from Cuba by way of Venezuela. From his earliest years, Carlos was a gifted guitarist and loved skateboarding. Excelling in academics in high school, he attended Miami Killian Senior High School and the School for Advanced Studies, where he took dual enrollment classes for college credit. In 2006, he graduated with summa cum laude honors and as a National Hispanic Scholar. However, looking back, he feels that his work at that time was not his best, and he could have done better.

Entering high school, Carlos felt as though a "switch" had suddenly turned on, and he experienced feelings of isolation and loneliness. He was drawn to musical groups like Nirvana and other grunge artists. In hindsight, he realizes that sometimes artistic or creative lifestyles come with their own risk factors, including more latitude with substance use or disrupted sleep patterns. Some of the musicians he identified with endorsed the artistic subculture of the "stoner" guitar player or skateboarder, and yet he remembers that the music provided him with a sense of identity and validation of feelings that he was unable to fully articulate.

Carlos was exposed to marijuana as a young teenager the summer before high school. He began experimenting with cannabis for the first time, unknowingly searching for a coping mechanism he could not find in normal relationships. At first, it was a weekly activity, but soon, it turned into a daily habit. Daily drug use only aggravated his feelings of isolation. He was unable to fully concentrate, continued to struggle to find his identity, and could not connect with a healthy peer group where students were not using drugs.

At age 18, Carlos remembers his thoughts were like a "broken radio switching between channels." Carlos was going through the "prodrome" phase of schizophrenia (a phase in schizophrenia prior to the first psychotic episode) with behavior changes that would soon progress into a full-blown psychosis. However, like many families, he and his parents saw these behavioral changes as a normal expression of adolescence and were entirely unaware that he would soon spiral into full-blown schizophrenia.

Carlos did well enough in high school to be accepted early into The Ohio State University (Ohio State) College of Medicine for a joint bachelor's/medical school program. If he maintained a GPA of 3.2 in the degree program, he would be guaranteed a place in medical school. Though Carlos had dreamed of becoming an English professor, his father was a physician, and Carlos made the decision to follow in his father's footsteps.

But the subtle early signs of mental illness cast a shadow over his first year at Ohio State. Moving to Ohio presented new challenges. As a Hispanic male, Carlos also began to feel like he was a member of a minority group, though he had never felt "different" growing up in Miami, surrounded by other Hispanic families. He was not prepared for the rigor and responsibility of college and felt isolated again. At that time, he became depressed, found it challenging to get out of bed, and he gained 30 pounds.

In hindsight, he believes he needed to see a counselor, but the stigma of mental illness prevented him from seeking help. When his GPA fell to 1.8 in his second semester at Ohio State, Carlos made the decision to call his mom, ask for help, and move back home.

Back in Florida, Carlos benefitted from a support network including family and many close friends. He soon felt he was back on track. He reflects, "Just like it takes a village to raise a child, that same village is necessary to heal a child's mind."

In 2008, Carlos enrolled at Miami Dade College and completed his associate degree. Shortly after the completion of his associate degree, he won a scholarship to attend the New College of Florida in Sarasota to pursue a bachelor's degree in humanities.

However, while studying for his bachelor's degree, his mental health problems came back to haunt him. He struggled with concentration and memory. He stared at his computer screen, was unable to complete assignments, and was skipping class. He was getting into cars with strangers, obsessed with the party culture, and heavily using drugs.

During his senior year at the New College of Florida, he began laughing and talking to himself, and running or playing basketball for hours at a time, often into the early hours of the morning. While trying to manage his excess energy, he was wholly unaware he was dealing with psychotic symptoms. He soon became preoccupied with religion and changed his academic focus from literature to religion. Carlos remembers this time as the onset of his first psychotic episode.

Entirely out of touch with regular life, he began looking for discarded food to eat on the university campus, picking up partially eaten hamburgers and other trashed food and smoking discarded cigarette butts. He also neglected his hygiene.

At times he realized that he was not well and that something was not right. Yet, he had become like a homeless person on campus.

During that semester, Carlos attended a life-changing meeting with his thesis advisor and his mom. Though his advisor confirmed that Carlos had a right to privacy, Carlos recognized that his mother would always be committed to helping him find his life. Carlos's mother would also soon play a significant role in his journey to wellness.

Carlos's family also had a close friend working at Harvard who was a specialist in schizophrenia in adolescents and children. He recognized Carlos's behavior as a psychosis associated with schizophrenia. This friend emphasized the difference between "access to care" and "access to quality care," hoping to give Carlos the best chance at a return to normal life.

Back at home with his parents again, Carlos and his family assembled the "dream team," including a group of six researchers, physicians, and mental health professionals from the University of Miami. Initially, he received an inaccurate diagnosis of avoidant personality disorder and schizoid personality disorder from other providers, which delayed receiving care. Nevertheless, in December of 2010, at age 22, Carlos was finally diagnosed with schizophrenia. He was prescribed an antipsychotic medication, which enabled him to focus again. He also completely stopped using drugs and would never use drugs from that point forward. This was 13 years ago.

To this day, Carlos is thankful for his "dream team" and the recovery model. He was also empowered to be a part of his health decisions and doctors affirmed that it was still possible for him to have a happy life, full of meaningful relationships and work.

Carlos would not describe his recovery as an "on and off switch," but as a "dimmer." His symptoms gradually lessened. After two months on his medication regimen, his thoughts were clearer and his mood had greatly improved. Carlos found that having a supportive community of family and friends, including membership with the National Alliance on Mental Illness, was key in his recovery. Exercise, diet, and stress reduction techniques were also very important.

At one point, Carlos's doctor said "It's up to you, Carlos. If you take your medication and work towards your recovery, maybe you can still go back to school and graduate."

Carlos did not go back to the campus of the New College of Florida; however, he had already completed all of his classes and only needed to finish his thesis in order to graduate. His advisor arranged for him to be able to complete his thesis at home. Unfortunately, despite finishing his thesis and earning his BA, Carlos did not return to this college campus to collect his degree on stage or graduate with his peers.

After completing his degree, Carlos worked in the food industry, waiting tables and cooking hamburgers. He was also not fully well and would not feel fully recovered for several more months. Considering his future, he made the decision to take community college classes at night to continue his education.

The next year, in 2013, Carlos successfully landed a job with Florida Judge Steven Leifman as part of the 11th Judicial Criminal Mental Health Project, a project at the intersection of mental health and criminal justice. Judge Leifman is an internationally renowned professional working to establish south Florida jail diversion programs and crisis intervention teams, helping people in the criminal justice system transition into housing in the community. Carlos worked for Judge Leifman for nine months, helping disabled persons apply for disability benefits. He felt he had finally found his niche.

Working with the mentally ill in the community under Judge Leifman motivated Carlos to return to school, as he hoped to make a greater impact. He considered both law and nursing. Realizing that a nursing degree was much more accessible, only costing him a few thousand dollars, compared to hundreds of thousands for law school, he chose nursing.

Carlos started his associate of science in nursing (ASN) in 2014 at Miami Dade College. At the start of his bachelor of science in nursing (BSN) program, Carlos continued to learn about mental illness and criminal justice through working the night shift at a maximum security forensic hospital while studying nursing in 2015-2016. After six months, he would give up his position at the forensic hospital which he describes as a "pressure cooker," with Florida's forensic system being one of the worst in the country.

Following the completion of his bachelor's degree in nursing in 2016, Carlos found himself fully recovered and doing his best work. He decided to attend the University of Miami for his master of science in nursing (MSN) degree, graduating in 2017. Upon the completion of his degree, he worked as an adjunct and lecturer at the University of Miami, teaching nursing to undergraduates. Teaching at the college level had always been one of his dreams.

The following year, in 2018, he completed his psychiatric nurse mental health practitioner certificate.

In his recovery, Carlos also collaborated with Matthew Racher, who was in recovery from mental illness as well, to create a band they called "FogDog." To this day, Carlos is an active performer as a vocalist and guitarist with "FogDog." Carlos and Matthew found they shared a vision for a band that "represents a voice inside of every individual struggling with their own mental health."

In 2017, Carlos joined the Board of Directors of the National Alliance on Mental Illness (NAMI) after serving several years with NAMI-Miami Dade County.

Carlos has enjoyed working full-time seeing patients. During his evenings in 2018-2020, he also studied for the LSAT law school aptitude exam, scoring in the 97 percentile. The University of Michigan reached out to Carlos, encouraging him to apply to their law school, and he was accepted to the University of Michigan in 2020 on a partial scholarship. Carlos was also accepted to the Kennedy School at Harvard University on a Zuckerman Fellowship to study for a concurrent master's degree.

Today, while working to complete law school, Carlos studies and works part-time as a graduate student instructor at the University of Michigan. He is a member of the Global Scholars Program, looking at global social justice issues such as human rights, peace, nuclear proliferation, and environmentalism. These topics are discussed through a lens of cross-cultural dialogue within this diverse student cohort from different schools and STEM fields as well as the humanities. He recently gave a lecture on mental health and human rights.

As he looks ahead to graduating from law school, Carlos hopes to work in social justice, mental health advocacy, and human rights. He also hopes to someday find an academic role, working as a professor and is considering working in civil service as an elected or appointed official. This coming summer, he plans to work at a law firm in Washington, D.C.

Carlos never settled for less due to the diagnosis of schizophrenia and encourages others with the illness to dream big and never give up.

Today Carlos looks back on his struggle of dealing with the prodromal phase of schizophrenia in his formative years, at a time when young people decide where to go to college and start their career. Without early intervention, schizophrenia and related disorders can derail a young person. He feels the system of education in the United States lacks appreciation for what people with psychosis go through, and hopes that through sharing his story, there will be more compassion and accessible services to help struggling students achieve their best chance at success in school and at life.

On February 25 of 2023, Carlos married the love of his life, and began the next chapter of his journey.

2

LEIF GREGERSEN
From Hospital Patient to Hospital Faculty

Mental illness came upon me slowly from a young age. When I look back at my school photos, as early as age 9, I see depression written all over my face. My mom suffered all her life from a severe mental illness, experiencing symptoms of depression and psychosis. When I was 10 years old, she attempted suicide, though I was too young to understand what that meant.

At the age of 12, I heard my name called in an empty house where no one was present. This was my first auditory hallucination. I noticed it happened after an exciting weekend with the Air Cadets (a youth military organization based on and partially funded by the regular Canadian military) where I got very little sleep and friends were often calling my name. Over the next few years, it seemed a healthy eight hours of sleep would cause the voices and other symptoms to disappear and restore my sanity. I thought getting enough sleep would always solve the problem. However, it wasn't long before I was unable to bounce back.

Soon after the hallucinations started, and as they worsened, I began to experience mood swings. At one point, I felt high. I imagine this is how I would feel if I had abused drugs, though I never used drugs. I kept talking quickly and irrationally. My parents were alarmed and took me to see my mom's psychiatrist. This doctor suggested I come into the hospital for observation.

I am certain I was diagnosed, but I can't remember if anyone told me what my diagnosis was. My doctor started me on a medication to help me sleep. Upon my release, I was convinced I could do the impossible–use willpower to defeat mental illness. I threw out my medications.

During the next four years, I often experienced periods of deep depression with bouts of mania. I drank to excess, and I suspect some of my symptoms may have been brought on by alcohol consumption. After high school, I lived an erratic life: traveling, chasing my lost dreams of becoming a pilot, and moving in and out of psychiatric wards and hospitals. At about age 30, I relapsed into a deep psychosis and was sent to a hospital again for six long months.

It was during this extended hospitalization that I realized I had to change my life and that it had to be a drastic change. I had lost my home and all my possessions and had no more friends left. It also seemed my family no longer trusted me, and they certainly wouldn't let me stay with them. I realized I couldn't go on like this. I became very serious about my medications, went to all my appointments, and carefully listened to expert advice given to me by my treatment team. I took life skills courses and never missed an appointment with my nurse/therapist.

Eventually, my hard work and ability to teach and engage in public speaking led to employment as a creative writing teacher. In my spare time, I wrote and published my first book, *Through the Withering Storm*, about my journey. I found even more work through my local schizophrenia society, talking about mental health issues to groups such as junior high and high school students, university nursing classes, and even the Edmonton City Police recruit class. After faithfully taking medication and staying in treatment, things kept on getting better.

As my life kept getting better, I needed to stay vigilant with regard to my mental illness. Every two weeks I saw a nurse/therapist who gave me my injection and around once a month I saw my psychiatrist. My psychiatrist had been my doctor when I was first taken to the provincial psychiatric facility when I was 18, and I trusted him completely. One day I went in to see him and he told me there was a new medication given by injection that would work better, and I would need to take it less often. I was reluctant to change medications at first, but after a few weeks, I decided to try it. The medication was a good one, and it wasn't an attempt to save money, as the new medication cost around 20 times what the old one did. The problem was, though it worked well for many, it wouldn't do a thing to help with my psychosis, and the psychosis would come back with a vengeance.

I soon became delusional, hallucinated, and experienced extreme paranoia. About four months later, by Christmas, I had become so paranoid that I believed my neighbors in the building where I lived wanted to kill me. I barricaded myself in my room with a blanket over my head, eating canned meat and crackers to survive, believing that every little sound I made was enraging my neighbors even more. I also told everyone that I was going to move to Vancouver. In the state I was in, that could have been a train wreck. If I had moved, I would have ended up in a welfare hotel and had a very hard time getting proper medication, or even proper food, and I would have been completely alone.

At that time, I was still working a job teaching writing classes at a psychiatric hospital. Ironically, one day, I taught a class in the morning, and by that evening, my dad, who was horrified at my psychosis, called the police. I became a psychiatric patient in a different hospital in my city that night. I have no recollection of it, but my records show that I charged a security guard in a threatening manner. I was transferred to a very clean and comfortable hospital in the suburbs, but I was placed in the locked ward due to the risk of violence (or so they said).

Often, when the nurses came to check on me, they would find me lying behind my bed on the floor. I told them I thought someone was coming onto the ward with a gun to kill me, though they did their best to reassure me I was safe. I had many delusions, one being that a former friend was narrating my activities through the PA system in the hospital ward. Nothing I did or said went without ridicule and comment from my former friend's voice which I believed was coming through the PA. The commentary followed me from room to room in the psychiatric ward, and it took all my stamina to keep from lashing out. I also heard other voices that told me a young woman I cared very much for was being sexually assaulted somewhere on the hospital ward, and only I could stop it. I believed an older man on the ward who was very evil was putting ground-up glass in my food to kill me. I thought I smelled horrible.

While on that ward, I spent almost $5,000.00 on clothes, comic books, and a new phone from the nearby mall. I wanted to throw away everything that wasn't new, and I thought someone had breached the security on my old phone and could read and hear everything I was doing with it.

Even though the symptoms of schizophrenia had taken hold of me, this hospital stay was more pleasant for me than others I had in the past. I had a lot of visitors, including my landlady, my boss from the Schizophrenia Society, and two of my best friends. Once the staff understood I wasn't a threat to anyone, I was sent to the regular ward where I had a chance to play badminton and basketball. I got along well with the other patients.

When I got a chance, I bought a notebook and started writing poems in it. I later scanned these poems I wrote into my computer, and they became part of a book about my ordeal which ended in me being put back on my old medication with only a few changes. One of the things that turned out differently during this hospital stay was that I didn't make many enduring friends, though I had treated everyone with respect. It wasn't that my fellow patients were bad people, but they were dealing with either mental health or addiction issues, and I was ill-equipped to support them as a friend when I was released.

I named the book I wrote from this hospital experience *Alert and Oriented x3*. I got the term from notes my nurse made about me, which I had later requested permission to get copies of and scanned into my computer, and they became a significant part of my new book.

I now am back to living in my large, comfortable apartment and thriving again after my medication mishap. I hope to stay on my current medication which has worked well for me for many years. My days are full now; I have three part-time jobs plus I work as a freelance journalist. One of my jobs still involves teaching creative writing as a wellness skill to people who have psychiatric disabilities, though I no longer work at the psychiatric hospital. My book, *Alert and Oriented x3* has done well, selling a few hundred copies. Currently, I have also published a short story collection that I am hoping will prove I can write fiction with the best of them.

I do not consider schizophrenia to be the end of my life. With medications and treatment, I have academic ambitions again and a real future ahead of me.

I wish my psychiatrist had never changed my medication and that I had never relapsed and ended up back in the hospital. But I would encourage anyone struggling with psychosis to know that psychosis can be overcome with patience, effort, medications, and group and one-on-one therapy. If you are struggling, reach out to a medical doctor or psychiatrist; be as open, honest, and descriptive as you can about what you are experiencing; and get the treatment you need.

With proper care and a good treatment team, recovery is always possible!

edmontonwriter.wordpress.com

3

LIZ RAPP
Managing a Nonprofit and a Family of Five

I grew up in a small town in upstate New York. My childhood was normal, uneventful but happy. However, even in elementary school, I perceived I was different from the other kids, which made me uneasy, and I struggled with weight gain. By high school, I was having delusions, believing there were monkeys living in my parents' home. As I grew older, I thought of suicide, but I hid these feelings from my family.

High school was difficult, but there were bright spots. I studied photography, excelled in English, and was editor of the school's small paper. I was also secretary of the AIDS Committee for the school. Looking back, I believe I was experiencing a mania that enabled me to accomplish all these things. Some days, I would crash hard and go into a very dark place. Fortunately, I had two terrific friends who knew I was struggling.

I managed to graduate high school in 1988 and started college the next fall at SUNY Farmingdale where I studied graphic design. Far away from my family, I experienced an increase in symptoms. I thought my roommate was trying to kill me and that my room was bugged with cameras that were monitoring me.

Needless to say, I didn't do well my first year in college. I came home in mid-April before the school year ended without finishing my freshman year. When I arrived at home, I felt healthier in a safe and familiar environment with my family. But my parents thought I came home early for another medical reason, as I disclosed to them that I had been having migraines, and did not suspect anything was wrong with my mind.

The summer after my freshman year, I started working for a florist, and I loved it. I assisted with orders during the day and learned how to design arrangements. I also learned how to make the perfect bow and many other skills that I still find useful now. I worked there for four months.

My girlfriend introduced me to my future husband who I married in January of 1990, about eight weeks after we met. I became a mother the same year. During this time, my delusions were ever-present and increasingly annoying, but I still held it together.

After my second son was born, my husband started noticing something was not quite right with me. My husband was in the Navy, and we moved to Italy when I was 26 and pregnant with my third son.

Italy was fantastic. The country and people were amazing. We lived on a small island in the middle of the Mediterranean Sea. I was generally happy, but at the same time, my mental health began to spiral downhill. I was unpredictable and edgy. My husband was walking on eggshells, unaware of what would set me off. He did not realize that my delusions were increasing and that I believed there were people watching me with cameras in my house. These delusions were getting more prevalent with each passing day.

After we moved back stateside from Italy, my husband finally convinced me to seek help for erratic behavior, as I had begun to experience both depression and mania and was spending money we didn't have. I was hiding my true symptoms from everyone, aware that most people did not think there were monkeys in their homes. I finally went to a doctor who started me on medication for what she thought was bipolar disorder. I did not stay on the meds she prescribed because I did not think they were helping me, and I hated the way they made me feel. I stopped going to the doctor altogether. I believed I could manage my symptoms on my own as I had done most of my life. My family moved to Ohio from Washington state that same year, in 2004.

My husband and I were not doing well as a couple. The stress of my untreated mental illness was taking its toll on us, though we did not yet know it was schizophrenia. One day, after an argument with my husband, I revealed to him that I was suicidal, and he took me to the hospital. This was the first of many stays in the behavioral health unit.

Shortly after my first hospitalization, I had my first psychotic break. I was actually seeing and hearing the monkeys in my home. I thought they were in the basement keeping me from doing laundry. I was on the phone with a friend of mine and mentioned to her I couldn't do laundry because of them.

I was in and out of the hospital over the next few years, trying to find the right meds and the right treatment team. I was still not very forthcoming with my doctor about all my symptoms, so it took about four years to find the right medications for me. It took another three years to find a treatment team that I felt I could trust and that I liked. Finally, my team identified my hallucinations, delusions, and depression, and gave me a correct diagnosis of schizoaffective disorder.

The transformation after finding the right diagnosis and a great treatment team was amazing.

Following my recovery, I became the loving and present mom that my three sons badly needed. I also began going to school for massage therapy while we were living in Washington state. Then we moved to Ohio, where I started working for a wonderful massage therapy company.

But despite success in both my work and family life, I was still not taking my medication consistently. I would take it until I felt better then stop, thinking I didn't need it anymore. I was hospitalized a few more times but still did not understand that I was only temporarily doing well because of my medication. During my final hospitalization, I realized that I did not want to ever relapse again and began to faithfully take my medication.

In 2013 I went back to school again to be an esthetician (specialist in skin beautification) and I started my own business.

It was hard but I was relatively successful. I loved being an esthetician almost as much as I loved my new job as a massage therapist. I ran my esthetics business successfully for two years.

By 2015, I was working at another massage therapy company as a lead esthetician. But finally, the stresses of working two jobs for almost 60 hours a week along with raising a family became too much for me to handle. In 2015, I wound up having another bout of hallucinations and delusions, seeing monkeys again and believing strangers were taking pictures of me, and I had to close my business.

I was devastated. I hated giving up what I loved doing and a business that I was working hard at.

This time, I worked closely with my doctor and was not hospitalized. I also joined a support group for people with psychotic illness. It happened to be a step group similar to Alcoholics Anonymous (AA). I took the steps to heart. I practiced them every day, and I came to the realization that I needed to change my life and get my illness under control once and for all.

This included many things, but the top three were...

1. **My weight loss journey**, as weight gain had been a problem since high school,
2. **Starting a journal** which gave me a place to express my thoughts, struggles, and feelings without being judged, and
3. **Discovering the world of daily planning.** Daily planning gave me a sense of control over my life and my illness as well as a creative outlet. As I focused on these three things, I was truly doing well for the first time in my whole life.

That same year, I was approached by the leader of my support group and asked to come to the hospital where he was a volunteer to tell my story of success. I have been telling my story of recovery for almost five years now, and I

AWAKENINGS

enjoy it immensely.

In 2019 I started Project Daily Pages, which is a non-profit organization that helps those with mental illness live in recovery to the best of their ability by providing tools, materials, instruction, and support. The goal is to allow them to live more stable, more productive, and more successful lives, as I have done personally.

I am living in recovery now. To the best of my ability, I hope to help others learn helpful techniques I have learned mostly by trial and error over the years. Today, I am happy, successful, and free from nearly all my symptoms.

As I do what I love, which is helping people, my family truly supports me. I would not know what to do without them, especially my husband of 30 years. We have been through a lot together. My boys are grown now. They give me a reason to take my medication. I stay healthy for my family.

What I want people with mental illness to know is you may not get well overnight. Your recovery will look completely different than mine. But that does not mean you are not WILL NOT BE successful. If you are doing all the things in your life that you can to aid your physical and mental wellness, such as taking medication and practicing good self-care habits, then that in itself is a great accomplishment.

4

BRANDON STAGLIN
President, One Mind

Brandon Staglin grew up in Lafayette, a small suburban town near San Francisco, California. At age 7, he remembers his feelings of excitement when his sister was born. He and his sister remain close today. Though Brandon grew up in a small-town environment, his parents often took him and his sister abroad, traveling to Europe, Hong Kong, Singapore, and Beijing. They also went on safaris in Tanzania and Kenya.

As a child, Brandon was advanced academically, and his teachers felt it was best for him to skip eighth grade. He remembers the challenges of studying with students who were all older and more advanced in their social development. He missed his former classmates.

At 14 years old, Brandon traveled to the Three Sisters Wilderness in Oregon where he would learn wilderness training along with 10 other teenagers as part of the Outward-Bound Program. He and his peers would guide rafts down rapids, climb glaciers, and hike to the top of the famous South Sister Peak.

He remembers his first solo trip during training where he was isolated in a wilderness campsite for a couple of days. Alone in the mountains, he began to reflect on principles to live by, realizing the need to believe in yourself and to believe yourself. He became determined to not fear the future and to not regret the past. He also realized that anything was possible and that he could accomplish great things. To this day, Brandon still thinks back to his meditation while alone in the wilderness and still holds these principles dear.

From his early years, Brandon was a science fiction fan and dreamed of building the world's first interstellar spacecraft. This motivated him to excel throughout high school, taking advanced placement classes during his junior and senior year and always achieving 5, the highest score.

In addition to academics in high school, Brandon participated in track and intramural soccer. He also served as captain of the soccer team during his senior year, playing center half back.

Brandon traveled to Switzerland at age 16 as an exchange student, staying for six weeks with a family that only spoke French. While in Europe, he enjoyed perfecting his French, as well as mountain climbing and integrating into a new culture. He also began to think seriously about his college plans. A friend who traveled with him to Europe was about to leave for Dartmouth College, and after some serious thought, Brandon made it his new goal to study engineering at Dartmouth. In addition to their excellent engineering program, he looked forward to living in an area near open wilderness.

Brandon's hard work in school paid off, and he realized his dream, winning a National Merit Scholarship to attend Dartmouth College following his senior year of high school.

Despite the excitement of beginning classes at Dartmouth, Brandon experienced serious culture shock in New Hampshire. The college environment was very different from the small town where he had grown up. He remembers the "prep school" environment, which he was not used to. However, he was able to make a few close friends. Brandon finished his first year in Dartmouth's engineering program successfully, achieving a 3.7 GPA.

Back home for summer, Brandon looked for a paying job, but found it much more difficult than he anticipated. He eventually decided to volunteer at the Oakland Zoo to study the behavior of chimpanzees. While at Dartmouth, Brandon had added a second major, anthropology, and he felt the study of chimpanzees would complement this other major.

In addition to a stressful job search, during the summer after his freshman year, Brandon broke up with a serious girlfriend. He experienced significant anxiety, and for the first time in his life, felt he could not stop ruminating on his thoughts. He found himself unable to focus on work and unable to communicate effectively with others.

Increasingly anxious and stressed, Brandon soon took a turn for the worse. He began to feel that all the stress and tension he was experiencing came to a point on the right half of his head, behind his right eye, and that the tension had snapped. Suddenly, all the emotions that he was used to feeling about people in his life and memories from the past became inaccessible. He could not even recognize his feelings anymore.

With the sensation that half of his mind had disappeared, he felt that any new experiences and the awareness of his surroundings would only form through the right side of his body, and this would create a new personality. He recalls his mind becoming a "dark vortex of dread."

Unable to sleep, Brandon began wandering around his community looking for a place where he could close his eyes and not be distracted, hoping to bring back the "right half" of his mind by sheer willpower. This search for solitude culminated when he was driving the freeway at 2:00 in the morning with his eyes closed. Hearing police sirens, he woke up, found himself swerving in and out of control, and became afraid, unsure of what he would say to the police. He passed a sobriety test but was still apprehended for reckless driving.

Police suspected him of using alcohol or cocaine. He was mandated to stay the night in a holding cell until his breath test came back negative in the morning, when he was finally released. Even though he had not slept for five days, he had not been able to sleep in the holding cell.

Following his night in jail, he was given a free bus pass. He picked up his car, which the police had parked for him in a nearby parking spot. He spent the rest of the day wandering around the community, still looking for a quiet place.

Later that day, afraid that his heart would stop after five days without sleep and unable to recognize that he was having a psychotic break, he called for an ambulance. However, emergency medical personnel could find nothing wrong with him. He did not mention to them that he had been unable to sleep.

Brandon's parents had left on a trip to France a few days prior to his first psychotic episode. After his quick discharge from the emergency room, he decided to telephone a friend from high school, admitting that he was in desperate need of medical help, though he could not find the words to communicate what he was feeling.

Together with his high school friend, Brandon drove to a local psychiatric hospital in Walnut Creek, California. At first, Brandon did not want to admit he was struggling with a mental illness or enter the psychiatric hospital as a patient. However, following an evaluation at the hospital, he was informed that if he did not check in voluntarily, he would be involuntarily committed. Not wanting to have an involuntary commitment in his permanent legal records, he consented to enter the hospital for a three-day hold.

Because he appeared agitated, on his admission, Brandon was placed in an isolation room for an hour, which he found frightening. Meeting with other people who exhibited strange behavior felt uncomfortable, and he could not relate to them.

Following admission, Brandon was not seen by a physician for a day and a half, and then was offered no specific diagnosis, though he was told he had a thought disorder from a chemical imbalance in his brain. While in the hospital, he continued unsuccessfully to get back the right half of his mind through willpower.

Brandon was prescribed the medication thiothixene (Navane) which made him agitated. He remembers Navane as "stifling," as though there was "thunder and lightning in my head." The evening he started Navane, he tried to make a run for it and leave the locked ward. Tackled by a group of hospital staff, he was injected with a sedative for sleep. Brandon was then hospitalized again.

After his parents' return from France, they took Brandon home from the locked ward against his doctor's recommendation. Brandon and his parents managed to find a good psychiatrist who they could trust, though Brandon felt marginalized and resentful from the hospitalization. He was diagnosed with schizophrenia soon after, in 1990.

Brandon's new psychiatrist took him off Navane and tried another medication, trifluoperazine (Stelazine) which gave him a seizure. Despite nearly intolerable side effects, with his parents' encouragement, Brandon worked with his doctor to adjust his medications and consistently took them as prescribed.

After trying various medications for a few months, which were mostly ineffective, Brandon grew depressed and became suicidal, feeling he had lost everything. He experienced delusions, believing that if he made small mistakes, he would be thrown into hell forever. These delusions were very real to him and left him scared and exhausted. He hoped that he would make right choices and then die in his sleep shortly after. His medications did not help with these delusions.

He recalls a night when he was sleeping in his parents' front yard in a sleeping bag under the stars, hoping that he would die in his sleep on a moral high note to enter heaven. During that night Brandon suddenly remembered his primary goal—to build starships. He realized there was so much more in life to see, experience, and do. He left his sleeping bag outside and came back into his parents' home, determined to fight and not give up on his dreams.

The next medication Brandon tried was clozapine. After a few weeks, he found it to be the only medication he tried that was both tolerable and effective.

Thanks to clozapine, a sense of purpose, and a loving family unconditionally supporting him, Brandon began to get well. For some time, he could not feel his parents' love, but knew it was there, and knew he wanted to feel it again. He was determined to recover. On clozapine, he began auditing classes at Berkeley. He also contributed to his community by volunteering at the zoo again, and at the Marine Mammal Center near Sausalito, helping sick and injured seals and sea lions. Brandon's dream was to return to Dartmouth, which he successfully did in January of 1991.

Back at Dartmouth, Brandon carefully hid his diagnosis, expecting no one to empathize or understand, so he struggled socially. It took a few years for him to achieve grades as high as he had earned his first semester. But with treatment compliance and a strong will, Brandon graduated with his engineering bachelor's degree in 1993 with honors.

Following graduation, Brandon took a job at an engineering firm in Silicon Valley called Space Systems Loral where he designed communication satellites for various companies as well as the federal government. For three years, he worked successfully full-time, faithfully taking clozapine.

Ambitious for his future, Brandon finally decided to return to school to study engineering in a graduate program. He was accepted at Stanford as well as his dream school, MIT.

While on clozapine, Brandon slept nine hours a night. Planning for the future, he realized that he could not thrive in a master's degree program without regularly studying late into the night. He had been stable for years without a psychotic relapse and hoped to be able to live without needing any antipsychotic medications. Planning for life at MIT, he discontinued clozapine.

Six months after discontinuing clozapine, while working, Brandon suffered his second major psychotic break. He experienced tactile pain, feeling as though he was being stabbed with knives in his head and side. He began to experience what he had felt before — that the two halves of his brain were not working together. Because he could not sleep or concentrate, he was admitted to the University of California at San Francisco Hospital for a week in 1996. A retrial of clozapine was ineffective. This time, he was prescribed a cocktail of medications including olanzapine, lorazepam, paroxetine, and risperidone. Brandon describes himself as "stable" at that time, but not thriving. He would never begin graduate engineering studies.

Out of the hospital, Brandon moved into a small San Francisco apartment where he would be near his psychiatrist. He could not work or socialize normally, was unmotivated, and felt entirely alone.

About that time, in 1995, Brandon's parents founded the nonprofit organization International Mental Health Research Organization (IMHRO) which they later renamed One Mind.

From its onset, One Mind always supported research into better treatments for schizophrenia. One of the first initiatives of One Mind involved a clinical trial on cognitive training at the San Francisco Veteran's Affair's Medical Center, spearheaded by Professor Sophia Vinogradov. Brandon took part in this trial as a subject. The project involved brain training exercises on a computer an hour a day for five days a week over a period of two months.

Participating in the program took discipline, but Brandon hoped the cognitive training would enable him to feel better and progress in his recovery. He also felt he was contributing to science by helping others.

This experience was a turning point in his recovery. On completing the program, Brandon was able to focus better on conversations and in general, which researchers believed resulted from the strengthening of neural pathways. Cognitive training helped Brandon get past a plateau he had reached on medications alone.

Following completion of the cognitive training program, Brandon moved back from his apartment in San Francisco to the Napa Valley, where he would live at his family's home again. In 1998, he began to work for his family's vineyard. He taught himself HTML website coding from a book and created a website for the vineyard, working as the site's webmaster for a few years.

About that time, Brandon encountered a family whose son's journey through schizophrenia was remarkably similar to his own. Off medication, he had also had a similar relapse to Brandon's. Meeting this young man's family helped Brandon learn the value of mental health advocacy, and Brandon began to consider the injustice and inadequate treatment of millions of persons around the world struggling with schizophrenia. He developed a new goal: to help people with schizophrenia around the world improve their lives.

The medication aripiprazole was approved by the FDA in 2004, and Brandon was switched to this medication in 2005. At first, the medication made him restless, which he dealt with by exercising for hours at a time. But after committing to exercise, he lost 50 pounds he had gained on other medications. And with exercise, the medication was tolerable.

In 2005, hoping to make a positive impact, Brandon joined One Mind as the Director of Communications. That same year, in the fall, he met the love of his life. For the next decade, Brandon worked both for One Mind and the Staglin Family Vineyard. In 2015, he joined the Board of Directors of One Mind.

In 2017, Brandon decided to move forward in his career by earning a master's of science degree in healthcare administration and interprofessional leadership at the University of California in San Francisco. He was open about his schizophrenia with the university, and the university was welcoming and supportive. Halfway through the program, which lasted 18 months, he was promoted to President of One Mind.

Today, Brandon continues to serve as President of One Mind and helps with his family's vineyard on the side. He is celebrating 14 years of marriage and still lives near family in the Napa Valley.

Brandon has been symptom free since the early 2000s. In recovery, he sometimes experiences feelings of mild paranoia when not getting enough sleep or under a great deal of stress, but he easily recognizes it when it begins. With enough sleep and rest, it resolves quickly.

Today, Brandon is an avid guitar player. In 2017, he performed an original song he wrote about schizophrenia recovery at four events around the United States, including at Mental Health America's national conference and at One Mind's annual fundraiser. Today, as Brandon leads One Mind as President, he continues to balance his hard work with practicing guitar at home, which enhances his personal life's sense of meaning.

Brandon would encourage anyone struggling with schizophrenia to hold on to hope, have aspirations, and always make plans. He remembers that, even while ill, finding meaning was still within his reach with good treatment and family support. He also believes it is important for the patient to participate in their own care and recovery.

For family members, it is important to know that symptoms of illness can mask a loved one's aspirations and personality. But treatment can make a person's goals and personality shine through. It is vital to never give up on your loved one with schizophrenia. And it is also important for people living with schizophrenia to never give up on themselves.

Brandon believes in the power of purpose and of love from family and friends in his healing and eventual full recovery and is particularly grateful for his family for never giving up on him. He is proud of his and his family's contribution to the recovery of thousands through the work of One Mind.

Today, One Mind is a nonprofit catalyzing visionary change through science, business, and media to transform the world's mental health. Through Brandon's work with One Mind, he aims to create a world where all facing brain health challenges can build healthy, productive lives.

www.OneMind.org

5

CHRISTINA BRUNI
Thriving as a Librarian and Advocate

Christina Bruni was diagnosed with schizophrenia in 1987, soon after graduating college with a BA in English.

In 1987, when she was 22, her beloved Sicilian grandfather slipped into a coma and was hooked up to a respirator in an intensive care unit. The experience was Christina's breaking point.

At 5:00 pm on a Friday, she experienced paranoia and delusional thinking. Christina thought that the government was after her and that the world was ending. She thought a person would kill her and was fearing for her life, though she didn't hallucinate or hear voices. By 9:00 am that Saturday her mother had driven her to the ER.

Christina was given medication within 24 hours. Three weeks later she had no symptoms. Her current doctor lists her condition as paranoid schizophrenia in remission. She has been symptom free since that time, thanks to medication.

However, the mental health staff at Christina's day program held the belief that recovery wasn't possible. But even then, she believed in her vision of recovery. Her goal was to obtain a full-time job and live in her own apartment. She achieved this goal within three years of having her breakdown.

Christina and her psychiatrist made the decision to wean her off all medications in 1992. However, Christina soon found she was unable to function without the antipsychotic medication. Since that time, she has taken her medication everyday as prescribed. Christina credits her success to her ongoing treatment. Today, she has been in full symptom remission for over 30 years.

In June 2000, Christina graduated from Pratt Institute with a master's in library and information science (MS). Today, she is a member of the Beta Phi Mu librarian honor society.

She has worked for over 20 years as a professional librarian in an urban public library. Fifteen years ago, she found her niche to be career services, helping others find jobs that fit well with their skills and interests. More than 85% of the individuals she created resumes for over the last 15 years have obtained job interviews that led to job offers.

Since 2005, Christina has been the *"Bruni in the City"* columnist for City Voices, a peer-to-peer mental health newspaper. In 2020 she started to alternate this original column with her new Career Corner articles. These articles are available at www.cityvoicesonline.org.

Christina understands that life can be hard for everyone living on earth. Her early life was difficult, and she prefers to keep this private. In July 2000, when she was 35 years old, her recovery took off when she started her librarian job.

She has been a motivational speaker since 2002, talking with peers, family members, college students, teachers, counselors, and the general public. Christina wants you to know that you can have a full and robust life of your own design while living in recovery from schizophrenia. An optimist, she firmly believes that your greatest pain can be the catalyst for figuring out your life's purpose. Her goal is to advance joy, love, peace, and understanding in the world.

In addition to being a speaker, author, and librarian, Christina is an athlete. The achievement she is most proud of is her ability to deadlift 205 pounds at the gym.

Christina's full recovery is documented in her first book, *Left of the Dial: A Memoir of Schizophrenia, Recovery, and Hope*. The premise of *Left of the Dial* is that getting the right help right away resulted in a better outcome. Christina healed via medication and by engaging in creative pursuits with art, music, fashion, books, and writing.

Her second book, *Working Assets: A Career Guide for Peers: Finding and Succeeding at a Job Living with a Mental Illness*, was published in October 2022. It details real-life strategies, first-person accounts, and resources for finding and succeeding at a job that is right for you.

The best advice Christina can offer about living in recovery is that having a support network can make all the difference. It can be as simple as sharing a meal with friends. Finding what gives you joy can help when you're going through a hard time. Be open, curious, and receptive to new people and possibilities.

www.christinabruni.com
www.workingassetscareerguide.com

6

LAURIE RUSSELL*
When a Patient Becomes an Academic

Laurie's first contact with mental health services took place in 2005 when she was still at secondary school, and she cut her hand with a craft knife for no apparent reason. At the beginning, nobody suspected anything more than a "teenager's mood disorder" or even a kind of "typical" self-injurious behavior found in girls of her age. Laurie, however, did not carry out the act out of distress, impulsivity, or sadness. Instead, she had always claimed that she was not the one who did it, that she was not in control when it happened–someone else told her to cut her hand. Even her child psychiatrist dismissed her claims as manipulative excuses indicative of an emerging borderline personality disorder, and this "someone else" in her mind was a sign that she was "communicating her distress clearly." Her child psychiatrist found her difficult to diagnose and determined she had clinical depression.

Disillusioned and severely let down by her first adult psychiatrist, as she started her undergraduate studies in pharmacology, Laurie's condition deteriorated. The other person from outside her own mind told her to injure herself more and more severely to the extent that it became life-threatening. Still, Laurie denied that she wanted to do any of this. She developed the idea that her blood was contaminated with messages "from the air," that her thoughts were not hers but were accessible from her handwriting, and that none of these belonged to her own self. None of these were of her own volition. She was a puppet under the control of some sinister force.

Laurie's other symptoms included somatic passivity, thought interference (especially thought insertion) and associated self-disturbances. Delusions of persecution and auditory-verbal hallucinations were present although they were not as severe as the former three. As she continued to spiral downwards, she hit her lowest point, a serious suicide attempt in November 2008 that she insisted was not her own behavior.

When she was found by the police, she was forcibly committed (called "sectioned" under British legislation) to a psychiatric hospital. And sadly, Laurie was

---
*The name has been changed to protect the privacy of those involved in the story.

handed back to the same psychiatrist who discharged her with no follow-up care at all. Her future husband (then partner) arranged for her to seek a second opinion, and she was finally diagnosed with schizophrenia and put on an antipsychotic medication. This, for Laurie, was absolutely life-saving. She also requested a new psychiatrist in the National Health Service. Despite a few more hospitalizations and changes in medication in 2009 and 2011, she has not been an involuntary patient for over 10 years.

Although she had to take a whole year away from her undergraduate studies, she managed to gain the highest mark in her final year research project and a year later she was awarded a distinction in her master's degree (the highest classification) in psychiatric research methods. She thinks her psychotic break helped her choose her future career in psychiatric research. In 2014, she was able to secure a UK Medical Research Council-funded PhD studentship focusing on studying cognitive neuroscience of early psychosis, including the early stages of schizophrenia. She successfully passed her PhD oral exam three years later with only minor corrections. Although she continues to take her medications, she is also no longer in need of psychiatric care. Today, she works with a general practitioner and no longer needs psychiatric care from mental health services.

More recently, Laurie secured a tenured permanent academic position in mental health research at a prestigious British university. While her personal experience, especially that of a fragmented self-consciousness, inevitably informed, if not inspired, her own research, she views herself not as a psychiatric patient but as an academic and researcher who stands on equal footing with everyone else at her stage of the career. She does tend to downplay her psychiatric history, not always because of potential stigma (despite this being a sad yet relevant concern), but because she does not wish to be defined by a label (either given by psychiatrists OR by other patients). And there is so much more to what she can offer than simply being a psychiatric service user.

When a patient becomes an academic, it means that nobody should be limited by their experiences of mental illness alone. It means that it is still possible to thrive despite a lifelong diagnosis such as schizophrenia.

Laurie hopes she will continue to contribute to her beloved scientific field and to the wider society and engage in influential research that has real-life benefits so that more patients, should they choose to, can become academics.

7

MATTHEW RACHER
Musician and Peer Specialist

I have fond childhood memories of my early years growing up in South Miami, Florida. On weekends I would play with kids in the neighborhood. One day, a water line broke and flooded the streets. My local neighborhood friends and I built mini boats and rafts to float alongside the parked cars.

I went to high school down the street at Gulliver, a college preparatory school with excellent faculty and an array of extracurricular activities. I became heavily involved in musical theatre, casting for lead roles in Grease, Into the Woods, and Once Upon A Mattress. After graduation from high school, I went off to college in Cleveland, Ohio, at Case Western Reserve University in fall 2004. I was interested in studying business and connecting with other like-minded students who had an interest in music.

During my undergraduate studies, in the winter of 2005, I began to experience noticeable feelings of depression and anxiety. I started to sleep through classes and stay up all night. I was becoming socially distanced.

I remember in my freshman year I auditioned for an on-campus a cappella group as a baritone singer. I was so ecstatic to have been offered a position. But as my depression kicked in, I became less and less interested in singing and all my other musical interests. When my depression started to hit full force, I began to self-medicate with drugs and compulsive gambling. I entered a dark hole: one in which I couldn't stand to be present in my life. I felt I had to escape by any means possible.

In 2006 I transferred to the University of Miami near my parents' home, and I lived with my parents. When I moved back in with them, I took all my escapist coping tools with me, including marijuana and compulsive gambling. Drug addiction and gambling became my closest friends. All my dreams and hopes seemed to be a distant and unreachable dimming flicker of light.

While living with my parents, they noticed I was experiencing a decline in my mental health. I was more isolated than ever, shuttered in with a mind filled with incoherent thoughts. I would sleep all day with the window shades down. I recall a decline in my personal hygiene. My depression had taken over, and I felt as though my life were over, as if I were trapped in an existence that was merely a shell of who I once was.

My parents brought me to see a psychiatrist. I began engaging in psychotherapy two to three times per week. Several medications were prescribed including bupropion, sertraline, and lamotrigine. I started taking the medications, and although they helped for a short while, I would always resort back to old habits and my own ways of escaping reality. I began to mix the marijuana use with the medication and spiraled down even more.

In 2009, while still living at home with my parents and attending classes locally at the University of Miami, I suffered my first psychotic break. I recall feelings of intense paranoia that compelled me to obsessively look through the blinds of my window. I was convinced that the FedEx delivery driver was sent to my house by the FBI. I remember pacing back and forth with racing thoughts consuming my mind. I thought the world had ended, and it was my fault.

My parents noticed that my behavior was off, and we met again with my psychiatrist. He recognized that I was experiencing psychosis and prescribed aripiprazole (Abilify). On this medication, my symptoms started to slowly abate. A year following my psychotic break, I was able to focus more on school, and I graduated from the University of Miami (UM) in May of 2010 with a BA in psychology and a minor in music business. I was only able to graduate from UM because I was adhering to medication and determined to make it through my undergraduate studies.

In 2010 I suffered a life-shattering loss. My closest friend from high school died by suicide. When I heard the news, it felt like an earthquake to my body and soul. I'll never forget sitting in my room completely shaken by the news of this loss. Unfortunately, this drove me to escape into my negative ways of coping instead of embracing a process of mourning the loss.

After continuing to sink further into depression and marijuana use, I experienced another severe psychotic episode in 2011. I recall waking up and feeling a powerful surge of newly found energy. I called everyone in my contacts and apologized to them, letting them know how much I loved them. Delusional, I remember feeling a strong sense of guilt, believing that every family member or loved one in my life had been negatively affected by every decision I had made in the past.

Soon after, while acutely psychotic, I ran away down the street, barefoot, as my father chased me. I was taken to the psychiatric hospital in South Miami for nearly three weeks. To this day I still believe that a significant catalyst for my second psychotic break was my avoidance of processing, embracing, and mourning the death of my friend. While in the hospital, I endlessly searched through the dimly lit corridors for my friend who I had lost to suicide.

Today I am thankful to have had insurance and the resources to cover such an extensive hospital stay.

After this stay in the hospital, I returned home to what was a long road ahead, a road in which my family and support network tried everything possible to reintegrate me back into a level of connection within my community, and I continued taking Abilify. My parents drove me to doctor's appointments, peer support groups, and local clubhouse events. My father offered me a job in his office so I could develop and build on work-related skills. My mother drove me to NAMI (National Alliance on Mental Illness) meetings and became passionate about volunteering with the Miami-Dade affiliate. She and a few other NAMI members helped revitalize and grow the local chapter into the remarkable organization it is today.

At that time, I also made a friend named Carlos who had similar mental health challenges. Carlos and I discovered our shared love of acoustic rock music and eventually formed a band, known as "FogDog." To this day, we travel to different communities, spreading the message of hope through original music.

I have never felt more grateful for my recovery than I am today. I feel a sense of purpose in giving back to a community that has allowed me to grow to where I am now.

I am currently working as a certified peer specialist and was recently awarded state certification through the Florida Certification Board. I recently graduated with my Master of Social Work degree and look forward to continuing work in the field of mental health and harm reduction counseling. I plan on working toward licensure to support individuals in achieving their mental health and substance abuse recovery goals, especially within the field of early intervention treatment and care for psychosis. I hope to continue my work to improve the reach of sustained community-based mental healthcare.

I would not be in a position today to help and serve others within my community if it were not for medication, the support of my family, and NAMI Miami-Dade.

When I look back on my experiences from the dark depths of isolation and despair to the light of hope, support, and connectedness, I can only hope that others find it within themselves to never give up and to know that they are not alone. Only together can we discover the strength to quiet this voice and instill a sense of belonging and purpose.

I hope others can find the support and resources to pave a path towards their own light, purpose, and path of self-discovery and realize that recovery, in the face of pain and adversity, is, in fact, an actualization of our most unique, courageous, and resilient qualities. If we hold onto this path and never give up, our individual stories will serve to guide others.

8

J. PETERS*
Author and Social Worker

Schizophrenia snuck into my life in college. I was starting my last semester at Binghamton University in upstate New York. I had no idea I was getting sick (a common symptom of schizophrenia called anosognosia). Something seemed wrong with everyone else, primarily Binghamton University and the English department. I was so confident in my perception that when people suggested I was sick, I didn't listen to any of them.

It was my last year of college, so most of my friends had already graduated the previous semester. There had been 8 or 10 of us friends living together for 4 years, and I missed them. I panicked after spending the summer before my senior year with my remaining two friends. I realized I didn't have a real plan after graduation. After all, I was going to graduate with a degree in English. The job prospects and reality of beginning my life were daunting. In hindsight, I realized my anxiety at that time was beyond normal in its intensity.

I spent the last summer in Binghamton taking classes. After spending the summer and almost the entire year at school without returning home, it became clear that I had a real fondness for the university and being a student. While many say college was the best years of their life, I took it a step further. I began preparing to become a lifetime student when I applied to the English PhD program while completing my last year as a bachelor's student. Though many of my friends and peers were applying to PhD programs, they could envision life after the program and saw more education as a stepping stone to a career. I planned to be a student forever.

I was enthusiastic and eager to learn about language, new words, and philosophy in college. Though I always planned to be a student, I had other lofty ambitions. After getting my PhD, I would use my newly found language understanding to become an English professor.

I was just one semester shy of getting my bachelor's degree. To finish my degree early, I planned to complete 19 winter credits in 4 weeks at 4 universities.

---

*The name has been changed to protect the privacy of those involved in the story.

This was an unrealistic and unhealthy pace, as many students were reluctant to take more than four credits at the same time. The anxiety involved in taking on so many credits would eventually contribute to my first full-blown psychotic break.

Shortly after the winter session began, I received an email informing me of my rejection from the doctoral program in English. I was left in total disarray, feeling betrayed and increasingly confused about the events unfolding around me at the university. Despite being rejected and without a workable plan to keep studying at Binghamton, I hoped for the best for my status as a student. My determination to stay optimistic and keep pressing forward in the face of rejection was becoming delusional. The delusional system at work in my mind would only grow more complex as the spring semester unfolded.

That was when I angrily emailed the department to petition my entry into graduate classes. My presence in the department became increasingly visible. The staff started complaining about the course petitions and that it seemed like I was forcing my way into the graduate program. While I had the best intentions, my behavior was becoming increasingly erratic. The department eventually contacted the dean and the university ombudsman. According to the dean of students, I was described as "alarming." They enacted rules to establish boundaries between the department staff and my ongoing presence in the office. I wasn't allowed to enter the graduate school area of the department office, a restriction put into place by the university ombudsman.

My biggest problem at the time was the paperwork involved in petitioning the program for permission to begin graduate classes. At one point, I would need to hand the English department secretary a piece of paper signed by the professor of the petitioned class. All this was before course registration took place on the Internet.

At the time, I experienced symptoms impacting my mood. I was becoming increasingly grandiose. I was entitled to be admitted to any academic program I chose. I developed an obsession with English history, especially King George III, the king in power during the American Revolution and during the aftermath after England lost. In my mind, I had a special relationship with the English language, like how King George had control of all facets of English life, including language, as a monarch.

I invented a word on my own, "meta-power." This was when my delusions began to develop, and I became fixed on specific themes that seemed to consume my thinking. One of these delusions was that I could write a new journal article I intended to publish. It was titled "Contesting Admission." This journal article would feature my new word, "meta-power," and I believed it would turn around the recent adverse events in my life. I expected the paper would overturn the admission. I had such high hopes for the article, I conceived it as a "super weapon" as is used in war, changing the tide of my circumstances.

I entered the English department office before the deadline passed to add classes. In my hand was a course petition. As I knocked on the door to the office where I was not welcome, I compared my situation to the American Revolution. I remembered the shots heard around the world in Lexington and Concord. This knock was heard around Binghamton University, but nothing significant came out.

That was when the graduate secretary of the English department picked up the phone and called the police. I still remember walking into that office, looking up, and watching the secretary as she picked up the phone and said, "I am calling the police."

Believing I was a victim, I didn't think the police would do anything or respond to her call. I was wrong again. Within minutes, the university police arrived. They handcuffed me in the department corridor and walked me out of the building, only to put me in the police car and take me to the university barracks. Very much visible and now on everyone's radar, I found myself handcuffed to a pole in the university police barracks.

I was left handcuffed for hours in the barracks, crying uncontrollably. The police gave me a citation for loitering. While in custody, I was still lucid enough to interact somewhat sensibly. Fortunately, the only infraction I had committed was disobeying the ombudsman's rule. The district attorney dropped the charge when my case went to trial months later.

The police incident frightened me. I was anxious about my status at the university after I was arrested. I was preoccupied that the university would take further harsh action against me. I started to get paranoid at this point. I felt like I could not turn to the university for clarification on moving forward with my education, and I was left isolated and agitated. Unfortunately, in my case, the trauma of my arrest and isolation from support, including losing my friends and staff members at the university, only hastened the progression of what would be later understood as symptoms of schizophrenia.

At that time, it was as though I went into exile, losing touch with many more friends and staying away from campus. My symptoms improved somewhat with less intense stress, but these symptoms would soon return in full force. I began to hear voices in the upstairs area where I was living. I was confused and didn't know if I was an undergraduate student or a graduate student or if perhaps, I had even graduated. I thought I might be in a unique program for only the most gifted students, which was not communicated to me for a critical, unknown reason.

I began to think I could transmit thoughts from myself to another person's mind and influence their thinking. I was soon convinced I could read people's minds. Anytime I saw literature posted on a wall in the community, I believed it had to do with me and my situation as a student.

AWAKENINGS

As my symptoms worsened, it became harder and harder to study. In my final class, I was hallucinating and hearing so many voices that I wasn't sure if it was the teacher talking to me or voices. Ironically, the class was titled "Voices of Foucault," which didn't help. I was already normalizing the onset of what were auditory hallucinations. I thought to myself, "This is intense! A whole new world!" In hindsight, I was making up my reality to cope with feeling disconnected, unaware that I was floridly psychotic.

The voices manifested as old friends: faculty members, sometimes as my parents, and as various other people I had known throughout my life. I often heard my mother and women I had had relationships with in the past. Eventually, I could not tell the difference between different voices and often wondered who had spoken.

At one point, I sensed I was in a courtroom, and a judge and witnesses (my professors or old friends) were speaking. They talked about what was happening in the English department and whether I should graduate or be a student.

I heard the police and emergency personnel beckoning me over a loudspeaker, threatening to enter my building by force. I also heard the CIA and the FBI. The CIA told me I was in a training program, but they later said I was in a CIA witness protection program and that I needed to be in the program for protection because everyone was trying to harm me. Then, the voices of the FBI told me not to listen to the voices of the CIA.

As my voices grew more frequent and louder, I was still convinced the experience was average. By the end of my final semester, I had lost most of my ability to communicate, was unkempt, and was utterly delusional about what I was doing at the university and my status as a student. Despite this, I graduated from Binghamton University with a bachelor's in English in 2008.

Shortly after graduation, I began wandering around the community, loudly talking nonsense. Suddenly, the CIA or FBI (I can't remember which) told me to throw a rock through my car window to retrieve something from inside. I broke the window, climbed inside, and then, after throwing a rock through the other side, I climbed out. At that point, the police came, determined I was unwell, and took me to a hospital.

My parents were generally unsurprised, as they had watched me deteriorate for half a year. However, they were shocked when they saw how sick I had become. When they visited me in the hospital, I could barely speak and could not converse with them for more than five minutes.

While hospitalized, I did not know where I was, believing I was probably in an FBI/CIA training lab. After three weeks in the community hospital, my clinicians decided I had "failed" their inpatient program and sent me to a state hospital where I would stay for nearly two months.

I regularly moved furniture around the hospital to cover the electrical outlets, fearing the hospital would use them to monitor me. I was placed on a "one-to-one," where a staff member monitored me around the clock. This lasted for weeks.

Initially, I refused medication, unsure of what it was and paranoid it would contain a microchip that would always monitor me. I began an older medication, which began to clear my mind.

However, eventually, during one family meeting, the psychiatrist in the hospital and my social worker emphasized the importance of taking medication to treat my new diagnosis of schizophrenia. Until then, I had no explanation of how or why I was in the hospital. The diagnosis made everything much more straightforward. That was when I agreed to begin injections of aripiprazole (Abilify), which were highly effective. I remember my hallucinations dissipating, becoming harder and harder to hear. Finally, my medication had wholly cleared my mind.

In terms of my healing from schizophrenia, finding the proper treatment fit can be difficult. Not all therapists are a good match. Facilities, programs, and treatment centers are not one-size-fits-all, and finding the right setting for some people may take some time.

I began outpatient mental health treatment, psychotherapy, and medication, being discharged from the state hospital center in Binghamton, New York, and coming home. Shortly after returning home, I began treatment at a local hospital with a partial hospitalization program. I completed the program within the usual length of stay, two weeks.

My experience in the partial hospitalization program was pleasant enough. The staff was friendly and skilled, and I was moved through the program quickly enough. Referred to the hospital's outpatient mental health program, I would do a seven-year stint with various therapists and psychiatrists over the better half of a decade of recovery.

During the initial phases of treatment, I made incredible gains. By 2009, I was connected to a motivating therapist at the hospital back home in Westchester and a clinically savvy psychiatrist. I was adherent to my treatment, medication, and therapy. I was still on an intramuscular injection (IM) that worked well for me, aripiprazole (Abilify Maintena). Today, I have been on Abilify Maintena for 15 years.

Don't get me wrong. There were setbacks, but they were my learning moments. Eventually, I learned about my disorder, gathered insight and better judgment, and returned to the classroom after a year at the local community college, where I completed a paralegal certificate. Even through my psychosis and treatment, my goal was always to pursue higher education. Using references from my paralegal program, I re-applied to Binghamton University. I knew I would never be admitted to the English department again. After all that I had been through, it also would have been an extremely unhealthy decision to do so.

I wanted to continue healing from my illness and not re-invent the unfortunate experience in college. So, I decided to apply for a master's in social work (MSW) instead of another English degree. Since Binghamton University has several schools, my reapplication to the university was swift and without incident. I was admitted to the MSW program without problems in 2010, two years after getting sick. No one investigated my former issues as an undergraduate student.

I liked my treatment team at home and didn't want to begin with a new therapist and psychiatrist upstate. I also wanted to stay on my injection since it controlled my symptoms. To do so, I traveled to and from the hospital at home to Binghamton every month to obtain my injection, though the round trip to and from the hospital took six hours. I had proper support for my education despite the distance in treatment. Despite commuting, I never missed an IM injection, which enabled my full recovery. I graduated with my master's on time, exactly four years after I had graduated with my bachelor's in 2012.

Graduate school was also vital to shaping my concept of healing. I began thinking about self-management while studying social work in graduate school. I still remember sitting in class one afternoon when I was a student. I was 27 at the time. It was a seminar on the theory of human behavior. Students were debating how everyday people could best self-monitor their mental health. In doing so, students and faculty suggested that self-awareness will lead to better mental health. Throughout graduate school, using the skills and information I learned, I constantly applied them to my health and recovery and would recommend these techniques to clients following my graduation.

For over a decade after my initial "break" or "the first episode of psychosis," I spent time in therapy and self-guided reflection, thinking about my mental health. After graduating with my MSW, I returned home, began working as a social worker, and practiced in the community where I grew up.

I passed my initial social work licensure exam (LMSW) two months after graduating. That fall, I began working in Westchester County for a local agency as a mobile mental health therapist for the Mental Health Association. DCMH, the Department of Community Mental Health in Westchester, funded the program. As a family specialist, I later worked for an ACT Team (Assertive Community Treatment Team). After my time with ACT, I began supervising social work MSW students from various universities in New York City in an Article 31 licensed clinic.

My passion for mental health reached beyond practicing as a social worker. I wanted to create a blog different from others I had seen online. I launched my *Mental Health Affairs* blog in the autumn of 2016. *Mental Health Affairs (MHA)* evolved into multidimensional and blended peer and clinical research elements.

My blog was an experiment to merge "two worlds." Indeed, the common theme I settled upon to bridge the peer and clinical gap was self-management. Under the auspices of self-management, clinicians and peers can benefit from better teaching and self-employing techniques to better regulate their emotional and behavioral health.

By 2017, my blog had gained the attention of the mental health community across the pond. In 2017, I was asked to speak at a blogging conference in England on mental health blogging. With my parents by my side, I crossed the Atlantic on the *Queen Mary Two* to Southampton, England, and spoke about healing, blogging, and self-management in London.

In 2019, I authored a memoir about my experience in college titled *University on Watch* (pseudonym, J. Peters). Today, my blog, *Mental Health Affairs*, is the most significant player in my healing and contribution to mental health. As noted in my book *University on Watch*, "This is why, after 10 years of recovery, my parents continue to support my writing on mental health and understand how this act of writing on mental health, spreading awareness to others through blogging, and learning self-management skills is used by people carrying a mental health [psychiatric] diagnosis to self-soothe, and to diffuse and disrupt their new or active symptoms" (J. Peters, 2019). *MHA* brings readers the most critical and rigorous analytical commentary on the status of medicine, psychiatry, social work, psychology, and allied fields intersecting with mental healthcare today.

Through my work as a social worker, therapist, and disability rights advocate, I've fought for those without a voice in the system. Currently, I chair the Consumer Advisory Board (CAB committee) for the New York City Department of Mental Hygiene (DOMH). I've been a member of the CAB since 2020. The mission of the CAB couldn't be more essential to the rollout of a significant new initiative impacting mental health in New York City (NYC).

CAB members and I meet periodically with a liaison from NYC DOMH and other high-level managers and program directors, including managers from programs including Assisted Outpatient Treatment (AOT) mandated treatment programs. We all sit at the CAB committee to review new initiatives in NYC that will impact mental health services and people with psychiatric diagnoses.

In 2020, I was awarded the Bold 10 Under 10 Award from the Binghamton University Alumni Association. I gave a speech at homecoming about my success as a social worker in the first 10 years of my career after graduating. The following year, I partnered with OnTrackNY of Binghamton. I talked at the university about early intervention for people experiencing first-episode psychosis, as I had experienced in college.

When I am not blogging, teaching, or speaking at an event, I am busy running

AWAKENINGS

a private mental health therapist office, Recovery Now, LLC, which I opened in 2021 and where I practice as a psychotherapist. Ultimately, schizophrenia aside, nothing worthwhile in my life came easy, but it has been an incredible journey, and I wouldn't give it up for any other life.

https://mentalhealthaffairs.blog/

9

LESLEY MCCUAIG
Athlete and Mental Health Counselor

Lesley McCuaig grew up in a village outside of Halifax, Nova Scotia where she lived with her parents and two older brothers. Her dream was to ski, and during high school, she placed third in a Canadian National Competition in Banff, Alberta. Lesley later became a skiing instructor in British Columbia.

Lesley attended the first independent high school in Canada, Kings-Edgehill School, where she won the 2000 Bronze Millennium Governor Generals Medal. She also learned Irish step dancing and studied at the Gaelic College. In 2006 she completed her bachelor's degree at Acadia University in kinesiology.

Her journey with mental health started in 2009, when she first sought help for depression and anxiety. What she didn't realize at the time was that her depression and anxiety were the result of a substance use disorder, causing her to consume alcohol daily. From 2007 to 2013, Lesley worked successfully for a real estate and insurance company as an accounting technician. However, in 2013, when she was in her late 20s, she began to suffer from a growing addiction to alcohol. She attended a residential treatment facility for alcoholism in Maple Ridge, British Columbia in the spring of 2014 and has remained sober and in recovery to date.

In 2015, Lesley's mother suffered from heart failure and slipped into a coma while fighting for her life. The stress was difficult for Lesley. During her mother's recovery, she experienced her first symptoms of schizophrenia, hearing voices in her mind. After two weeks, the voices worsened. She was unable to sleep for days at a time and finally checked into a hospital. Lesley was released quickly with no diagnosis and no medication.

When Lesley returned home, she experienced paranoia, changing all the light bulbs in her house and believing someone was spying on her through the glass. She experienced delusions that her neighbors were conspiring against her, and she called the police on them multiple times. Every time she called the police, she was apprehended under the mental health act and put under psychiatric evaluation.

After her first hospitalization, in June 2015, Lesley left home, wandering the nearby neighborhood. Perhaps the most significant hallucinations she has experienced to date occurred on that evening. She remembers standing on vehicle tires because she thought she would be electrocuted if she remained on the ground. She was experiencing both auditory and olfactory hallucinations, which led her to believe this. When a citizen noticed her standing on their vehicle's tires, she quickly moved to the ground and collapsed with fatigue. Police soon found her confused and sleeping in a public place, and she was retaken to a hospital.

She would be hospitalized several more times in the summer of 2015 for behavior relating to auditory hallucinations. The police came to her house several times for mental wellness checkups, called in by both family members and mental health professionals. This was a tumultuous time for both Lesley and her family.

Finally, in January 2016, Lesley was given the opportunity to meet with a new mental health nurse. He was very upfront, earned her trust, and listened intently. It was here that Lesley became honest with the mental health nurse about her auditory hallucinations and began regularly seeing a psychiatrist.

Later in 2016, Lesley celebrated a year and a half of sobriety and several months of remission from schizophrenia. That same year, Lesley decided to start a non-profit organization in British Columbia called Connected Through Sports Society. The Connected Through Sports Society was a non-profit entity designed to provide a safe environment for people in recovery from addictions to participate anonymously in community sports.

She also founded her own for-profit business, Lesley McCuaig Consulting and Research, and was successfully self-employed. However, in 2017, Lesley was still struggling to live independently and decided to move back to Nova Scotia to be closer to her immediate family.

It was at that time that Lesley began to thrive personally and professionally. She decided to make a career change and pursued a master's degree in counseling psychology. She began her master's degree program in January 2019, studying full-time and working full-time in an accounting firm in Halifax. Lesley graduated in 2022.

Lesley's life today is unrecognizable from the life she was living in 2013 — isolated, alone, and suffering from alcoholism and schizophrenia. Today, Lesley still skis, golfs, hikes, kayaks, plays the piano, fiddle, and guitar; and enjoys photography. She has many close friends and loves to spend time with her family. With the completion of her master's degree in counselling psychology, she recently began her own private practice, Coastal Hope Counselling. Coastal Hope Counselling currently offers mental health counseling for addiction, psychosis, trauma, grief, anxiety, and depression. Lesley also is a peer supporter with Hope for Mental Health.

Her advice to anyone who has schizophrenia is to "open up about your symptoms as soon as you notice them, so mental health teams are able to provide early intervention."

www.lesleymccuaig.com

10

DARRELL HERRMANN
Computer Programmer and Volunteer

INTRODUCTION

Hi, my name is Darrell. I am a retired United States Army officer and a retired computer programmer. I am happily married and share my love of attending live jazz performances with my wife.

I grew up on a small family farm in western Kansas about 30 miles east of Dodge City. For those of you who are western fans, this is the real Dodge City. I can literally say I got the heck out of Dodge.

Growing up my life was typical of farm boys of that era. I learned to drive a tractor by the age of 6 or 7. I milked the cows before and after school. I spent my summers working on the farm. After high school, I went to Kansas State University to study physics. I graduated in May 1976 and was commissioned as a second lieutenant in the United States Army through the ROTC program at Kansas State University.

Today I am going to tell you a little about how mental illness has affected my life. I am living proof that although having a serious mental illness changes your life, it is still possible to live a relatively normal life despite that illness.

WHAT HAPPENED

In 1984 I was a captain in the United States Army. My specialties were field artillery and nuclear weapons. I began to believe that I had been drugged with an experimental medicine as part of a secret conspiracy to produce super soldiers. I believed that this was why I was mentally falling apart, having trouble sleeping, and generally unable to cope with my daily life. Because I believed I had been drugged, it seemed logical to seek medical help. So I went to the army hospital emergency room asking for help. They quickly realized that I was delusional and becoming psychotic. I soon found myself on a military psychiatric ward. At this point, it was obvious that my military career was over because nuclear weapons and psychosis just don't go together very well. I spent my 30th birthday on the psychiatric unit, and it was a real bummer of a 30th birthday because I knew my military career was over, and I had no idea what my future held.

After I was released from the psychiatric ward, it was approximately six months before the army finished the process of deciding what to do with me and released me from active duty. During this six-month period, I had no assigned duties and was placed in a medical holding company. I needed something to do to occupy my time, so I volunteered at the Red Cross office on my base. When I started volunteering, I didn't function very well. I could answer the phone, take a message, and do minor clerical duties. Because the staff was supportive and encouraging, I began to do more things as time went on. By the end of the six months, I was doing virtually everything that a paid worker would do at that office. I firmly believe that this six months in a supportive environment and the chance to rebuild my coping skills were crucial to my later success in dealing with my illness.

I decided to go back to college and become a professional computer programmer. In January 1985, I began studying for my computer science degree at Kansas State University. In December 1986, I completed my BS in computer science. During this time in college, I was again learning to cope with demanding work and schedules. After my first semester, I had to have a medication change as the antipsychotic medication I was taking called trifluoperazine (Stelazine) did not allow me to think as clearly as I needed to. On the new antipsychotic called perphenazine (Trilafon) which I had been on briefly and liked while I was on active duty, my thinking was much clearer. To this day I still use that antipsychotic medication to treat my symptoms. I also found that I had to work a lot harder at my school work than the first time I was in college. I think my mental illness slightly lowered my IQ. I have learned to deal with occasional symptoms, such as hearing voices that aren't there, that still occur despite the fact that I am properly medicated.

In January 1987, I began working as a professional computer programmer. I did that very successfully despite the fact that computer programmers are often laid off and have to move to other locations to find work. In April 1995 I moved to Columbus, Ohio, for a new job and have stayed in the area ever since. In February 2000 I was laid off from the job that I had moved to Columbus for. I will share my experience with this layoff as it was typical of other layoffs that happened to me. My employer had given me my annual review in January. The review was outstanding as usual and said that I was an exemplary employee and programmer. In February, the day arrived for the announcement of annual pay raises. Previously word had leaked that layoffs were happening to some of the company. I was called into the vice president's office to learn my fate. I was told that because I was such an outstanding employee, I was going to receive a 5% pay raise. This was well above inflation and probably the best raise the human resources department would allow. Then I was told that I would also receive two weeks of extra pay as a cash bonus. In addition, because I was a top-performing employee, I would receive two months' pay in stock options. Then came the bombshell. "We have decided to shut down this department and outsource all the work. You have 60 days to find a job elsewhere in the company or your employment will be terminated." Although I was unable to find a job elsewhere in the company, I did find employment with another company in Columbus within the 60-day window and was able to bank the six weeks of severance pay I was due for being terminated.

In 2004 the stress of working was causing me to have mild delusional thinking and some hallucinations even though I was on a very high dose of antipsychotic medication. I describe what happened to me with that employer as being "The Dilbert Syndrome" after the comic strip Dilbert. Just like the character in the comic strip, I was dealing with impossible coworkers, unreasonable schedules and deadlines, confusing and conflicting guidance from management, and computer users who never knew what they wanted but wanted it yesterday. When I delivered these users programs doing exactly what they had requested the programs do, they were never satisfied and wanted something else. It reached the point where I could not see a win in the situation for anyone: not me, not my coworkers, not my management, and certainly not the company I worked for. At that point, after a lot of discussion with my psychiatrist and psychologist, I decided to go on disability because my work experience at several different companies over 18 years showed that the Dilbert Syndrome is endemic in the American corporate environment. Although I could have tried to find a job in another company, in short order due to my illness, the Dilbert Syndrome would likely strike me again and once again severely impact my ability to work successfully.

After going on disability, I needed to find ways to productively occupy my time. In January 2003 I started volunteering one hour a week at the Riverside psychiatric unit talking to their patients about how to live and cope with a mental illness. I decided to expand my volunteer efforts and with the help of Mental Health America of Franklin County, I expanded to other hospital psychiatric units in Columbus. In the 10 years prior to the COVID pandemic, I spoke to more than 30,000 people in those hospital groups. In November 2019 I published a book of essays about the things I had learned that hospitalized patients had questions about and needed answers to. This book was a product of my many years of volunteering and has been very well received. The title of the book is *Straight Talk About Living With A Severe Mental Illness*. It covers the basic information that anyone dealing with a severe mental illness should know but all too often don't know. It is now available in paperback, Kindle, and audiobook formats.

Another highlight of my years volunteering occurred in 2007. A very special woman attended a few of my groups while she was hospitalized. She decided to check out the community support group I worked with, and we quickly became friends. After a year or so we became best friends. Later still we started to talk about getting married. We decided to see a marriage counselor to make sure we were really compatible and to discuss how our illnesses (mine schizophrenia and hers schizoaffective disorder) might affect our marriage. The marriage counselor felt that we were one of the most compatible couples he had ever seen so we decided to get married. We married on October 23, 2010, and are still happily married over 12 years later.

WHAT HELPS

The key element and foundation of my recovery from schizophrenia is my antipsychotic medication. When I first became ill in the army, I was placed on an antipsychotic medication called thiothixene (Navane) that quickly brought my symptoms under control but had some bad side effects. Specifically, I felt a little stiff, my feet hurt mildly when I walked on them, and I ached and felt sort of like you do with the flu. I was sent back to my apartment and put on sick leave. One day I forgot to take the medication. I felt much better and realized later that it was because I was not taking my medication. I decided that I wouldn't take the medication anymore. When I saw the army psychiatrist a couple of days later and told him what had happened and that I didn't want to take the medication anymore, he said, "That's fine." A few days later he returned me to duty. Approximately two weeks after I stopped taking the medication, I once again became fully psychotic and wound up back in the hospital. I was placed on a different antipsychotic medication called perphenazine (Trilafon) and my symptoms were once again quickly brought under control. From this experience I learned that I needed medication to stay out of the hospital and because I want to stay out of the hospital as much as possible, I have never gone off my medications again. I need to point out that everyone's experience with medications is different. A medication that works wonders for one person may be pure poison to someone else.

Another key thing in my recovery has been learning as much as I can about my illness. While I was in college, I researched schizophrenia extensively in the college library but found very little of help. Almost all of the research I found was based on psychoanalysis. Medication was rarely if ever mentioned as a treatment for schizophrenia in that research. Then, in 1985 I found the new book *Surviving Schizophrenia* by E. Fuller Torrey, MD. It was one of the first books written for lay people about schizophrenia and treatment of it as a medical illness. This book and the information I received from it gave me a good foundation in my recovery from schizophrenia. The first edition of that book was part of the beginning of treatment of schizophrenia as the medical illness, which today we know it is. That book is currently in its seventh edition and still a valuable resource.

The third and final major piece of my recovery is a support group that I became involved with in Columbus. This support group was the first time I had friends I could openly share with and talk about my illness and coping with it. I find it extremely beneficial to be able to discuss coping skills and current issues with friends who have been where I have been and where I am today. We help each other cope.

WHAT'S NEXT

For me success means that I am living as full and rewarding a life as possible. I enjoy helping others learn to better cope with a mental illness. As the COVID pandemic winds down, I am looking forward to hospitals once again being open to volunteers. It is my goal to return to doing as many weekly sessions on hospital psychiatric units as I can manage comfortably. My goal is to see at least another 30,000 people over the 10 years after hospitals fully reopen to volunteers.

I would like to thank you for reading my story. I hope I have given you a better perspective on mental illness and what is possible than you had before. I want each of you to know that although your interaction with a mentally ill person may at times seem pointless, your efforts might be the key to setting that person on the road to recovery through your words or actions. I am a prime example of recovery at its best and want to emphasize that your role in someone's recovery should never be underestimated. You can play a key role in their recovery, and there is always hope for recovery.

11

MEGHAN CAUGHEY
Artist, Professor, and Author

I felt invincible when I was a little girl growing up in Atlanta, Georgia. My big brother would take me on hikes by the creek near our home. I played violin and cello and was a page in the Georgia State Legislature, where I lobbied for civil rights and against the war in Vietnam. I didn't understand that my father had alcoholism or that anything was different in my family.

I assumed that I could do anything, but when I was 12 and my family moved to San Antonio, Texas, I was suddenly in what seemed like a strange and foreign land. In high school, I spent most of my time drawing and playing my cello, and I loved to spend time in nature. When I was 16, I discovered Zen Buddhism and explored meditation, and I spent most of my time alone.

When I selected a university, it wasn't about the academic qualifications, but about how easily I could access the wilderness of the Rocky Mountains. I believed I needed solitude in the wilderness at the high altitude near the tree line. That was how I began college at Colorado State University. I studied art and spent as much time backpacking in the Rockies as possible.

Early in my first term, I had an experience I could never have predicted and will never forget. One afternoon in an art history class, I heard faint, intrusive, cruel voices that no one else could hear. When I struggled to return to my dormitory, the people I saw didn't look normal — their faces looked like enormous insects. When I was finally in my dormitory room, and I looked at myself in the mirror, I was no longer human. I had turned into an awful beast. Although I tried my best to continue my studies and backpacking trips, my world was fearsome. Finally, one snowy night, some other students who saw how disturbed I was took me to the student health center. I was given the medication chlorpromazine (Thorazine) there, and I slept in a darkened room. Eventually, I was taken to see the psychiatrist. He sternly looked at me across his desk, and pointing his finger at me, he condemned, "You have schizophrenia." Although I didn't know what schizophrenia was, it was clear that I was doomed.

In the following years, I struggled to complete my studies and was often hospitalized for my symptoms, which were visual, kinesthetic and auditory hallucinations. I returned to San Antonio, where my parents were, and enrolled at Trinity University. I switched my major from art to psychology because I needed to understand what was happening to my brain. At one point, I was deeply discouraged and contemplating suicide, and I was able to do an independent study course in suicidology. I got college credit to obsess about killing myself. The irony of this was inescapable. My doctor would give me antipsychotic medications, but I hated how the side effects made me feel, so I usually would stop taking it and then end up in the psychiatric hospital. I would have to stay in the hospital until I could be stabilized by retaking the medication again. I went in and out of various hospitals but eventually graduated with a bachelor's degree in psychology.

I decided on becoming an art therapist to combine art and psychology, so I went to graduate school in Vermont. It didn't take long for my psychotic symptoms to become severe, even though I was working as an art therapy intern at the Vermont State Hospital. There, I saw a patient who had full-blown tardive dyskinesia, a serious movement disorder caused by the same medication I was taking. The sight terrified me. I ended up in the psychiatric hospital and, for the first time, was tied down with four-point leather restraints on my ankles and wrists. I had no memory of how I ended up in restraints, but it would not be the last time. Being tied down for hours is a profound experience.

I was told I would have to leave school and be treated in a residential psychiatric program. I resisted this, but eventually, it became unavoidable. Because I detested psychiatric medication, I ended up in an unusual program in Oakland, California. It was called the Cathexis Institute, and they claimed they could cure schizophrenia without using medications. Instead, they believed that psychosis was caused by faulty parenting and the cure was in "reparenting patients." They physically held adults in the therapists' laps and gave grown adults baby bottles of warm milk. They even would put adult patients in baby diapers, and the adults would regress to infancy and be cared for, including having baths and diaper changes. There was also the practice of corporal punishment if a patient broke a rule. My mother was told she was "schizophrenogenic," meaning she had created my illness, and the program blamed her for inadequately nursing me when I was less than three months old, and said she was what had caused my disorder.

I stayed in this program because I was very motivated to get well, and they didn't make me take medication, but eventually, I ran away. I ended up living in a cabin in the coastal mountains south of the south San Francisco area, and I intensely focused on my art.

I went in and out of psychiatric hospitals. I detested the medications because they caused movement problems, shaking, blurry vision, swelling of my breasts, lactation, dry mouth, and excessive sleepiness. And I especially detested the inevitable weight gain — this all made it very hard to draw and paint which was my passion, and I felt ashamed of myself — I didn't understand why I had these side effects.

Eventually, I was determined to go to art school, and I finally completed an MA in drawing and painting and then an MFA in pictorial art. I did this despite the frequent hospitalizations.

I met a young man and fell in love, and we got married and moved to Santa Cruz, California.

In the first year of our marriage, I made a significant suicide attempt — being married could not ease my emotional pain. We moved to Oregon and, after seven years, were divorced. This was followed by years of many hospitalizations and suicide attempts. I have been hospitalized well over one hundred times, sometimes in the Intensive Care Unit, after trying to kill myself.

When not in the hospital, I attended a day treatment program. One day in the waiting room, I found a medical newsletter that listed schizophrenia medications that were being researched, and one caught my attention. It said it didn't cause weight gain like most other medications, and it was in Phase III trials. I immediately had the feeling that this medication was going to change my life. I was 48 years old, and no one thought I would ever get out of the wards of psychiatric hospitals. With many calls to the drug company that made the medication, I got into a Phase III clinical trial in Southern California. I faithfully made the 16-hour trip from home to the California hospital every month for two years. I lost over 70 pounds, and my psychotic symptoms disappeared. And, remarkably, I started to experience a new feeling — I felt pleasure, for the first time in many years.

I stopped going to the hospital. The drug company trained me in public speaking. They paid me to fly across the country and travel in limousines to give presentations at medical conferences and mental health advocacy events.

Eventually, I pursued a career in mental health advocacy and peer-delivered services, services in which persons who themselves have recovered from their personal mental health challenges get special training and are able to work as peer specialists helping other persons who are still struggling with their problems. The peer specialist can sometimes empathetically connect with others who are having a hard time and because of their own experience, the peer specialist knows viscerally how to help.

No one had ever thought I could work, but my career began at age 50, even though my psychiatrist said I "was too sick to work." I designed and directed mental health programs in Oregon as well as nationally. I finally ended up in Portland, Oregon, as senior director of peer wellness services at a large health nonprofit.

Now I am also a clinical assistant professor at the Oregon Health and Science

University, Department of Psychiatry. I train psychiatry and doctoral residents in the Public Psychiatry Training program and also work with a suicide prevention program. I also have a consulting business.

In 2021 I had Neuroleptic Malignant Syndrome (NMS) caused by the antipsychotic medication that had saved my life. Because I can no longer take it, I have occasionally had ECT (electroconvulsive therapy). I am a survivor.

I continue to make art, play the cello, and write. I write poetry and essays. My memoir, *Mud Flower, Surviving Schizophrenia and Suicide Through Art* (2021) has won 12 book awards. My work has been shown and published internationally. I'm currently working on *Making Art from the Lap of the Universe*. In 1998 I received a Buddhist lay ordination and was given the name, Jisho, which means compassion for all living beings. This describes the motivation and purpose of my work.

Last year, I trained a cohort of peer wellness specialists in Cape Town, South Africa, and this year they are calling me the "Mother of the Program" which pleases me immensely.

Is it possible to heal from schizophrenia? I honestly must say that sometimes things can still be challenging, but it is possible to do something that may seem impossible to the average person. One does not have to accept the label of "mental patient' if one insists on imagination and perseverance. It may not always be easy, but it is worth claiming one's freedom!

www.Mudflowerbook.com
www.Meghancaughey.com

12

ROBERT ROSS*
IT Expert and Poet

My name is Robert, and I was born in a small town of modest means in Jackson, Michigan. My mother was a dietician at a hospital, and my father worked for the local government. I have a twin sister and an older brother, born nine years before us.

My parents struggled to make ends meet financially and my childhood home left much to be desired, both in comfort and in activities. I remember cold winters. Our house was created by a World War II veteran with stone and cement and heated by a fireplace. Naturally, it was drafty.

I remember much about my childhood. Growing up in the country, I was often isolated. My sister and I shared a room until around the age of 9 when my brother went to college. We naturally butted heads often as we both struggled for limited attention from our parents. My father was out of the home most evenings after school. He would bowl or visit friends on weekdays. My mother would often be upstairs working on projects or on long phone calls.

My earliest schizoaffective symptoms started to manifest when I was in middle school. I remember reading a book about Albert Einstein and imagining Einstein's essence or spirit was permeating in the sky as I thought about him. My mind would often wander.

My first psychotic breakdown occurred in high school around my sophomore year, after I smoked a cigarette that may have been laced with marijuana. I kept thinking the same thoughts repeatedly. I had been bullied mildly in school, but I could not let it go, and it devastated me. I was extremely sensitive, and my emotions were inappropriate. When I should have felt happy, I felt sad. When I should have felt sad, I felt happy. As my symptoms worsened, I developed disorganized speech, and it seemed obvious to others that my words/thoughts were jumbled. My parents finally picked up on this and decided to send me to a medical professional.

My first doctor didn't know what to make of it. I was prescribed lithium for my erratic emotions and olanzapine for my disorganized speech. At that time,

---
*The name has been changed to protect the privacy of those involved in the story.

my doctor believed I was bipolar with psychotic symptoms. These medications caused massive weight gain (which I would eventually work off playing on the tennis team). My psychosis continued until I was placed on aripiprazole (Abilify) and sertraline (Zoloft) which, fortunately, insurance was able to cover.

Once I was placed on Abilify and Zoloft, my grades started to improve. I went from a C student to an A student. I eventually finished high school, and though I had missed substantial class time my sophomore year, I still graduated with my senior class. I remember the meeting with teachers who stated, "he is ready for college," as they were aware of my intention to continue my education.

I started at a community college where I was awarded a Michigan Education Assessment Program (MEAP) scholarship. I then transferred to Michigan State University (MSU) with around 50 credits. Despite this success, I felt alone and abandoned, like I was damaged. Though I channeled this academic success to further increase my self-esteem, I felt in some ways I was a fraud. I felt alone. Academics was my temporary escape.

Despite my feelings of confusion and isolation, I flourished at Michigan State. Looking back, I believe that my medications enabled me to keep my grades up. But I began to question whether I had a mental condition at all.

My junior year, I was awarded a scholarship to study abroad in Tanzania, Africa. I also had a girlfriend I met the prior semester, though we broke up upon my return to the United States.

Back from Africa, I decided to take less and less of my medication as I "felt fine." Out of my six semesters at MSU, I only missed the dean's list twice, including my last senior semester. I attribute the last semester issues to not taking meds appropriately, but I still ended up with a 3.8 major and a 3.5 cumulative GPA.

After college, I followed my parents to Florida, where they had moved from Michigan. However, my family began telling me something was "wrong." Although I was entirely unaware of it, off medication, my disorganized speech had resurfaced, my emotions were inappropriate, and my behavior was erratic. My parents wanted to take me to another psychiatrist, but rather than comply, I decided to move back to Michigan.

In Michigan, I started working at a web host IT company. I worked there for around a year before I realized my symptoms were returning, worse than ever before. I returned to live with my parents in Florida, where I was hospitalized. I was unable to explain the situation to my employer.

In Florida, I was placed on all kinds of medicine until my parents contacted my old childhood, board-certified doctor in Michigan. Then I was placed on Abilify and Zoloft again. My diagnosis was now schizoaffective disorder. After realizing I had a lifelong condition, I have taken my medicine faithfully for over a decade.

Currently, I work in IT for a global industry leader in digital signage. I have a great group of friends who understand my condition, and I have hobbies that I enjoy in my free time. I play pickleball, tennis, and the trading card game *Magic: The Gathering*. I am under the impression that people have little idea I even have a condition. I write poetry and dystopian science fiction, and I hope to one day be a source of inspiration for others with similar conditions.

I believe with proper and consistent treatment many people can recover the life they had prior to their diagnosis.

My parents have been helpful in my recovery and though part of any illness is nature and nurture, I hold no ill will. People often do as much as they can when they can.

13

ASHLEY SMITH
Author, Advocate, and Mom

Imagine a 20-year-old college student living life on campus, studying, working internships, going to events with friends, and visiting family. Suddenly, they're facing felony charges. And, admitted into a psychiatric hospital.

That's my story. It was unreal — rough, chaotic, and sudden for me and my family. However, the incident spearheaded my recovery. It established a new beginning and understanding of myself and my role in advocacy for peers and their families. I developed insight on how to articulate my story and practice a variety of coping tools to manage. I've learned how to master resiliency.

Having experienced a wide range of dreadful symptoms, my diagnosis was traumatic in itself. I became suspicious of everyone including family and those in my close circle. I believed friends and fellow students whispered and gossiped about me. I believed a relative tried to kill me by poison and put something in my pancakes. I believed they tapped my phone and put a tracking device in it. I was also convinced that neighbors and others spied on me and strangers followed me everywhere. The world was against me, and I couldn't escape.

I did not know what hallucinations were. But the voices and ghosts frightened me — they wouldn't stop. The male and female voices joined in with the evil cartoon characters in my head. They were shouting and criticizing me for what seemed like hours. I was alone, vulnerable, and falling apart — losing myself and the Ashley everyone knew.

Then I thought I found relief, even though irrational thoughts continued to dominate my mind, moods, and actions. These ill thoughts led me to steal a truck in hopes of saving myself from family, strangers, and everybody that came near me. The truck was military property, and my legal battles would consume my family's life. Consequently, I was at risk of being charged with felonies and facing prison time. Soon, my symptoms became worse than ever before.

The prolonged legal process worsened my symptoms, escalating the deterioration of my mind. Then I received an official diagnosis and a description of the symptoms I was experiencing. I had many symptoms. Doctors used words I had never heard of: catatonia, delusions, psychosis, and hallucinations, to identify a few. These were foreign to me and my family.

I was catatonic, literally still. I would not move an inch. I sat in a daze for hours or lay in bed for days. I was told later that the jail health team sent me to the emergency room a few times because I wasn't eating or drinking. I had scrambled thoughts, racing thoughts, and no thoughts. I couldn't keep up, let alone understand what was happening. Despite me shutting down, my family endured the battles.

Ironically, the legal interventions helped me. Mandated medication compliance brought me back from that place in my head which made me stuck, with a lack awareness of time and minimal closeness and connections with family and others. It restored my ability to function.

When my doctor told me I had paranoid schizophrenia, I didn't understand the diagnosis. I had heard of all the scary myths and stigmatizing stories in movies and in the media. Now, that description applied to me, but I realized that was not me! The doctor nodded his head up and down repeating how the voices were another symptom. He compared my diagnosis to diabetes in that it would require ongoing treatment. He reassured me I could go back to school and manage as long as I took medication and controlled my stress.

His advice and enthusiasm for my recovery undoubtedly lit a fire in me and motivated my family to keep trying to help me get my life back. We wouldn't accept the discouraging perception that recovery isn't possible and that I would have limitations in life. We braced ourselves and got ready to fight these invisible wars no matter how severe and how long it took.

When I was diagnosed, my family and I quickly researched for ways to cope. We did our homework online and met with my doctor to learn how to control the illness. While I would never compare schizophrenia to diabetes, I wholeheartedly agree that recovery is possible, and there is hope for me and my peers in treatment. Despite this diagnosis and related conditions, we can live a quality life.

Hope. My definition of it has been revolutionized. I live it every day: to have faith in the possibility of achieving better.

My recovery includes getting a lot of support from family, friends, and my health team. We became involved in a behavioral health program. Participating in these programs and in various organizations helped me reduce my feelings of stigma about my own illness. However, stigma from others persisted, and I wasn't immune. I've experienced discriminatory attacks. For example, I've been called demonic by strangers during my presentation for my advocacy work. This happened even though my faith is important to me and is a part of my coping tools.

At the beginning of my recovery journey, I learned about Mary Ellen Copeland's Wellness Recovery Action Plan (WRAP) which is a crisis plan similar to a psychiatric advance directive but more informal. It provides people with instructions on how to treat a person during a crisis by providing preferences and medication history among other helpful information. And my family joined NAMI, the National Alliance on Mental Illness.

Part of my advocacy has included sharing my recovery journey on my blog, Overcoming Schizophrenia, which I established in 2008. I titled my blog Overcoming Schizophrenia because I view my condition as a health concern that is manageable. My blog looks at the cup half full. I share my experience with an optimistic outlook.

Getting involved with NAMI Georgia, Inc., has propelled my advocacy efforts. Through NAMI I've undergone extensive training, which has helped me to share my story with countless audiences. For example, I have presented to the crisis intervention team training for law enforcement through the In Our Own Voice NAMI presentation. Today, I serve in various capacities at NAMI Georgia, Inc., including state board member, state trainer, group facilitator, and resource coordinator for their non-emergency helpline.

Now that I've been in recovery for over 15 years, I understand the importance of repeatedly applying my coping tools along with practicing medication management. For example, having a routine helps to reduce symptoms.

Over the years I've created self-care rituals, for example, journaling, exercising, meditation, affirmations, listening to motivational talks, therapy, medication management, and pet therapy. My dog also contributes to my wellness, as he helps me combat challenges with depression every day.

Another strategy I use is my creativity. I blog and create fun projects. I enjoy writing and sharing my story to support recovery in other people. I developed blog books, which are a collection of organized articles from Overcoming Schizophrenia. My two blog books are *What's On My Mind? Volume I, Revised Edition* (2022) and *What's On My Mind? Volume II, Coping Takes Work* (2019).

Through my support system, treatment, coping techniques, and advocacy, I am able to press forward with pride but also humility.

Still, I have challenges. Reflecting on my health crisis reminds me of how fragile I can be, but how resilient I am too. I'm renewing my focus daily. I look at my mind wars as battles to be overcome. I've lost my mind but have come back stronger. My definition of recovery and strategies to cope continue to evolve. I define recovery as applying coping tools to stay in a good place. My family and friends hold me accountable in my recovery. They help me maintain wellness.

My top three pieces of advice for peers with this condition are to develop a support system, engage in therapy, and maintain hope. Every peer has a piece of wisdom to share because living with schizophrenia is hard, but recovery is possible.

Finally, despite recurring symptoms, I keep hope alive for better days. Currently, I work as a peer counselor, otherwise known as a certified peer specialist (CPS). My job is to share my story to support my peers on their recovery journey. Also, I teach them more about the diagnosis and the importance of medication management. To date, I've self-published five books on inspiration, prayers, and hope for recovery. My son, Big Boy, is my joy and motivation to keep striving for wellness no matter what.

I continue to share my story on my blog to offer hope for my peers and those affected and to support the anti-stigma movement. Living with a psychiatric illness can raise significant challenges but they can be overcome. I'm proof.

www.overcomingschizophrenia.blogspot.com

14

REBECCA CHAMAA
Writer and Wife

Rebecca Chamaa graduated with a liberal arts degree from Evergreen State College in 1989. Originally from Washington state, she attended an American high school in Cairo, Egypt, where she met her future husband.

Following her college graduation, Rebecca began her career as a social worker, in which she thrived from 1989 to 1993. However, in 1993, at 28, Rebecca began to struggle with paranoia. Believing that her food contained poison and that people in her life were conspiring against her, her symptoms worsened. When Rebecca's mother and aunt noticed her paranoia and that she could not sit still, they convinced Rebecca to obtain a psychiatric evaluation.

Rebecca went voluntarily to the emergency room and started inpatient treatment in the psych ward. She was initially diagnosed with bipolar disorder. Her doctors began her on an older antipsychotic medication. It helped significantly with her symptoms and would keep her stable for most of the next 13 years, with a few instances of psychosis. From 1993 to 2006, Rebecca was busy with many jobs as a library technician, marketing coordinator, salesperson, and caterer.

Following her marriage in 1998, Rebecca and her husband purchased a condo in the Los Angeles area. She and her husband have enjoyed traveling the world throughout their marriage, including trips to Paris, Abu Dhabi, and Dubai. In 2006, they took six months off to tour the United States, and on their return, they settled in San Diego.

That same year, one of Rebecca's doctors believed she had no mental illness and convinced her to discontinue all her medications. After stopping her medications, Rebecca became acutely psychotic, and her symptoms lasted for several months. Finally, after several medication changes, Rebecca began a newer medication she takes today. Her new doctors diagnosed her with chronic paranoid schizophrenia.

On medication, Rebecca again resumed an everyday personal and professional life. She landed another job as a social worker, where she worked from 2006 to 2011.

In 2015, Rebecca found the courage to share how she was preparing to jump off a Seattle bridge when two strangers interfered and persuaded her to return to safety. Rebecca sought to find these strangers and thank them. Her story and a call to find these strangers was on the site of *People Magazine* on December 24, 2015.

Although Rebecca lives with symptoms of schizophrenia and an anxiety disorder daily, she finds purpose by sharing her story about living with schizophrenia. She has written articles for *Teen Vogue, Good Housekeeping, Glamour,* and *Women's Day*. She writes regularly for the finance section of *Insider*.

Today, Rebecca aims to start conversations about schizophrenia in the mainstream media. Her most recent article was in the personal section of *Huffington Post*. She also works as a public speaker for NAMI (National Alliance on Mental Illness) and talks about life with schizophrenia to law enforcement, nurses, therapists, and other people who work with those with a mental illness.

Rebecca considers herself a lifelong learner and recently completed a certificate program in Narrative Medicine from Columbia University. Although her symptoms give her significant limitations to working full-time, she continues to seek out work that is both meaningful and gives her a sense of purpose.

Rebecca's motto and motivation come from the saying, "Life is both tragic and beautiful." She finds that statement to be true for her in her journey to live successfully with the symptoms of schizophrenia.

RebeccaChamaa.com

15

ZACH FELD
Finishing College and Seeking a Career

My schizophrenia story starts in fall 2008. I started school at Kenyon College right after high school. My high school was a small, gifted program, and I had done well enough to get in the year Newsweek called Kenyon a "New Ivy," so my future seemed bright. At first, things seemed normal for my freshman year. I was going to class, doing my homework, etcetera. After a while, however, things took a turn for the worse. My grades slipped dramatically; I struggled socially; and I began having thoughts of paranoia regarding my friends and roommates. At one point I believed they were conspiring to drive me to suicide or at least have some kind of angry outburst.

By spring of my freshman year, I withdrew from school and went home. Kenyon followed me in a sense. I began hallucinating my friends and other ghosts of Kenyon in my childhood home. During that time, I tried to continue my education by taking courses at a community college, but the paranoia and hallucinations were large roadblocks. Around the same time, my grandmother on my mother's side passed away, and I hallucinated her for a while. I remember being so sick that I giggled at her funeral because of intrusive thoughts.

Eventually, I had an outburst due to a major psychotic break. The outburst was a culmination of distress from changes in the way my mind had been operating, including increasing visions and other imaginary phenomena. When I saw my mother one evening, I felt as if she was invading my mind. In frustration, I smashed a plate on the floor which was filled with blintzes Mom had made for dinner. I yelled, "Get out of my head!" at her, and she called the police.

I wound up at the Lindner Center of Hope (a psychiatric facility in Mason, Ohio) for about a month. I wasted away at the Lindner Center, watching the charge nurse write the date every day on a large display pad. This helped me regain a sense of time I had lost from spending days at home not knowing the time or date. They put me on medication, but when I got home I had anosognosia (lack of insight) so I was non-compliant with my meds.

I lasted a short period of time off meds. Before things worsened, I took some woodworking classes, played a lot of Call of Duty, and worked a summer gardening job my high school friend got for me. By the end of summer 2011, after my job ended, I was at the Lindner Center again. While I was getting help, I missed my brother's wedding, and I had few visitors because everyone was preoccupied with the wedding. When I was discharged, I had my head shaved to a two-inch haircut from the shoulder length curly hair I had and was sent off to a work therapy farm in Massachusetts called Gould Farm. It is not too far from the site of the wedding I missed.

At Gould Farm I participated in farm work as therapy. I started on the forestry and groundskeeping team and eventually moved on to work in the kitchens and with livestock. The age-old medicine of chopping wood and carrying water to build one's self up was a very literal part of my treatment. There's nothing else like hard outdoor physical labor to ground you and force you out of your head and into the environment. I did physical labor not only thanks to work therapy but by my own volition. I had started out randomly doing pushups at the command of hallucinations and by the end of my stay at Gould Farm, I was a regular user of the farm weight room, and I was hallucination-free thanks to being stabilized on meds. A self-motivated exercise routine that was my own idea was an important step in my recovery because it gave me a sense of control over my own self-improvement that wasn't being handed to me from an outside source. Others self-medicate with cigarettes and drugs. I was lucky those had never appealed to me. Whatever sparks of self-starting in the recovery process one has are important to keep and nurture because, otherwise, you're left with other people's motivations and no motivation of your own, which leads to non-compliance.

The prescribed meds were a problem for me, however. The psychiatrist noticed some tardive dyskinesia and it upset me so much I started "cheeking" my meds (storing my meds in my mouth rather than swallowing them) in the medication line. I regularly butted heads with the resident psychiatrist and was also getting fed up with the work program. Something had to change so I took drastic measures. I made an attempt on my own life by drinking Simple Green—the cleaning solution—which as luck would have it is non-toxic. I was rushed to the hospital after immediately alerting the night staff of my impulsive behavior. I spent a week at the Pittsfield Mental Hospital until I ended up back at the farm. Later that year, I eventually ended up back in my hometown.

Back at home, I was treated by the Assertive Community Treatment (ACT) team at Greater Cincinnati Behavioral Health (GCBH) around the time of my fourth and final hospitalization. The ACT team helped me get resituated in my hometown. They reminded me of psychiatric appointments and assisted me as I searched for my first apartment. Another thing they did was get me involved with GCBH job coaching. They were a series of friendly, caring, and understanding faces that kept me from isolating at home by visiting me regularly or having me drive to them at the GCBH office. I was hospitalized this one last time and during my hospitalization, the ACT team had a hand in continuity of care between the hospital and GCBH. I stabilized on a four-week injection of paliperidone (Invega Sustenna) so that I didn't have to think about taking oral medication. I ultimately ended up taking daily divalproex sodium pills as well, but the Invega does the majority of the work, so if I miss a day of the oral medication it's not a tragedy. I also have a PRN (as needed dose) of oral risperidone today, in case of occasional flare-ups in symptoms.

Things were neither here nor there for a while. I reunited with my biological father who sought me out (I was adopted at birth), and I learned that schizophrenia was inherited from that side. It is a part of the mosaic of contributing factors to my illness. I gave cognitive enhancement therapy a shot and worked a little bit of retail. Eventually, I went back to college, Xavier University, when I felt recovered enough in fall of 2015. The university provided accommodations to work around my illness and learning disability from high school, and I finally graduated in summer of 2022 with a degree in economics and sustainability. For my capstone project, I chose to write a 20-page paper about Gould Farm and present it over Zoom. I looked at the recovery program from an economic, environmental, and social perspective. A big part of my capstone was highlighting the need to return to work after going on disability for a mental illness and showing how meaningful work is important to recovery, finances, managing mental illness, and becoming less of a burden. There is an economic story to be told about disability, work, and upkeep of standards of living that can, sadly, include stories of joblessness and poverty when personal and community failures happen. There is also a beacon of light when successful treatment is administered.

Towards the end of my educational career at Xavier I returned to Gould Farm for an alumni weekend and spoke on a panel about some of the triumphs in my recovery. Revisiting places of recovery can be hard because they are so charged with memories of traumatic times, but it can also help the healing process towards later stages of recovery as a reminder of how far you've come.

These days I spend my time volunteering at a food pantry where I've been working for a year now. I bring my mom's dog to the dog park, paint, chauffeur an elderly lady, job hunt, and look for ways to further my career after my recent graduation. I don't know what the future holds, but I have learned how to manage my illness and feel it is largely behind me now. There are so many institutions that have helped me find hope, including the Gould Farm, the Lindner Center, and Greater Cincinnati Behavioral Health. I particularly like the Gould Farm slogan, "We harvest hope."

AWAKENINGS

I still go to doctors' appointments and work with a case manager, but I no longer am involved with Assertive Community Treatment because I have graduated from that. I still have occasional residual symptoms, but for the most part, I am more comfortable and compliant than when I started. Some of my breakthrough symptoms lately include animation of paintings I have up on my walls when it's getting close to my injection time and other hallucinations like the occasional voice. Schizophrenia is a thief of sanity, but with the right treatment, care, and management it can be caught. The mental soundness lost from schizophrenia can be recovered and returned; damage can be mitigated.

www.gcbhs.com
www.gouldfarm.org

16

LIZ GRACE[*]
Conquering Deafness and Schizophrenia

Liz Grace describes her childhood as happy, up until she was 10 years old when her mother died from breast cancer. Afterward, she remembers life as lonely and difficult. Following her mother's diagnosis, her maternal grandparents moved closer to Liz's family and were always loving, supportive, and emotionally close to Liz throughout her whole life. However, she was not close to her three siblings after her mother's death.

Liz remembers doing satisfactory work in elementary and high school, but it was not her best. She was smart, and though she often didn't do her homework, she sometimes corrected her teachers' academic mistakes in math classes.

Liz decided to add another year of high school, often called a "victory lap," because she had failed three of her classes during her fourth year due to lack of motivation, which was caused by her declining mental health.

Staying in high school for an extra year was difficult because all her friends had graduated and moved on to college. During that year, Liz sank into a deep depression. She hated herself and was unhappy. Her memory was failing her, and she struggled with basic memorization in classes.

At times, while in high school, she experienced voices in her head, laughing at her like a laugh track on a TV show. Fortunately, these voices disappeared for many years and would not bother her again until adulthood.

In October 2005, during her fifth year of high school at age 17, Liz experienced her first suicidal thoughts. Her grades dropped, and she chose to see a counselor without telling anyone.

Thinking that her conversations with the counselor were strictly confidential, Liz confided that she was still thinking of killing herself and had a plan to do it by overdosing on pills. She was immediately hospitalized for her first time, for three days. Upon discharge, Liz made a promise to her counselor that she would not hurt herself. But Liz was unable to keep her promise. That afternoon while at school, Liz swallowed a bottle of Tylenol. She expected to die, but instead,

---
[*] The name has been changed to protect the privacy of those involved in the story.

became very sick.

Soon after, a teacher found her feeling severely ill and called an ambulance. Though it was too late for her to be treated with charcoal, she still made a full recovery.

From age 16, Liz also struggled with rapid hearing loss due to a genetic condition. Looking back, Liz believes that her hearing loss exacerbated her struggle to blend in socially. At that time, she volunteered with teenagers with special needs, and some of her closest friends were in a local youth group.

Liz would be in and out of hospitals five times during her last year of high school. At times, she was incorrectly diagnosed with borderline personality disorder and post-traumatic stress disorder. And though she was struggling with psychosis, her treatment team failed to recognize it, thinking that she was simply seeking attention. During her third and fifth hospital stays, she was forcefully restrained during a meltdown, which is still traumatic to her today. She also was put on an antipsychotic medication which did work well for her, but it had bad side effects such as weight gain.

Just prior to her fifth year of high school, Liz was told that her father was about to be remarried to a woman she barely knew. The stress of this and still coping with the loss of her mother led to her third hospitalization, which would last six weeks.

While her dad was busy preparing for his wedding, he had no patience for Liz's psychotic outbursts, and he kicked Liz out of their house. Since 2006, she has had no contact with him. Fortunately, Liz's grandparents took her in and were loving and accommodating, meeting all her needs.

Liz was excited to graduate from high school and finally move on to enjoy the independence of being an adult. After high school, she enrolled in college in Toronto where she lived in a dormitory on campus. At this time, she was taking an antidepressant, but she went on and off of it. Finally, she realized she needed the antidepressant, and in treatment, she lived in nearly full remission. She excelled in college without any hospitalizations for the next eight years.

After two years, in 2008, she graduated from college with an occupational therapy assistant diploma and enrolled in undergraduate studies. As an undergraduate, she worked as a dormitory resident assistant and always scored high grades. She completed a bachelor's degree in child health in 2012.

Unfortunately, while doing her best in school and scoring high grades, Liz's hearing loss progressed, and she developed profound hearing loss by her third year at the university. Over several years, she learned American Sign Language and benefitted from a large Deaf community in the town where her university was located. She would spend every Friday night learning and practicing sign language. She eventually used both sign language and captions to make it through her college studies.

In 2012, Liz began studying for a master's degree in occupational therapy, which would take two years.

During Liz's last year of her master's program, in 2014, she had surgery for cochlear implants, enabling her to eventually regain some of her hearing. Though hearing again was a breakthrough and radically changed her life for the better, the stress and excitement of getting the implants led to her first clinical manic episode, though Liz had not had a psychiatric break since her fifth year of high school.

Just as she was finishing graduate school, Liz's psychosis returned. Approaching graduation with her master's degree, she began to make some poor and reckless choices. She walked nine kilometers over four hours through unsafe neighborhoods, desperate to lessen the extra manic energy she was experiencing. She could not focus or sleep.

Weeks before her next hospitalization, when she was diagnosed with bipolar disorder, she landed her first job as an occupational therapist. On her discharge from the hospital, her doctors felt confident she could handle her new job. She left the hospital on the antipsychotic medication quetiapine as well as haloperidol, valproate, and lithium.

After leaving the hospital and beginning her job, Liz quickly realized she was unable to perform. Liz's first occupational therapy job gave all new employees a three-month probation period. She was fired only one week later for manic behavior.

Plunging into depression, Liz found she could not eat, sleep, or even shower. She needed friends to call her to remind her to go to bed or to eat. Soon after, her friend drove her to a psychiatric emergency room.

Unfortunately, hospital staff did not allow Liz onto the psychiatric floor with her service dog, who had helped her for years through her hearing loss. Liz was quickly discharged from the hospital against medical advice to get her dog back. Still manic, talking too fast, and unable to focus, a few days later she was readmitted to another floor where she could be accompanied by her dog.

While in the hospital, Liz remembers the walls "bleeding." She kept washing the walls to try to clean up the blood, though the walls were clean. She slept at night clinging to a plastic knife which she felt she needed for protection. She also believed she was working with Steven Hawking, to solve mysteries of the multiverse, and she was actively looking for black holes.

A few weeks after the completion of graduate school and after her hospitalization, Liz moved in again with her grandparents. She entered a day program at a Toronto psychiatric hospital from the summer of 2014 until early 2015. She continued to take medications throughout this whole period.

Although Liz was very medically compliant, she remembers not being able to take her medications for a few days when she ran out of them. Off medications, Liz felt more awake and alert, but her psychosis quickly returned. After one time briefly discontinuing her medications, she realized how badly she needed them and would never discontinue them again.

In the summer of 2015, Liz determined that she was well enough to work again. She landed a new job in occupational therapy with flexible hours located an hour and a half away in a small town. Her grandparents were worried about her, feeling she was not ready to work.

By the beginning of 2016, while working, Liz began again to believe that she was collaborating on a physics project with Steven Hawking. She heard someone shouting her name, and there was noise in her head, like a quiet radio where she could not make out the words. Her hygiene suffered and she did not frequently bathe or brush her teeth. At this time, she had no mood symptoms. Her diagnosis was changed from bipolar disorder to schizoaffective disorder.

She decided to take a two-month leave of absence, spending several weeks in another day program. Fortunately, at her new job, she was considered an independent contractor and her hours with the job were flexible.

Finally, thanks to effective antipsychotic medication, in 2016, Liz had achieved recovery. From 2016 until 2022 she worked about 30 to 40 hours a week in her field, living independently. In 2017, she bought a house in a rural community about an hour and a half outside of Toronto.

Liz began another new job at a pain clinic in January 2022. Initially, the stress of changing jobs landed her in the hospital again for four weeks, but that hospitalization was to be her last, to date.

Over the years, many of Liz's friends have had difficulty understanding and accepting what has happened to her through her challenges in her mental health. She finds that while friends after graduate school often do not understand, she has kept several relationships from her undergraduate and graduate years, where she was excelling academically and personally. She sometimes struggles to go the next step in relationships, moving on in her relationships from acquaintances to friends.

Today, Liz has insight. Prior to a manic episode, she feels fidgety. If she starts to experience a great deal of stress, she may become slightly paranoid. In the past, she suspected her colleague of trying to get her fired but quickly recognized this as a delusion, and with rest and a medication change, the delusion went away. Recently, she found herself driving too fast and recklessly and realized the need to rest and discuss it with her treatment team. When she experiences mild paranoia or other symptoms, she is quick to share this with her case manager, therapist, and physician.

Today, Liz has achieved recovery on the antipsychotic cariprazine, bupropion, and the mood stabilizer lithium. She is surviving, thriving, working full-time while being the primary caregiver for her grandmother. She also has her own small business and participates in various community activities.

Liz is the author of the book *Resilient: Surviving My Mental Illness* (2023), which is available on Amazon. She is actively pursuing speaking engagements in order to share her book, her message, and her story.

RECOVERED ON CLOZAPINE

The following individuals are recovered on the medication clozapine, which is highly underutilized around the world, particularly in the United States. Clozapine can work when all other antipsychotics fail, and is considered a "gold-standard medication." To learn about clozapine, see Part Three of *Awakenings*.

17

BETHANY YEISER
President of the CURESZ Foundation

My name is Bethany Yeiser, and thanks to clozapine, I have been fully recovered from schizophrenia for the past 15 years. Two days after my first admission to the hospital, my parents were told I was permanently and totally disabled. But today I live in full recovery.

MY HISTORY AND RECOVERY

I experienced a happy childhood with loving and supportive parents and a brother who was a year and a half younger than me. I thrived in high school, and my passion was the violin. At age 13, I began practicing for four hours a day, joined the Cleveland Orchestra Youth Orchestra, and was accepted as a violin student of a music conservatory professor in downtown Cleveland.

When it was time for me to consider colleges, my first choice was the University of Southern California (USC) in Los Angeles. As I traveled there to visit, suddenly, it felt as though the whole world had opened up to me. I could be a geneticist, or an engineer, or a mathematician, or a physicist. When USC offered me a half tuition scholarship, I was sold. My new dreams were unfolding.

The summer before I was to begin classes at USC, a family friend arranged for me to volunteer in a medical research lab focusing on antibiotic resistance. My research that summer would become a part of two journal articles on which I was listed as an author.

In fall of 1999, at age 17, I left Ohio for USC. Soon after my arrival there, I earned the privilege of becoming the community orchestra concertmaster. I signed up for challenging classes. I also began working with a scientist who had discovered an error-prone DNA polymerase (DNA replicator). Error-prone DNA polymerases were later found in humans and were associated with certain types of cancers.

I remember going to lab meetings every Friday afternoon. At one meeting, the professor explained that if a certain experiment led to another desired result, which led to yet another new breakthrough, a Nobel Prize could be within his reach.

I'm sure everyone at the lab ignored these comments, as they were unrealistic. But they became my world. This was first spark that began a long journey to delusions.

My second semester at USC, I gave up my concertmaster position in the orchestra to spend every minute I had free in the lab. Eventually, I found myself working in the lab regularly until the early hours of the morning. Surprisingly, I had made an unexpected and very promising discovery about the importance of a certain error prone DNA replicator, and then I dreamed of publishing my research in one of the best journals in the field.

My grades were nearly straight A's my first semester, and I felt my classes were easier than expected, but during my second semester my grades sank because I was spending all my time in the lab. I remember getting a C- in my second semester of freshman biology, which covered biology that I had not encountered in the lab. As I became obsessed with the lab, I lost track of my priorities.

During the start of my junior year, in 2001 when the September 11 (9/11) terrorist attacks happened, my world began to look different. At that time, I began to wonder if I could make a world-wide impact by sending struggling people who lived throughout the world funding for their basic needs, as well as working somehow toward world peace.

That semester, my church sent a team of female college students and recent graduates that included me to China to visit the poor. After landing in Kun Ming, China, the young women and I traveled into one of the poorest areas in the country. I remember thinking: "Can I help a million people in poverty in China?" "Can I help millions?" Suddenly, I had a new goal for my life, and I was convinced that, yes, a worldwide impact was within my reach. In hindsight, I realize this was one of my first delusions.

On my return from China, I was on fire to visit Africa — specifically a region afflicted with poverty in a slum area. I decided to go to Africa alone during the following summer. My parents were greatly disturbed and worried by this decision. I promised to provide them my contact information, but while I was in Africa, I felt guilty for not taking care of myself, and I was also afraid my parents would make the trip to Kenya to find me. I had no address in the slum area, and I never gave my parents a certain African woman's phone number who could have helped them find me. I was in Africa for two and a half months. The last month, before leaving the country, I spent a week in Nigeria where I visited a prominent businessman and his wife.

On my return to USC, with renewed determination to do well academically, I moved into my dorm room, bought books for my classes, and faithfully attended lectures. I remember my first exam in an advanced molecular biology class. I thought I aced it, and I was encouraged that I was back to my high-achieving "normal self." However, when my exam was returned to me, I found I had failed it, because all my answers were gibberish.

My mind had become a thick cloud of ruminations, like a damaged vinyl record skipping back to the same place again and again. I found that I could think of nothing but Africa, and I could not move on. At that time, despite my failure in school, I worked together with a friend to establish a nonprofit organization which we called Innovative Medicine International. Through the organization, I raised and sent thousands of dollars to professional friends I had made in Africa, but as my mental functioning deteriorated, I would be unable to continue raising money.

A few months later, I officially dropped out of USC, moved out of my dorm room, and began sleeping in the university library. With a shattered mind, I was totally unable to study or work. I had dropped completely out of contact with family and friends. My parents tried contacting my church, my friends, and my professors in an effort to reach out to me, but I was resolute in refusing any contact. They sent me a large package which I refused and returned to them. They offered to allow me to pay for basic needs and food on their credit card. I refused. I was afraid they would somehow stop me from making a worldwide impact.

Because I had a USC identification card that still appeared valid, I was not asked to leave the library, and I slipped through the cracks for two and a half years. I also started making friends with students who regularly studied or wrote computer code in the library all night. I became an expert at washing up in public bathrooms and looking for discarded food to eat at two or three in the morning.

During the first three years of my homelessness, my delusions were the center of my existence. I continued to be paranoid of my parents. I did not realize that schizophrenia was taking over my life, as my behavior had not yet become bizarre enough to be picked up by police.

Everything in my life would drastically change on January 28, 2006. I found myself sitting on a park bench resting when suddenly, I heard some voices that I soon realized were actually coming from my own mind. I would soon experience more voices that sounded like a chorus of young students. Visual hallucinations came next. I remember looking in the mirror to see my reflection, but instead, I saw an image that consisted of a cross between my face and the character Lisa from the show *The Simpsons*.

Once the voices began, I gave up hiding in USC libraries and began living outside. My first night in a churchyard near the university, I put on three changes of clothes in layers to stay warm. Months later, when trespassing on the USC campus again, I was picked up by police and jailed for two days, which was a horrible experience. The jail was extremely crowded and dark. On my release from the jail, I experienced command hallucinations telling me to scream and shout profanity. March 3, 2007, I was again picked up by police and this time taken for evaluation in a psychiatric ward.

When I was admitted to the emergency room for psychiatric evaluation, my parents were notified. I wondered why they even wanted to speak to me since I had dropped out of college and was homeless. But I consented to talk with my mom. Over a phone call I noticed that she said, "You are my best friend." Not "you could be" or "you were," but "you are." She said she missed me. My parents arrived at the hospital within 24 hours. Their compassion touched my heart.

I was adamant that I did not need an antipsychotic medication, but after a few days, I consented to start taking risperidone. Risperidone was what some might call amazing. The visual hallucinations disappeared. Paranoia of my parents and friends was gone in a few days. Many of my auditory hallucinations also disappeared, as well as my command hallucinations. But even though my serious symptoms were gone, I still heard loud voices in my mind, like a radio blasting between channels. I never believed I had been sick or was improving.

No one pointed out the positive effects that were noticed by my treatment team on risperidone. I do not remember being told my diagnosis, or what side effects I might encounter. I did not know there were other medications that could be tried. One staff member simply told me that I would probably be on that medication for life. At the same time, I was not convinced that I even needed it. I believe he did not know me or was confused.

After two and a half weeks in the hospital, I flew home with my parents to recover at their home in southern Ohio. While I was in California, they had moved from Cleveland to Cincinnati. My parents' friends were generous and kind to me, never asking questions about how I had spent the prior five years of my life.

However, when I arrived in Ohio, the side effects of risperidone became problematic. I was sleeping 16-18 hours a day, which I had not noticed in the hospital, thinking I was just resting because I was bored. My muscles became increasingly rigid, and I experienced akathisia, an extreme restlessness. I had a blunted affect (flattened emotional expression) and could not enjoy my favorite music or my favorite pictures because the medication had dampened my ability to experience pleasure. The absence of feeling pleasure, or "anhedonia," was the side effect that bothered me most. I also had an uncontrollable appetite and quickly gained nearly twenty pounds.

Confident of who I was, certain that I did not need an antipsychotic medication, and unaware that the medication was helping at all, I stopped my risperidone. After a few days, I began screaming that I had to go back to California. Off medication, all I wanted was to be homeless again and "free." I again lapsed into florid psychosis with command hallucinations and agitation, and ended up breaking an expensive violin. A friend of our family called 911 for medical intervention for my condition, and I was again hospitalized.

During my second hospitalization, a psychiatrist offered me a lifeline. He said, "Do you remember playing violin at a high level and studying molecular biology?" He said that I might be able to have these things back, but that to do so I must always stay on antipsychotic medication. He also told me that every time an antipsychotic medication is restarted it can become less effective, even at higher dosages, and that discontinuing medications was what eventually would lead to disability. I believe this is something every patient should be told on the day they begin medication.

I left the hospital after about five days, now knowing that I always needed antipsychotic medication, although a different one.

I spent the next several months totally disabled and felt like a shadow of whom I had once been. I was unable to attend school, work a job, or even participate in meaningful volunteering. My life involved sleeping, resting, and captive listening to the voices in my mind. I lived as a totally disabled person for 12 months, even while enduring trials of different antipsychotic medications.

At that time, when all hope seemed lost, I was referred to a schizophrenia expert named Dr. Henry Nasrallah. From the start, Dr. Nasrallah was different than any other psychiatrist I had worked with. He carefully reviewed the history of my life accomplishments, including my three scientific publications from the Cleveland lab and from USC. He knew about my history of playing the violin at a high level. He also knew that I wanted to finish my molecular biology degree but had been told it would be impossible.

Dr. Nasrallah started me on the medication clozapine, which I had never heard of. Dr Nasrallah informed me about the potential side effects of clozapine which included weight gain, sedation, and the need to have blood drawn every week to check for white blood counts, which may drop in 1% of patients and may be potentially fatal.

After a month on clozapine, I could see real progress. I experienced a significant drop in my auditory hallucinations which I had not made on any other antipsychotic medication. After about four months, I had entered full remission from the illness. I had many long conversations with Dr. Nasrallah about my future goals and plans. He encouraged me to reenroll and complete my college education.

In 2009, a year and a half after beginning clozapine, I moved from my parents' home in the Cincinnati suburbs into an apartment a few minutes' walk from the University of Cincinnati. In December of 2011, I graduated with honors in molecular biology [magna cum laude] from the University of Cincinnati. It was a very emotional time for my parents who attended the ceremony with Dr. Nasrallah.

SHARING WITH DOCTORS AND FAMILIES

After I graduated from college, Dr. Nasrallah encouraged me to document everything that had happened. My life story became a memoir which I published in a book titled *Mind Estranged: My Journey from Schizophrenia and Homelessness to Recovery*. My mom also wrote a companion book with her perspective as a mother and a nurse. Her book is titled *Flight from Reason: A Mother's Story of Schizophrenia, Recovery and Hope*. Both books were published in summer of 2014.

Following the publication of *Mind Estranged*, I began traveling extensively to make presentations to families and mental health professionals about sustained, full recovery through faithful medication adherence and, for many persons with schizophrenia, treatment with clozapine. What I learned through these interactions was that families were often told there was no hope for recovery from schizophrenia. And I met doctors all the time who also believed recovery was impossible and never even considered using clozapine for patients with lack of improvement on other antipsychotic medications.

One of the highlights of my advocacy was meeting with a doctor who heard my story of recovery on clozapine and decided to radically change his practice — to never give up on his patients, and if appropriate, use clozapine. This doctor now serves on our CURESZ Foundation Board of Trustees.

I began a new career of writing and giving national presentations, initially with Dr. Nasrallah at medical conferences and later by myself. I found myself quite busy and felt I was making a difference in the lives of people with serious mental illness. Today, my mind is clear and my life has a purpose.

ESTABLISHING THE CURESZ FOUNDATION

In 2016, Dr. Nasrallah approached me with another idea, which was to establish a nonprofit foundation which we called Comprehensive Understanding via Research and Education into SchiZophrenia, with an acronym of CURESZ. The CURESZ Foundation now serves thousands of families who have a loved one suffering from serious mentally illness. CURESZ programs include our caregivers mentoring program, a support group, Ask the Doctor events, and on-campus clubs. These programs are described in Part Three of *Awakenings*. We are also proud of the "Survivors" we feature in Part Two who are thriving despite schizophrenia.

I have learned over the years that it is vital for psychiatric physicians to never give up on individuals struggling with schizophrenia and for persons with schizophrenia to never lose hope or give up on themselves. I will never forget my first psychiatrist telling my parents that I am permanently and totally disabled, even after knowing me for only about two days.

For those patients like me who are treatment-resistant, clozapine is the most effective antipsychotic but is an underutilized medication option. At least 1 in 3 patients with schizophrenia who fail other antipsychotics qualify for it, but in the United States, only about 1 in 25 actually are prescribed this medication. This means that there are hundreds of thousands of individuals living with schizophrenia in America who are disabled due to persistent delusions and hallucinations — in many cases, totally disabled — and they have never even heard of clozapine. There is a reasonable chance that clozapine could eliminate their psychosis and bring many of them back to their healthy baseline, as it did for me.

In 2018, the CURESZ Foundation established a Clozapine Expert Panel to help families find a clozapine prescriber whose office is near them as shown on CURESZ.org.

As I move forward with my life, I am extremely grateful for my parents who refused to give up on me, even when everyone else in my life did. I am also grateful for my former psychiatrist and coauthor of *Awakenings*, Dr. Henry Nasrallah. He has devoted his life to helping people like me whom many clinicians have either forgotten, neglected, rejected or deemed beyond help.

Through the essays I have written in Part One of *Awakenings*, and through this personal story, I would like to assert that I do not believe my schizophrenia diagnosis to be a life sentence or permanent disability. Thanks to my full medication adherence with clozapine, and support from family, friends, and Dr. Nasrallah, I have recovered. Today, I live a very happy, busy, and full life.

I am confident that my future is bright. Today, I am honored and humbled to serve as President of the CURESZ Foundation where I spend several hours a day executing its operations.

BethanyYeiser.com

18

DANIEL LAITMAN
Working as a Stand-Up Comic

Daniel attended SUNY Purchase University where he studied screen writing and playwriting and founded the Standup comedy club, graduating in 2015. He currently works as a comedian in Manhattan and helps run the nonprofit "Team Daniel Running for Recovery from Mental Illness" with his family.

Daniel Laitman was born in the Bronx, New York, to a mom who worked as an internist and a father who was a nephrologist. He has three sisters, one is older and two who are younger. Growing up, Daniel felt he was always "a bit different." But overall, he enjoyed a mostly happy and normal, upper middle-class childhood in the northern Westchester hamlet of Bedford, New York.

Daniel had his struggles and had occasional "meltdowns" in middle and elementary school. In fourth grade he started to see a psychiatrist and was treated with medication for anxiety and ADHD. He had an IEP (individual education plan) and a tutor and with this support he did well. During eighth grade he took a vacation to Italy, and after a visit to Murano, he developed an intense interest in glass blowing.

After many hours of research on where he might study it, he discovered a summer camp in Connecticut named Buck's Rock. It was a perfect fit for him. Not only did he learn more about glass blowing, but it was here that he was introduced to stand-up comedy. The clown shop became his second home. He spent four weeks there that summer, and that was his first time away from the family. It was a dramatic success. He would subsequently spend eight weeks there the following three summers.

Daniel's freshman year of high school went very well, but in retrospect, he noted that he was starting on rare occasion to hear voices. The summer between freshman and sophomore year he went back to camp for eight weeks, but as the summer progressed, the voices became more pervasive. At first, the voices told him they would help him with his comedy, and he remembers them as neither positive or negative, but "benign." However, a few days later, they began to order him to do strange things, altering his behavior.

The voices mandated he hold his arm at a constant right angle, which later he referred to as his "tard arm." They threatened him that if he did not continue to hold his arm in this uncomfortable position, something terrible would happen. He worried the voices might "take away" his comedy. He also began to see "trails" behind people who were walking by and heard voices in his mind telling him that if anyone passed him by, he needed to wait 15 seconds before continuing to follow them. After his parents picked him up from camp, they went on a short vacation to Canada. While in Canada, Daniel knew something was very wrong. The tard arm and other unusual behavior were quite apparent. Despite this, he interacted with his siblings and parents and had a good time.

Daniel returned to school after the summer vacation. As he had done after every summer, he restarted his ADHD medication. But within a few days he looked and felt sick. The light had gone out of his eyes, and they were blank. His parents felt that he was disappearing in front of them.

It was at that time he first told his parents that he had been hearing command voices and was not only afraid of losing his comedy but also of losing his soul. Soon after, Daniel saw his psychiatrist and was placed on his first antipsychotic medication, aripiprazole.

Unfortunately, his first experience on antipsychotic medication was negative, and over several months, he experienced severe side effects that resembled Parkinson's disease (which often presents with antipsychotic medications). The medication also did not resolve his symptoms. Ziprasidone and quetiapine were also tried and ineffective. In the fall semester of Daniel's sophomore year of high school, he was taken out of regular school and began an intensive outpatient program at a facility called Four Winds. During the spring semester, he was back in school at a special BOCES program (Board of Cooperative Educational Services), which provided Daniel with smaller classes and more individualized instruction. During this year and the next, Daniel tried other cocktails of meds including another antipsychotic medication, paliperidone. He remembers seeing his father cry.

As Daniel continued to suffer on partially effective medications, his parents did extensive research. With tremendous help from Deborah Levy, head of McLean's Psychology Research lab, they read everything they could find and discovered information about the only FDA-approved medication for treatment-resistant schizophrenia, clozapine. Finally, in March of 2008, with the help of Daniel's psychiatrist Charles Kaufman, he began clozapine on his grandfather's birthday.

Daniel does not remember his first few weeks on clozapine well, though he does recall sleeping for many hours during the days. He remembers taking a video course through school soon after and sleeping through it with his head on the keyboard. But with time, it was as though Daniel woke from a deep sleep. A few months later, while at lunch in school, Daniel began to wander from table to table, practicing his comedy. He quickly earned the reputation "comic boy."

Daniel's parents were dismayed that many psychiatric clinicians simply "did not know what they were doing" when it came to treating psychosis. They were outraged at the tremendous underutilization of clozapine and were further disappointed that psychiatrists did not "do the medicine," a catch phrase Dr. Laitman uses today about trying clozapine, to mitigate predictable side effects in those rare occasions when clozapine was used.

Over the years his parents slowly started to treat other patients who had psychosis with approaches that were originally developed for Daniel. Over the last 15 years they have transformed their practice to be psychiatric internists with special expertise in the optimal management of clozapine. They now have treated several 100 patients, founded a charity called Team Daniel Running for Recovery from Serious Mental Illness, written a book titled *Meaningful Recovery from Schizophrenia and Serious Mental Illness with Clozapine*, and continue to deliver regular lectures on their approach and their results. Currently, they are trying to train several psychiatric DNPs (NP, PhD) in their approach.

On clozapine, Daniel successfully graduated from high school and began studying for a film and a TV degree at Westchester Community College. He graduated with honors in 2012. Following the completion of his associate degree, he started performing standup comedy at open mics in various restaurants and clubs in New York City. Following his community college graduation, he attended SUNY Purchase University where he studied screen writing and playwriting and founded the Standup comedy club. In 2015, he graduated on the Dean's list. He then moved into the city to live in the East Village in order to pursue his career in standup comedy. He continues to write and work on his craft and has a large network of friends and admirers. His dream today is to write for a late-night host such as Stephen Colbert, Seth Meyers, or John Oliver and to continue to perform standup in continually larger venues.

Daniel is thankful for the medication clozapine which has given him his life back. He is also grateful for his two committed parents who were willing to do whatever it took to bring him to recovery and who now work tirelessly as advocates for other young people like Daniel who are struggling with schizophrenia, many who have never been offered clozapine or even heard of the medication.

Daniel is happy with his current work and looks forward to a bright future as a comedian.

www.TeamDanielRunningforRecovery.org

19

CHELSEA KOWAL
Back to School

Chelsea Kowal has lived with schizoaffective disorder, bipolar type since beginning college. Despite several hospitalizations and refractory symptoms, she is now recovered on clozapine. She graduated with her master's degree in biomedical engineering in 2013.

Chelsea was born in 1989 in Newark, New Jersey, and is the youngest of three siblings. Her mom was a teacher's aid and craftswoman. She had two older brothers.

Chelsea experienced a difficult childhood filled with abuse and neglect. At age 15, Chelsea was suicidal. This led to her first hospitalization, and what would be only one of many. While hospitalized, she met a person around her age who was hearing voices. At the time, she had no idea that many years later, she would experience the same symptoms.

Chelsea's oldest brother committed suicide at the age of 25, when Chelsea was only 17. A few months after his suicide, she spoke at her high school, encouraging students to not do drugs or drink and to seek help if experiencing thoughts of suicide.

In high school, Chelsea and her mother were evicted and became homeless. Chelsea "couch surfed" at night during the summer before her senior year and into the fall, staying off and on with about eight different families. During the summer, she helped build and fix homes through an organization with her church called Appalachian Service Project. She also volunteered as a Junior Camp Counselor at a camp for children and adults with special needs. The camp provided her with food and somewhere to sleep.

She was eventually notified that a permanent residence was required within the school district boundaries if she wanted to continue studying at her high school, which was one of the best in her area. To meet the requirement, she decided to move into a friend's family home and stay in their basement until she and her mother moved into an apartment together. She and her mother were homeless for about six months.

Chelsea dealt with her homelessness and abusive upbringing by directing all her effort toward her studies, and remained drug and alcohol free, after seeing how abusing these substances took a toll on her family. In her first year of high school, she had taken remedial courses including biology and social studies. But during her senior year, she would take five advanced placement courses and two honors courses, graduating tenth in a class of 300 students.

However, about that time — at age 17 — Chelsea attempted to take her own life, overdosing on her prescribed antidepression medication, only a month after losing her oldest brother to suicide. Fortunately, she recovered quickly after a hospital stay. After this, she was diagnosed as "probable bipolar." She was also diagnosed with Asperger's Syndrome (on the Autism spectrum) at age 22 and again at age 32. Due to her challenging upbringing, she was also diagnosed with post-traumatic stress disorder (PTSD).

In spite of her diagnoses, she looked forward to making a new start in college, living independently as a young adult, apart from her family. Despite her unstable family situation and unpredictable mental health, Chelsea was ambitious for her future. After applying to universities, she was waitlisted at MIT, Columbia, and Johns Hopkins, receiving correspondence from these universities while homeless. Nine different colleges across the nation granted her admission. She finally settled on starting at Syracuse University in 2007 to major in bioengineering.

Throughout her life, Chelsea always had a photographic memory. Starting college, she managed to memorize tens of pages of class notes in less than an hour. She would finish an exam scheduled to last over an hour in 10 to 15 minutes. She managed a course load of over 20 credit hours, over the normal limit of 18, and maintained close to straight A's. After her sophomore year, her GPA was 3.986.

In addition to studying full-time during college, Chelsea worked a variety of jobs for up to 60 hours per week. This included tutoring calculus classes. She remembers tutoring as a happy time when she enjoyed going the extra mile and taking any possible opportunity to help her students.

Along with working during school, Chelsea also performed research at two other universities as part of summer research internships. In the summer of 2008, she engaged in cancer research at University of Virginia. In the summer of 2009, she engaged in spinal cord injury research at Case Western Reserve University.

Looking back, Chelsea recognizes that during college, she was experiencing a "manic energy," always working or studying. At that time, her efforts were successful, and she was unaware that she was on the brink of developing a full-blown mood disorder and eventually psychosis.

Despite great success in school and work, during the beginning of her junior year, Chelsea's abusive upbringing came back to haunt her. She eventually attempted to take her own life again by jumping off a 40-foot building. Fortunately, a large tree braced her fall, and though she had broken her back, she survived. After two days of hospitalization, she was able to walk again, which friends and family considered to be a miracle. She would wear a body brace for the next three months to allow her broken vertebrae to heal.

Following her recovery from the jump, she was transferred to a psychiatric ward and mandated to take a 10-month leave from college. At that time, Chelsea heard from some of the calculus students whom she was teaching. They were encouraging, missing her, and wanting her back. She hoped to soon return to normal life.

Unfortunately, Chelsea's first antipsychotic medications negatively affected her exceptional photographic memory. Her clinicians tried risperidone, among others. These medications had bad side effects including weight gain and akathisia (restlessness). Following the suicide attempt, her diagnosis was changed to schizophrenia.

Following her hospital discharge, Chelsea spent the next 10 months in an intensive outpatient program (IOP). She tried various medications. While there, she enjoyed crocheting scarves, which she later distributed to the homeless in New York City. With her history of being homeless herself, helping the homeless has always been incredibly important to her. She also made friends in the program.

In fall of 2009 and spring of 2010, she unsuccessfully reapplied to return to Syracuse University. Finally, in fall of 2010, she was readmitted.

Back in school, Chelsea went from straight A's to A's and B's, as her memory was not as sharp as it had been prior to antipsychotic medication. She took fewer courses but enjoyed doing research in the Department of Orthopedics at the Upstate Medical University, where she worked on a project studying the anatomy of the human shoulder. Chelsea realized that she still had a bright future and promising career.

Chelsea also resumed working other jobs while in school, including washing dishes in a cafeteria, which she enjoyed for the fast pace. She tutored calculus and differential equations and worked as a math grader. She also volunteered at her local community center, helping students learn math and science.

In addition to studying for her undergraduate bioengineering degree, she added two minors: mathematics and general management studies (including marketing and accounting). Chelsea graduated magna cum laude from Syracuse University with a GPA of 3.736 and in the Honors Program. She also received several awards.

Upon Chelsea's college graduation in May 2012, she had worked in research for nearly three years. She decided her next step was to study for a PhD degree in biomedical engineering, and applied to the University of Florida, where she received a full tuition scholarship to attend in the fall of 2012.

However, during the beginning of her graduate studies, she began to experience her first delusions. She expected to win a Nobel Peace prize. Friends told her that she was one of the smartest people alive, and when voices in her mind confirmed that it was true, she believed it.

At the University of Florida, she developed an idea to cure cancer by using quantum physics. Chelsea soon expected to help cure cancer herself and wondered if there was anything in life she could not do.

Her closer friends and family quickly noticed that something was wrong. She was in and out of the hospital in Florida throughout her degree program, and her diagnosis was changed to schizoaffective disorder, bipolar type. At one point, a physician told her it was impossible for her to finish graduate school, and she should not even try. Despite the voices and delusions, Chelsea successfully graduated with her master's degree in biomedical engineering in December of 2013 with A's and B's.

Following her graduation, her psychosis returned, worse than it had ever been. She would not work again for 10 years.

She returned to New Jersey and entered another partial care program through the local psychiatric hospital while living at home with her mother. She remembers art therapy classes where she was encouraged to do simple art projects. Though she appreciated art, it was devastating to realize how far she had fallen from her success in biomedical engineering. Still, she held onto her goal and dream of returning to engineering.

Her doctors tried yet another medication, aripiprazole (Abilify) but she developed a rare side effect, becoming unable to swallow. Eventually, she was moved to a group home in Sussex in 2015 after another hospitalization. While living there, she would be closely monitored in a partial care program.

In 2017, Chelsea was finally admitted for a long-term stay at Greystone Park Psychiatric Hospital until August 2019. At Greystone, doctors tried lurasidone, among many other medications, which initially helped with her memory, but seemed to aggravate her psychosis. Haloperidol was unsuccessful. Chlorpromazine (Thorazine) made her more suicidal. The list goes on…

Chelsea remembers hearing voices all day, from the time she woke up until the second she fell asleep, and she recalled that she would often sleep only an hour per night for months. She even had two periods during which she recalled that she did not sleep at all for about nine days each time.

Chelsea was afraid of the staff, believing they were trying to kill her because she was too smart. At times, she refused to eat. She also believed she was working for the FBI, police, CIA, FDA, and Department of Justice. Everything she learned in college and graduate school was speeding through her mind. She wrote letters to various organizations with ideas for inventions.

Upon her discharge, she was still acutely symptomatic and delusional, believing she was the President of the United States. She also believed she was Jesus making a return back to earth. She remembers visiting a pier at the waterfront, believing rescue workers there were resuscitating people who had drowned many years prior. She thought she had invented a vaccine that would save all humans and animals from COVID. Chelsea also struggled intensely with "cybertelepathokinesis," a term she created for hearing other people's voices in her mind.

Chelsea finally accepted and made peace with her psychiatric diagnoses. It was about a year after being discharged from Greystone when a doctor prescribed a new medication, clozapine, when things really began to improve.

Chelsea began clozapine in the fall of 2020. After one month, she saw a significant reduction in her voices and delusions, which she had never imagined possible. She recalls that her voices were reduced from constantly to about 5% of the time. Within a few months, Chelsea had gained a high enough level of recovery to grasp a firm hold of her dream of working again, and she began a new life.

She began a volunteer internship in January 2021 for the National STEM (Science, Technology, Engineering and Mathematics) Honor Society to help students increase their awareness of STEM fields. She worked in seven departments, serving as Director of Market Research/Email Marketing, Director of Member Care, Department Manager of Sponsorships and Partnerships, and an intern in e-commerce, public relations, business management, and social media.

In January 2022 Chelsea resigned from her internship, focusing instead on the training she needed to become a peer support specialist.

Throughout her life, Chelsea always abstained from drugs and alcohol, having seen the negative effects the substances had on the lives of some of her family members. She committed herself to live differently. Fortunately, drug and alcohol use did not complicate her recovery.

Today, Chelsea has been in nearly full recovery for three years. In recovery, she finds herself busy again. She volunteers as a peer support specialist and a recovery coach in training. She also volunteers at her local library and YMCA, as well as a few other organizations. She currently suffers no side effects and experiences very limited symptoms.

Clozapine was different than any other medication she tried because every other medication either was ineffective, intolerable, or stopped working after a few months. Chelsea reflects that "Clozapine totally changed my life and enabled me to move forward in ways I never thought I could again… Now, I want my life to matter, especially because I nearly died a few times in my life. I am just grateful to be alive. Every day is a blessing."

AWAKENINGS

She recalls choosing biomedical engineering because there are so many projects in the field that would allow her to make a difference in the world. Her dream is to continue to make a difference in the lives of as many people as she can.

Chelsea recently became engaged to be married and is excited to see what life has to offer her next.

20

RHEA
Researcher on OCD and Early Psychosis

I was born in Potsdam, New York. When I was growing up, I showed warning signs of my illness, but they were dismissed as "spunk" or an overactive imagination. I graduated from high school early because I was academically advanced and I felt out of place in the rural, conservative town. I needed a change and chose to attend the University of Southern California (USC), where I received a full-tuition scholarship, and where I could pursue both my mathematical and musical interests.

My first semester was wonderful, and I made friends quickly, but I was soon diagnosed with mononucleosis and had to withdraw. During my second semester, my "spunk" and active imagination evolved into a full-blown psychotic disorder. By the time I returned home for the summer, I was convinced I was a computer and that the rest of the world was possessed by aliens trying to eliminate me.

I began to have the dual and seemingly contradictory symptoms of extreme suicidality and fear of getting killed. I would spend all day in a chair, trying not to kill myself, but when I was spoken to, all I wanted to do was to run away. Paranoia was all too present, with my beliefs that everyone was talking about me and conspiring against me. I frequently heard disparaging whispers and had visual hallucinations of a man threatening me. I often "switched dimensions" and had experiences in other worlds that existed only to me. I remembered different things than what the people around me recalled, or I failed to remember many events. I wasn't safe in the world, and I wasn't safe in my mind.

The psychiatric care in Potsdam was inadequate, and my doctor, one of the few if not the only outpatient doctor in the county, informed me that her next available appointment was in three months, despite the severity of my suicidality. The psychiatrist told my parents that I would need a friend for the long road ahead and recommended a dog. I named the dog Kiwi. He would become the center of my life, as well as a major support for my mother when she would later be alone in Los Angeles caring for me.

It didn't take long for me to wind up in the processing room for the closest psychiatric hospital, which was 40 minutes away. I contracted for safety (signed a document where I said I would not kill or harm myself) and was allowed to go home. But, soon after that, I found myself at risk for suicide. I told my parents and was brought to the second-closest psychiatric hospital, two hours away, because my parents were unhappy with the kind of care I had received at the other hospital.

During the first activity of the first day of my stay, I was told: "We see kids like you all the time. You will be in here three days and won't ever have to worry about it again." If only! It was years before that lack of worry was within reach.

I was insistent on returning to USC as if nothing had happened. My mother came to Los Angeles with me, supposedly just to get me settled in. She never left, afraid for my safety. I went to an intensive outpatient program every day, had an active extracurricular schedule, and took 18 units of classwork at USC. I have often looked back at that semester and wondered how I managed to juggle all that, but I think I had to. I had to stay as busy as possible or I would be alone with my thoughts, and my thoughts were scary.

One night, when I was at my mother's apartment, I began to get angry. Then, according to my mother, I stopped making sense. Random words were coming out of my mouth, and the fact that she couldn't understand them was making me more agitated. I began to cry. My mother took me to the hospital, where I was held involuntarily, given the prognosis of "grave," and diagnosed with bipolar-type schizoaffective disorder.

I would stay there for a month, on a one-to-one for much of that time (I had a nurse watching me 24/7, even when I showered, used the bathroom, and slept) because I tried to hurt myself in the hospital. I took my final USC examinations in the hospital, receiving 4 A's and a B+. I was in the hospital for Thanksgiving but out before Christmas. I briefly stayed in a residential program afterward but found it unhelpful.

I took the next semester off, relocating to Boston for programs at McLean. Doctors recommended electroconvulsive therapy (ECT), but the anesthesiologist would not sedate me due to my gastroesophageal reflux disease (GERD) and his fear that McLean, as a psychiatric hospital only, would not be able to help me if I were to be sick during the procedure. I was admitted and stayed inpatient at McLean for a bit, until they found a bed at Newton-Wellesley Hospital. I received 20 treatments of ECT, working with an anesthesiologist over a two-month period. I consider this to be one of the big mistakes of my treatment journey because my brain felt "different" afterward and I was still suicidal. I also gained 50 pounds during this hospitalization because I was bored and spent my days snacking in the pantry.

Post-discharge, I began a program at Boston University's Center for Psychiatric Rehabilitation called NITEO. The program aims to aid college students on leave due to mental illness. I went back to USC for an unremarkable semester but returned to Boston afterward for transcranial magnetic stimulation at McLean. I received this treatment outpatient, so I was able to intern at NITEO, serving as a mentor and confidante for other students and teaching the music and Photovoice classes. I found that even though I wasn't better, I was a master of compartmentalization. I was able to talk to the students and keep the attention off me. It was also very helpful that I knew all the adults there and they were very understanding if I simply couldn't be present for a day.

I realized USC was just not going to work, as much as I wanted it to. I transferred to Columbia University and began ketamine infusions. Initially, they were remarkable. Suddenly, I did not want to hurt myself anymore. And while my depression was not gone, I stopped feeling like life was pointless. The psychosis remained unchanged, but life was much easier without the constant suicidality. The effects started to wane after a bit, and ketamine lozenges were added to supplement the infusions. After one terrible treatment that left my brain feeling "broken" for a short amount of time afterward, I decided not to continue with the infusions since they were no longer efficacious, and I feared their effects.

I got by for a bit, not thriving in school and needing constant care from my parents, but managing to stay out of the hospital.

Then I began clozapine and everything changed. It took a while to get me stabilized on the dosing, but after a few months life got easier for me. I could suddenly manage my schoolwork, my hallucinations decreased, and most notably, my previously persistent paranoia waned significantly. No longer was I afraid to go to class, thinking my classmates were poisoning me or that strangers on the street were plotting to eliminate me. My suicidality also decreased even more. I began to get A's, which I hadn't managed to do previously at Columbia. There were downsides: side effects like excess saliva production and extreme fatigue, which required more meds to control. I still had significant depression, which I managed by staying busy, trying to stay out of the apartment, and spending more time with Kiwi. I eventually graduated in May 2020 with a BA in sociology.

I had planned on going to vet school, but after volunteering at a clinic, I found I got too attached to the animals. I began a master's in disability studies at the City University of New York, graduating with a 4.0 in May 2022.

I now live alone with Kiwi, do research on OCD and early psychosis at the New York State Psychiatric Institute and look forward to applying to PhD programs. I try to take Kiwi to the dog park at least twice a day so he and I can both socialize. I don't have a perfect life, but there are moments when I look around and am so glad that I am alive.

21

KIRK REITELBACH
Celebrating Fifteen Years as a Paralegal

My childhood was happy. I was born in Ohio to a family that had financial resources, and my parents deeply cared about me. I was the first-born. My family had one other child — a daughter — who was born three years after me. My sister Karen and I enjoy a fulfilling relationship to this day.

In high school, I did very well academically and excelled athletically. Upon my graduation, I was nominated as the most outstanding scholar-athlete. I was also accepted at an Ivy League school, Dartmouth, where I planned to major in philosophy.

In 1972, at the age of 18, I moved to Dartmouth. I did very well in my coursework for a year. However, most of my friends smoked marijuana, and I began to smoke with them regularly. I also experimented with LSD.

On New Year's Day of 1974, I arrived in Frankfurt, Germany, where I studied for 10 weeks as a foreign exchange student. On my arrival, I took a train to Amsterdam, Holland, where I met a Dutch girl who invited me to live with her when I finished school. I later wrote her a letter from the United States, as I was interested in maintaining the relationship. I promised to return but never did.

During my German language studies program, I developed severe paranoia. I became suspicious of other people, worried that they wanted to harm me. I neglected my studies and was regularly smoking hash. I was living with an old German widow, and she threatened to call the police on me because of the drug use.

My language program was scored as pass or fail, and despite learning very little German, I passed and boarded a plane back to America.

But on my return, my paranoia worsened. Everywhere I went, I thought people knew who I was and were "out to get me." If I stopped at a grocery store to buy food, I was worried that the cashier was going to kill me.

None of my friends from college or even from high school knew how to react, and I lost all of these friendships. I was unable to continue my studies at Dartmouth. When I returned home to live with my family in Ohio, I was devastated.

For two years, beginning in 1974, I worked for my dad's printing company doing odd jobs, earning minimum wage, and not functioning well. I lived with my parents, who were very concerned about me, but didn't know what to do. They sent me to a psychiatrist who couldn't give me much time. He put me on trifluoperazine (Stelazine) which I stayed on for a year. I strongly disliked the Stelazine as I felt it "numbed" my emotions and feelings.

I was still taking Stelazine when I experienced my first psychotic break at age 22 in 1976. That day, while at a friend's apartment smoking pot, I started hearing voices. The first voice I heard was the voice of the girl I met in Holland.

When my parents noticed my behavior, they were even more worried, but I was already seeing a doctor and on medication.

During the next four years, I barely managed to get through each day. But despite my struggles, I finally decided to return to school. I was just two quarters away from graduating.

On my return to Dartmouth, I was still smoking pot and abusing alcohol. I soon had another psychotic episode while in my dormitory, hearing voices, and yelling back at the voices. Police took me to Dartmouth's mental health center. After I was there for a couple of weeks, I was discharged and prohibited from continuing my studies.

Fortunately, at that time, my mother intervened. She was desperate to get me help, and she convinced me to completely stop all alcohol and drug use. I never used alcohol and drugs again.

Over the next 10 years, I continued living at home and working for my dad. During that time I also frequently moved in and out of hospitals due to my voices and erratic behavior. After that, my mother and I moved to Tennessee where I participated in a program for people struggling with mental health issues. For the next 15 years, I moved with my mother from place to place, trying many mental health programs, desperate for help.

Finally, at the recommendation of a psychiatrist named Henry Nasrallah, MD, a Florida hospital offered me the opportunity to try an experimental drug, clozapine. Unfortunately, inpatient hospitalization was required for the duration of my time on clozapine. Making the decision to give up my freedom and live in a hospital for an extended amount of time was difficult, but Dr. Nasrallah and others strongly recommended that I try clozapine. They even suggested it might bring me to recovery.

Then something happened which I had thought to be impossible. After two to three months on clozapine, I began to stabilize. My psychosis and symptoms gradually started to decrease. I felt better both mentally and physically. After four to five months, I felt I was a new person.

Unfortunately, I was required to continue living in the hospital as an inpatient for two years while on clozapine. In 1989, clozapine was officially approved by the

FDA, and I was finally permitted to leave the hospital and to begin a whole new life.

After my discharge, I began to dream again about finishing college. I contacted the president of Dartmouth University, asking for permission to take my last five courses at a Florida university near where I was living, and transfer the credit for them to Dartmouth. I was granted permission.

I began college at a small school in Sarasota where I earned high grades. After I transferred the credits, I graduated from Dartmouth College. It was one of the proudest moments of my life.

Following my graduation, my mother and I returned to our family home in Columbus, Ohio. A doctor sent me for testing at a vocational rehabilitation facility to determine which career might be a best fit. He discovered I had a high aptitude for the legal field.

Eighteen months later, in 2007, I completed a certificate in paralegal studies, and I was hired by Disability Rights Ohio in 2012 as a full-time employee. I continue to work full-time there to this day. I love my work and enjoy meaningful relationships with my coworkers and family.

I'd like to say that if you manage your life properly and follow your doctor's advice, it is possible to recover from a major mental illness and have a happy and fulfilling life. I am living proof! Never give up, and keep trying various treatments until you have reached the highest level of recovery possible. You never know what breakthroughs are around the next corner.

22

MILLIE VINE*
Successful Chef

I grew up in a stable and loving household. I attended excellent public schools and played competitive sports, including soccer, swimming, basketball, and volleyball. After working hard throughout middle school and high school, I graduated with honors.

In 2010, I began college at a university in Oregon on an athletic scholarship for rowing, even though I had never done so competitively. I loved rowing on the erg machines (machines that simulate rowing on the water) as well as being on the water, but the pressure of a highly competitive collegiate sport was too intense for me, so I gave it up after a year.

I have always loved cooking, so I decided to focus on food science as a major. I landed a job working on campus in a dairy making cheese, where I was able to use my passion for the profession for the first time. I even came in second in a college-wide contest on creative ways to use whey, a byproduct of making cheese. While I had successfully transitioned off the rowing team into a life-long love of cooking, all was not well. My grades began slipping, and I spent my savings on home decor, kitchen items, food, and make-up, hoping it would make me feel better. Having grown up with dogs and cats, I recognize the emotional benefit they provide. Feeling homesick for family and my animals, I got a darling tuxedo cat.

During my senior year of college, I became anxious, and friends recommended marijuana gummies to ease my nerves. I did not use drugs, so I had no tolerance for marijuana. My doctors said that since I was suffering from depression and my mind was fragile, the marijuana precipitated a psychotic break. I went to the hospital multiple nights knowing something was wrong, but they just dismissed me as a drug user. Eventually, the psychiatrist called my mom and told her I had a severe drug problem. She and my aunt drove through the night for 10 hours and found me in the Janis House, a respite facility for drug and alcohol abusers. I was still in the midst of a psychotic break.

Because I was so embarrassed, afraid, and ashamed, I wouldn't see my mom

---

*The name has been changed to protect the privacy of those involved in the story.

for hours after her arrival. Following days of confusion and a failure of mental healthcare to recognize my immediate needs, I dropped my classes, and my dad flew up to get me home. I lived in a fog, feeling like a failure. The future I was hoping to build abruptly changed as my dependency on my parents increased.

Early in my diagnosis, I begged my parents to find help for me. I'd go anywhere. I couldn't handle the degrading voices and hallucinations. The medication also made me feel extremely disengaged with reality.

Inpatient mental health facilities are hard to find if one does not also suffer from addictions. I have learned that finding high quality mental healthcare is incredibly difficult in general, but it was even more difficult for me because I live in a state that ranks 51st in the nation for mental healthcare.

Fortunately, I have a loving family who have been able to fight for me even when I am not able. In California, we found a treatment facility which seemed to be a good fit. After a month, I was feeling less paranoid, so I went home. Unfortunately, this respite did not last. At that time, my psychiatrist retired, which launched me into a downward spiral.

I found another psychiatrist who had more respect for my illness and realized the importance of my connection with family. He also had higher expectations for my recovery. Rather than calling the police when I felt suicidal, he contacted my parents, who set the appropriate actions into motion.

In 2019, I attended an Elyn Saks Institute seminar at the University of Southern California where I learned that many people who suffer from severe mental health illness can live successful lives. From this seminar, I heard about the pros and cons of clozapine. Subsequently, I went to see Dr. Steven Marder who advised me to begin clozapine since seven previous medications had not alleviated my symptoms. I asked my treatment team to start me on clozapine. The blood tests have been arduous, but the results for me have been life changing.

While I am still learning to live with my illness, I have noticed a few things that help me stay well: taking my medication, honestly communicating with my family and healthcare team, and living a more active, purposeful lifestyle.

Besides seeing my psychiatrist, I work with a family counselor, a personal counselor, and an amazing general practitioner. They have all contributed to my recovery. I feel I present them with a challenge, but I am determined to not be an invalid due to my illness. My family and I are not satisfied with the idea that I will have to live in a facility or at home as I was originally told.

My twin brother, Scott, has been a constant support. He has moved several times for school, which is hard for me, but I know I can contact him anytime. He knows my strengths and weaknesses; he can sense better than anyone when I need help. I worry I am a burden to him, so this furthers my determination to get better.

Having a job provides a sense of accomplishment, as well as a means toward financial independence. After I moved home, a chef recognized my talent and desire to improve my cooking skills, so she offered me a job to work in a pantry on the line. This involved making all of the desserts, salads, and appetizers. The job gave me purpose. Fortunately, my colleagues recognized and appreciated my skill while also understanding my illness. I worked full-time including service at nights, but the stress caused my hallucinations to return with a vengeance. Over time, I have been learning to manage these hallucinations.

Unfortunately, due to COVID-19, the restaurant has closed and will not reopen. I have now transitioned to doing small, family catering. I also work 30 hours in a boutique cheese shop. I have lived on my own with financial support from my family for five years.

My goal is to either find another restaurant job or extend my catering into a full-time business, so I can become financially independent. I also plan to finish my college degree and get into better shape physically. Forming more meaningful relationships is also important to me, and I hope to become an advocate and stand up against the negative connotations people have of schizophrenia. I have achieved a life-long dream by adding a boxer puppy to my life. She will help me navigate between reality and hallucinations. Over two years, we attended classes, and she is now a registered therapy dog.

Today, I realize that my independence and freedom depend on my ability to make conscious decisions to take my medications, ask for help when I need it, and take care of myself both physically and mentally. I would encourage young people struggling with schizophrenia to look for purpose. Work in my field has helped me find myself and has been key in my recovery.

23

EMEKA CHIMA
Expert in Information Systems and Peer Support Specialist

Emeka Chima earned an associate of arts degree from Montgomery College in Germantown, Maryland, in 2020, and in 2022 he received a bachelor's degree from the University of Maryland Global Campus in the field of Information Systems. At Montgomery College, he was a Dean's List recipient twice and was inducted into the Phi Theta Kappa Honor Society. He currently works as a peer support specialist for an outpatient mental healthcare clinic for first episode psychosis adolescents and young adults.

Raised by his Nigerian father and his mother from Washington, D.C., Emeka experienced a happy childhood. As the oldest of five, he had the privilege to watch over his younger siblings. In high school, he played soccer and flag football, winning three trophies. His mother is currently a cybersecurity analyst for a Department of Defense contractor. Emeka would also like to work in such a field.

However, about age 15, Emeka began to hear voices. Initially, while in class, the voices would command him to look away in the distance. Gradually, the voices became more powerful, telling him to isolate himself from others, even family members whom he loved.

One night, the voices commanded Emeka to cut himself with a knife. He became delusional, believing that if he just hurt himself, "everything would be fine." He remembers panicking and screaming as he waved a knife into the air. Looking back, Emeka struggles to describe his thoughts at the time. He felt as though he needed to run away.

Emeka's aunt heard him screaming and de-escalated the situation, calming him, as she convinced him to put down the knife. Afterward, Emeka felt guilty for "acting out," unaware he was struggling with the onset of severe mental illness.

A few weeks later, Emeka had a similar experience, brandishing another knife, but this time he was alone. The voices commanded him to keep the knife with him at all times for self-defense. Although the voices sounded like a family member to Emeka, he realized that his family would never want him to harm himself. In the following days, Emeka confided in his father that he was hearing voices and stated that he might need help.

Soon after, during the night, Emeka began hallucinating again. This time, he heard a crowd of people, unexpected visitors who came without immediate warning and seemed closer in his imagination than reality. As the night went on, Emeka heard a voice consoling him and confirming that everything would be okay, as well as another voice telling him to hurt himself.

The next morning, when Emeka's father visited Emeka in his bedroom, he thought Emeka might be having a seizure. Emeka's paternal grandfather had struggled for many years with bipolar disorder, and his father suspected that Emeka was also mentally ill. Together, they went to the hospital.

While in the hospital, Emeka was diagnosed with paranoid schizophrenia. He was still only 15 years old. Despite the devastation of being told he had a disorder of the brain, Emeka learned that his symptoms could be explained by his diagnosis, which gave him relief. He also discovered there was treatment. After three weeks on the psychiatric ward, he achieved stability, was discharged, and returned to school. He was still a junior at that time.

The next year was difficult for Emeka. The first medications he tried left his eyes bloodshot, and he felt like he had a hangover though he never drank alcohol or abused drugs. He did not have a regular doctor and often forgot to take his medication. Over the next year, he was hospitalized four times for breakthrough symptoms, but the hospitalizations resulted in little benefit.

During September of Emeka's senior year of high school, however, he had a new start when he was accepted into a treatment program called EPIC (Early Psychosis Intervention Clinic) through Johns Hopkins Medicine. Through EPIC, Emeka began a trial of clozapine, a medication for treatment-resistant patients. Within a week, Emeka began to see great improvement. He recalls feeling like his recovery on clozapine was a "miracle."

On clozapine, Emeka finished high school with high honors, winning awards for every class. He did not know exactly what career he wanted to pursue, but he was confident that he would succeed.

After high school, Emeka completed his information systems degree and has recently received honors towards his bachelor's degree at the University of Maryland Global Campus. He has also been involved with the nonprofit organization, Students with Psychosis since April 2020 and serves as President on its Executive Board.

Emeka says: "When it comes to young people with brain disorders, I would advise not to hesitate to receive help because there is both a physical and emotional need to be surrounded by people who understand. Working through the recovery process can feel overwhelming, but we can develop the resilience to achieve mental wellness."

24

ALEXANDRA JOHANN*
Peer Support Specialist, Career Coach, and Volunteer

I never expected to develop schizophrenia. I also never expected that after receiving the diagnosis, I would be given so many opportunities to help others who have also been impacted by the illness.

I had always been a happy kid, until about age 12. At 12, I actually wrote a will as I had become suicidal and told a friend of mine about the will. My older sister found the will and confronted me about it, but I dismissed it. My parents noticed I was becoming depressed, which runs in my mom's family, and arranged for me to see a school counselor. She said I was fine.

In my second semester of my freshman year of high school, my family moved from Louisiana to a small city in Oklahoma. Following our move, I noticed I had become a negative and pessimistic person, but since I was not a danger to myself or others, I assumed nothing serious was wrong with me. The summer before my senior year in high school, I developed mono, and though my doctor noticed I was suffering from depression, I convinced my parents that everything was okay. I thought that my experience with depression was simply my lot in life.

In college, I began antidepressant medications and was abusing substances, but I successfully graduated in 1997 with a BS in psychology from Louisiana State University.

About the time I began graduate school in economics, my mom finally encouraged me to go to a therapist, where I disclosed that I was having mood swings and was diagnosed with bipolar disorder. I bounced around full-time and part-time work, and when I was unable to work full-time, I became homeless for a month, living in a homeless shelter in an inner city. I was content there, though it felt highly dangerous. About that time, I also became very paranoid that others would discover that I had been diagnosed with bipolar disorder and discontinued my medication. I would never finish my master's degree in economics.

For several years, I worked part-time teaching at a school in Houston. In 2007, I finally agreed to resume medication and moved in with my parents again. Soon afterward, in 2008, my mom feared I would attempt suicide and believed I could

---

*The name has been changed to protect the privacy of those involved in the story.

not take care of myself. She found an attorney to help her obtain guardianship. One day, the police confronted me and confiscated my driver's license. I was also deprived of my right to vote. Because I was paranoid of police and sirens, being arrested was traumatic for me. I was also hearing voices at the time, which cautioned me to be on my guard around the police.

The hospital I was taken to felt scary, as a fellow patient told me terrifying stories about electroconvulsive therapy (ECT). In hindsight, I am doubtful her description was accurate. I also did not know how long I would be there. Fortunately, the antipsychotic medication I was given began to work after a week. On medication, I became much less paranoid, but my doctor prescribed a very high dose of antipsychotic medication that was highly sedating for me and left me dysfunctional and disabled. I felt like my life was over. I expected I would always be on disability, and my perception of disability was that it was a road leading to nowhere.

Six months after this hospitalization, I experienced command hallucinations telling me to kill myself by swallowing a bottle of Tylenol. I nearly succeeded, but my dad discovered me in time. Soon after, I signed a contract with a counselor agreeing never to harm myself again, and I stuck to it.

For the next few years, I constantly felt disappointed with myself. I worked part-time as a GED teacher, for a nonprofit, and then a secretary. But I was unable to work full-time and was living on Social Security disability income.

My life drastically improved a couple of years later when I began clozapine. This antipsychotic medication eliminated the paranoia, voices, and suicidal ideation I continued to experience. I had not expected the clozapine to make a significant difference, but it did in a few weeks, just as my therapist, who also was a nurse practitioner, had expected. Of course, I had to get used to having my blood drawn weekly, and then only monthly. I also needed to sleep at least 10 hours each night. Unfortunately, for me, the dosage prescribed did not suppress my symptoms for a full 24-hour period. My psychiatrist provided an additional clozapine pill to take in the afternoon, which eliminated most of these symptoms. I have been recreating my life since then.

Following my initiation on clozapine, I began looking for my niche as a professional. In 2013, I discovered SARDAA (Schizophrenia & Related Disorders Alliance of America, which today is Schizophrenia and Psychosis Action Alliance) and its free support groups for people diagnosed with schizophrenia or related disorders. These groups are called SA or Schizophrenia Alliance: Psychosis Support and Acceptance. The Blue Book used in these support groups provided me with a new goal: "Perhaps the most obvious sign of recovering is the reduction and control of symptoms to the point of permitting one to have the ability to find and keep steady and structured activity" (the Blue Book, 2019 edition, page 24).

ALEXANDRA JOHANN, PEER SUPPORT SPECIALIST, CAREER COACH, AND VOLUNTEER

In 2015, after volunteering as a grant writer for SARDAA, I was awarded the Volunteer of the Year honor. A couple of years later, I decided to face my fears of being "found out" and went through certification as a peer support specialist, learning to tell my story to help others and aid them in finding resources. I was hired by SARDAA to coordinate the SA groups, and in July 2020, I was promoted to the director of community engagement. I am still in that position and have worked at SARDAA for over three years.

In 2017, I became certified as a peer support specialist in the state of Louisiana and as a career coach by PARW/CC, the Professional Association of Resume Writers and Career Coaches. I am currently working on my master's degree online in academic advising from Kansas State University.

I was once told by a psychiatrist that I would never be able to work full-time again. I took that comment as a challenge and began working more hours each couple of years. In December 2022, I earned my graduate certificate in academic advising from Kansas State University. I will continue working on my master's degree in academic advising. I have worked at S&PAA — Schizophrenia & Psychosis Action Alliance (formerly SARDAA) for over five years, coordinating free support groups, answering our helpline calls and emails, managing volunteers, and helping with advocacy projects. I still have my certification in Louisiana as a peer support specialist, and I continue to be a career coach through PARW/CC.

As of July 14, 2023, I no longer work handling outreach, answering helpline calls and emails, and managing support groups and volunteers. I have been hired full-time to help college students qualify for and maintain scholarships and grants at public universities in my state. I finally have met the goal I made in 2008 of going off disability.

I am confident that my broad experience mentoring others will help me to excel as I work with people from many different backgrounds.

I am grateful for my own recovery every day and hope to see others rebuild their lives as I have. In the future, I plan to continue helping with the support groups and help people with schizophrenia or related disorders in their job searches and/or schooling.

25

ROBERT FRANCIS*
Fifteen Years as a Social Worker

I experienced a happy, normal childhood, which was the best time of my life. I enjoyed playing sports like basketball and football. My dad coached many of my teams, and my mom attended all of my games to cheer me on. I have one older brother who I enjoy a strong bond with to this day.

I was greeted by schizophrenia at age 22. I had just graduated with my bachelor's of arts degree from SUNY Geneseo in 1993. Following my graduation, I moved back home with my mother. It was at this time that my behavior began to slowly deteriorate. I thought I had a microchip inserted in my brain by the government and that I was being surveilled. As these delusions worsened and intensified, I became very paranoid.

At that time, I also began to hear voices. They sounded like shouts from the skies. I could hear President Clinton speaking to me. Additionally, I thought people I saw on television were talking about me, saying where I lived and who I was. As my reality became persistently delusional, I thought the government was watching me and that I was being used in a malevolent conspiracy.

Schizophrenia was never more trying for me than during my first onset of psychosis. Many patients experience anosognosia, which is lack of insight and a common schizophrenia symptom. I also struggled with anosognosia. I knew nothing about schizophrenia and never would have dreamed that a brain disorder was the source of my troubles.

After close to a year of rampant and severe psychosis, I was ultimately brought by my family, via an intervention of sorts, to the hospital. My family would have acted sooner, but they also knew nothing of schizophrenia, even though they did notice my behavior was becoming erratic. It took a while for them to conclude that it was something greater than just quirky or atypical behavior. This was the first of my inpatient admissions.

My first hospital admission was difficult. I was given intramuscular haloperidol, which caused all my muscles to contract (a condition called dystonia). I could

---

*The name has been changed to protect the privacy of those involved in the story.

not walk and crawled my way down the hallway to find help. The staff gave me Benadryl and the contractions stopped. I was off to a rough start!

After this first admission, I then began outpatient treatment at a community clinic. My psychiatrist started me on olanzapine (Zyprexa). Everyone is different, but for me, Zyprexa was awful. I felt cognitively zoned-out and impoverished, and I was tired all the time. I later came to know the medicinal slang of being "snowed." And "snowed" I was! Zyprexa induced a lethargy in me, and I felt no motivation other than to watch TV and sleep.

Because of the side effects and the way it made me feel, I stopped taking the Zyprexa altogether. Then, I was on no meds at all. Some months later, I again was brought to the hospital by family members who noticed my psychosis was returning.

Initially during my second hospitalization, I was very confused. I would sit for hours just watching the activity in the hospital milieu without saying a word. I was scared and paranoid. But fortunately, during this second hospitalization, my doctor refused to give up on me and was committed to my recovery. He suggested a medication I had never heard of before, clozapine. I was warned that there were many potential side effects, however, we determined I had to try it.

Three days after initiating clozapine, I felt like my healthy self again. All those around me were astounded at my return to lucid and rational faculties. A host of my symptoms subsided. I returned home feeling much better. Clozapine truly felt like a miracle.

After this second and final hospitalization, I moved on and started attending Continuing Day Treatment (known as CDT). I attended CDT for close to a year (unfortunately, this treatment modality has now been eliminated). CDT gave my day structure and the opportunity to be around others with similar problems. I learned a lot at CDT about the various mental illnesses. It provided me with invaluable psychoeducation.

Finally, after months of stability on clozapine, a social worker at CDT encouraged me to apply to become a peer counselor. She thought I had the capacity to help others.

I eventually became a peer counselor and really enjoyed the job. As a peer counselor, I worked in a hospital providing peer support to patients on the inpatient psychiatric units. I enthusiastically communicated that recovery is possible. I tried to serve as a role model for patients who were struggling.

After six months as a peer counselor, I applied for a full-time job at a group home for people with mental illness and was hired. After one year, I was promoted to assistant manager. Six months later, I was promoted to program manager, and I held this position for three years.

With the desire to further a career in human services, and specifically mental health, I decided to apply for a master's of social work (MSW) program at a nearby university and was accepted. I attended college full-time for two years and received my MSW in 2006. In 2009, I earned my LCSW (licensed clinical social worker).

I have now been a mental health therapist for close to 15 years. Over the last two years, I have written two books about my life living with schizophrenia, including my most recent book, *The Essential Schizophrenia Companion*. These books have been cathartic for me. They have provided me an opportunity to share my story with others. I write for those with schizophrenia, their families, and for the professionals who treat them. If one person benefits from my efforts, I have met my goal.

I cannot say I do not have ongoing symptoms. I do. But my recovery boils down to this: I have learned to function despite my symptoms. I have capably adapted. It took me a long time to learn to live with schizophrenia, but I have indeed learned, and I continue to refine my coping skills.

Above all, I have learned acceptance. I accept its daily provocations and I do not grumble. I know I can gainfully persist no matter the challenge schizophrenia may extend.

Schizophrenia has forged a strength in me I never knew I had. And for me, this is what I call recovery.

26

LUCAS PELUFFO
Spanish-English Translator and Secretary

Lucas was born in Buenos Aires, Argentina in 1963. He immigrated to the United States when he was 14 years old. As a child, he recalls that Argentina was not safe in terms of democracy and freedom of expression. Yet, Argentina has, over the last few decades, become safer for its citizens. To this day, Lucas loves to spend time in Buenos Aires with his family members who remain there.

In 1980, Lucas graduated from Edgemont High School in Scarsdale, New York. He then began college at the University of Vermont and very much enjoyed his years here. He had all A's in his premed courses and was a member of the track team, setting a school record for the indoor 500 meters. He also was a member of a 4×400 indoor relay team that set a school record in Boston.

Lucas graduated from college in 1984 with his BA degree. He later began studies to obtain a PhD in neuroscience at Columbia University in New York, but he never finished his degree program.

From 1988 to 1990, Lucas experienced two one-month psychiatric hospitalizations following the emergence of his first psychotic symptoms. Lucas remembers seeing angels, believing he could read minds, and experiencing a cognitive decline.

Prior to his hospitalization, Lucas had landed a job as a bilingual science teacher at a high school in Manhattan, New York. It had taken him a year to acquire the license to teach. However, his psychologist quickly determined that he was unable to work this job due to his mind-reading delusions and other symptoms. At that time, Lucas found himself unable to know what was true versus what was a hallucination, and he struggled with anger. Changes in his personality also led to conflicts with his family members.

During one of the hospitalizations, while psychotic, Lucas stole his mother's credit card. He intended to escape from the hospital to fly to Buenos Aires and hoped to finance his trip with the credit card. His father, a doctor, and a brother who later became a psychiatrist, were living in Buenos Aires at that time. Lucas remembers that the pathological drive to escape from the hospital included hallucinations, delusions, and paranoia. It was surely related to feelings of total hopelessness while foreseeing a grim horizon, including a financial burden for Lucas' family.

Lucas was unable to escape from the hospital, and since that time, his diagnosis has been schizophrenia. Unfortunately, he also felt traumatized by his experience in the hospital.

Fortunately, in retrospect, the hospitalizations were the beginning of a prolonged treatment that in the end proved fruitful. Lucas believes that it took 10 years of intensive psychology and medications to fully "resuscitate" him from his psychotic symptoms and other memories.

Twenty years ago, Lucas made a choice that turned his life around for the better: he began competing in track again. He spent 15 years doing track intervals and long-distance runs. In total, he completed about 160 veterans track races. Because he had smoked cigarettes quite a bit during his previous 10-year struggle, his times weren't competitive, but his motivation never declined. His overall health improved dramatically. He started sleeping better, holding onto jobs (like translating and secretary work in a medical center), and reading more. He stopped smoking.

Six years ago, Lucas found another welcome turn in his life: he started meditating. He stopped running track races, even though he continues to do regular exercise, especially long aerobic runs. On a daily basis, he hopes to strengthen his mind. Combining meditation with exercise provides Lucas with the hope of overcoming the psychotic symptoms by considering them as transient and not as important to health as other aspects of the organism.

Treatment with the rarely used medication clozapine was also key in helping Lucas to rebuild his life. As of today, Lucas has taken clozapine since 1998 with no relapse. He also believes that mindfulness has been important in his recovery.

Lucas currently works a job as a secretary in a medical center and is a freelance translator. He is fully bilingual in English and Spanish and has worked as a translator for 20 years. In his spare time, he writes and creates collages.

In retrospect he says, "When I recall the entire process I went through over my difficult 10 years of serious illness, I consider my being alive and even thriving as a great miracle."

27

ERIC SMITH
Social Worker and Advocate

My name is Eric Smith. I am a musician, composer, and a loving family member. I am also an alumnus of the University of Texas at San Antonio where I graduated magna cum laude in psychology in May 2018. I graduated with my Master of Social Work (MSW) degree in December 2021 and am now a licensed master social worker (LMSW) in the state of Texas.

    I was diagnosed with bipolar disorder in my early/mid-teen years, but I was also diagnosed with schizophrenia and schizoaffective disorder many years later while I was a psych inpatient. Along with the first diagnosis of bipolar disorder I received in my teens, my parents were told to not be surprised if I also developed schizophrenia or schizoaffective disorder later in life. In short, psychiatrists who have seen me at my worst (my most symptomatic) have diagnosed me with schizoaffective disorder and schizophrenia, and psychiatrists who have not seen me at my worst diagnosed me with bipolar disorder. Throughout that journey, it appeared I would never rebuild my life, let alone recover. My first medications had bad side effects and were not working.

    That all changed with Assisted Outpatient Treatment (AOT) and clozapine, both of which helped save my life. To understand how I eventually got there, let's go back to when I was a teenager.

    In 1997, at age 14, I was first diagnosed with bipolar disorder. In hindsight, it was clear I needed medical care for my mental illness, but neither I nor my doctors realized how serious my illness was. Able to function well enough, I convinced my doctors that hospitalization was not necessary. In my mid 20s, I experienced an extreme manic episode. At that point, I was hospitalized due to serious mental illness (SMI) for the first time.

    In the days leading up to my first psychiatric hospitalization, I was incarcerated for an entire month because of non-violent behavior stemming from an acute psychotic episode. About that time, I met with the FBI in person (in reality) on multiple occasions to let them know about codes I believed I had broken to prevent assassinations of world leaders that would stop World War III. They scheduled time to meet with me at their San Antonio headquarters (in reality) and also in a major business parking lot. Looking back, I am surprised they were willing to meet with me. Breaking codes that didn't actually exist kept me awake for several days straight. With the delusions, paranoia, and psychosis, I was about as far from perceiving reality as a person could be, which was scaring my parents.

I had been living out of my car at the time, for a few weeks, and showed up at their house agitated and out of touch with reality. At that time, the police were called, and they warned me that if I returned to my parents' house, I would be arrested for trespassing. Afraid and with no great alternative options, when I returned, my parents worked with the police to have me arrested for trespassing at their house.

My then-most-recent psychiatrist had told my parents the best chance I had to get the treatment I needed would likely come from me getting arrested for a low-level offense and then transferred to a state hospital bed if I was lucky enough for one to open up before the jail released me. While I was in jail, I was denied mental health treatment. I did not receive needed care for my mental illness until I was finally transferred to a hospital as part of a court order.

In jails and prisons, persons with SMI often do not get the treatment they need. Even worse, sometimes they do not receive any treatment at all, which was my experience. Jails and prisons are not designed to be providers of mental healthcare, nor should they be. Being mentally ill is not a crime. I see the real crime as the act of incarcerating those who need treatment for SMI. These individuals typically would never have been jailed had it not been for behavior stemming from unmanaged or poorly managed SMI. Thus, necessity for medical treatment should be the guiding principle of policy and practice for SMI without relying on the criminal justice system as a main entry point before treatment.

Prior to being prescribed clozapine, I was on the receiving end of treatment that was essentially trial-and-error, exemplified by a long list of failed medications over many years. All of the other medications — antipsychotics, benzodiazepines, anti-depressants, SSRIs, and others — had failed to meaningfully treat my symptoms. In 2011, while I was hospitalized for the third and final time, and as a last-ditch effort of sorts, my doctor prescribed clozapine.

Clozapine may not work for everyone, but for me it felt like nothing short of a miracle. Today, it is the only psychiatric medicine I require. I have been in meaningful recovery on clozapine for more than 10 years.

I was discharged from the hospital (for the third and final time) on clozapine, and then entered into San Antonio's groundbreaking AOT program (for the third and final time). The program required me to meet with a judge a few times per month to track my progress as I continued to build on my recovery. The goals of these hearings included ensuring I was taking my medication as prescribed and evaluating my mental health, confirming that I still no longer required hospitalization.

Today, I credit the AOT team, clozapine, my family, and my dedication to recovery for enabling me to regain my health and life. The complementary, symbiotic relationship between the judge, doctor, and the rest of the AOT treatment team completely changed my view of managing mental illness. This was the beginning of my realization that I should take ownership of my treatment, and my ability to do so. The way the AOT treatment team cared about me, and the fact that I finally found a medication that worked, allowed me to follow through on my medical care without needing to be court-ordered to do it. My AOT treatment team went from being a champion of my mental health and well-being to teaching me how to be my own champion, building upon my new-found ability to manage my illness.

The beauty of AOT is now something I have the capacity to more fully appreciate. Without AOT, I would at best be living under a bridge somewhere consumed by mental illness, but perhaps more likely than that I would probably be dead. Death is a tragic reality for many people suffering from SMI who do not receive the life-saving care provided by programs like AOT. Clozapine and AOT took me from a path of delusion and danger to becoming an accomplished, habitual honors student and graduate.

Today, as I continue my pursuit of helping others in a professional capacity, I hope to give back to the community. I am thankful for the second chance at life afforded to me by the treatment and care I needed: AOT and clozapine. Additionally, I thank all individuals and organizations who support AOT and other measures to help people like me and families like mine. I am especially thankful for the CURESZ Foundation for championing AOT and clozapine.

---

[1] See page 237, "Enough is Enough: The Case for Outpatient Treatment."

28

MICHAEL B
Managing Full-Time College

In my first two years of high school, academics came easily to me and I was an honors student. As a member of the National Honor Society, National Technical Honor Society, and student council, my future looked bright. I made plans to major in computer science in college.

However, during my junior and senior years of high school, I started struggling academically and losing interest in the hobbies I had always enjoyed. I began experiencing extreme anxiety and alternated between sleeping hours on end and being unable to sleep for days at a time. My teachers, family, and friends began to notice something was different, but they did not know what it was. At the time, no one in my life realized this was the beginning of my journey into the world of mental illness.

I barely managed to graduate from high school. Fortunately, due to my previous academic accomplishments, I had already been accepted at the College of the Ozarks with a full scholarship.

In 2016, during my first semester of college, I experienced my first delusions and feelings of paranoia. I thought my teachers were against me. I believed subliminal messages were being broadcast from the TV and radio. I had trouble falling asleep and couldn't wake up in time for classes. When I did homework, I found myself reading the same text over and over without comprehension.

Unable to concentrate, I skipped my classes and isolated myself in my room. I couldn't understand why schoolwork had become so difficult. I failed my classes and returned home that summer confused and discouraged.

Over the course of the next several months, my mental health continued to decline. I wasn't sleeping and I experienced cognitive issues. I began having visual, auditory, and tactile hallucinations: hearing voices and experiencing extreme fear. I was no longer able to study or work. My parents sought treatment for me, and in November 2016 I was diagnosed with schizoaffective disorder.

We tried numerous medications and treatment options for improved cognition and anxiety control: clean eating, gluten and dairy free foods, supplements, vitamins, and holistic and naturopathic medicine. Nothing worked. Finally, in my desperate and confused state, I believed that more medication might work better to relieve my symptoms, and I took a two-week supply of medicine all at once. This resulted in me being picked up by ambulance and hospitalized with multiple organ failure. This was my fourth and last hospitalization.

After 13 failed antipsychotics, numerous mood stabilizers and antidepressants, and four hospitalizations, my parents finally found a doctor who was unwilling to give up on me. This doctor started me on a rarely used medication called clozapine, for treatment-resistant patients.

On clozapine, my concentration and memory began to improve. I began to experience less anxiety and fear and I started to enjoy old hobbies like reading. Over several months, the delusions, hallucinations, and voices faded away. As these schizophrenia symptoms began to fade, my cognitive abilities slowly improved. I enrolled in community college and each semester proved a little easier than the last.

I have now been in meaningful recovery for five years. I am back at my previous college, which is three and a half hours away from home, and I am living in a dorm on campus again. I work 15 hours a week in the campus library. I have made friends and am enjoying college life. My grades are excellent.

In 2019, I founded a NAMI peer support group in my hometown for people living with mental illness (NAMI stands for National Alliance on Mental Illness). In 2020, I started a NAMI on-campus support group for the Metropolitan Community College of Kansas City. I am a board member of NAMI of Greater Kansas City and the program director for all NAMI on-campus groups in Kansas City colleges. I have been arranging Zoom meetings, and people from all over the United States attend virtually. I was featured on the PBS Documentary, "The Hidden Pandemic."

I recently changed my major from computer science to social work. After graduation, I want to work in the mental health field. I believe that people living with mental illness need help, hope, and understanding, and I want to work with patients to improve their lives. I want them to know that recovery is possible with the right medication and that they are not alone.

I hope that through sharing my story, more young people will seek appropriate treatment so they can rebuild their lives as I have.

PART THREE

PREFACE TO PART THREE

The following are resources offered online by the CURESZ Foundation. From our description of schizophrenia as a treatable brain disorder to underutilized and cutting-edge medications, to essays on schizophrenia, we hope this information will enable you to begin the conversation with your provider.

The resources provided in *Awakenings* do not include our online Clozapine Expert Panel of 125 psychiatric clinicians, or our Tardive Dyskinesia Panel of 35 clinicians. Please log on to CURESZ.org and click "Resources" to find clinicians who prescribe clozapine and medications for tardive dyskinesia. You can also access our CURESZ YouTube channel online and sign up on CURESZ.org for the programs described in this section of *Awakenings*.

1

SCHIZOPHRENIA AND ITS MANY IMPACTS

Although currently classified as a mental illness, schizophrenia is also scientifically accepted as a neurobiological brain condition.

A SYNDROME

Schizophrenia, a neurobiological brain syndrome, includes possibly hundreds of distinct brain diseases. These diseases are sometimes referred to as "schizophrenia spectrum disorders." Symptoms vary greatly among different people. The most widely accepted theory of schizophrenia is that it is a neurodevelopmental disorder, which means that normal brain development during fetal life or later is disrupted due to various genetic factors and/or environmental factors.

Schizophrenia usually first manifests in adolescence or early 20s in males and in the late 20s and sometimes early 30s in females.

A BRAIN DISORDER

While schizophrenia is clearly a neurological disorder along with stroke, Parkinson's disease, Alzheimer's disease, and others, schizophrenia is still classified as a mental illness. It should be emphasized that one of the most important jobs of the brain is to generate the mind, and thus all mental disorders such as schizophrenia, bipolar disorders, major depression, or panic disorder are actually caused by abnormalities in brain structure and function. As Thomas Insel, MD and former Director of the National Institute of Mental Health said, mental disorders are biological disorders involving brain circuits.[1]

There are hundreds of "biotypes" within the schizophrenia syndrome, but they all share a similar phenotype of psychosis, cognitive deficits, and negative symptoms.

---

[1] Insel, T. R. (2010, November 10). "Rethinking schizophrenia." *Nature*, 468, 187-193.

CLINICAL FEATURES OF SCHIZOPHRENIA

Schizophrenia affects about 1% of the world's population, (60 million people around the world). Symptoms of schizophrenia may include hallucinations (seeing, hearing, or smelling things that are not really there) and delusions (persistent false beliefs, such as believing they are a member of the CIA or that someone wants to harm them). These symptoms are referred to as "positive symptoms," though they are not positive to the person experiencing them. ("Positive" refers to manifestations of disrupted human thinking, perceptions, and behavior.) These symptoms are attributed to increased activity of the neurotransmitter dopamine in a certain region of the brain.

Social withdrawal, lack of interest in things a person used to love, and loss of interest in self-care (such as not eating or showering) are considered "negative" symptoms of schizophrenia. ("Negative" refers to loss or decrement of normal human social or personal functions.) Some of these symptoms are known to be associated with a reduction of the same neurotransmitter dopamine in the frontal region of the brain, affecting the ability to be motivated, display normal facial expressions, or to initiate an action.

Cognitive impairment is another important aspect of the illness that includes memory deficits and the inability to plan or make decisions. Additionally, patients with schizophrenia often do not realize they are sick and resist being hospitalized or refuse medications that can help them. This lack of insight is quite common in schizophrenia. Medications as well as counselling can help patients develop awareness that they do have a medical illness and that they should adhere to their medication in order to achieve remission and ultimately recovery.

While a complete list of schizophrenia symptoms may be extensive, most patients experience some but not all of these symptoms. It may even be difficult for one person with schizophrenia to understand and relate to what another person with schizophrenia is experiencing. For example, a patient with hallucinations may find it hard to imagine how it would feel to experience paranoia, or the voices of one patient may not resonate with the voices of another.

MEDICATIONS

Medications that reduce or eliminate symptoms of schizophrenia like hallucinations or delusions are called antipsychotics. Examples available today include risperidone, olanzapine, quetiapine, and aripiprazole. Clozapine is an antipsychotic that can work when several others fail to control the psychotic symptoms.

Some people with schizophrenia experience full recovery (becoming asymptomatic, or nearly asymptomatic) and work or continue to pursue higher education. A sizeable proportion will have at least partial recovery and may be able to function at some level in the community. These people may choose to not disclose their schizophrenia because of common misunderstandings of schizophrenia and the unfair stigma associated with it.

MISUNDERSTANDING SCHIZOPHRENIA

Typical symptoms of schizophrenia may be very different than sensational stories in the news media. The media sometimes wrongly portrays people with schizophrenia as impossible to relate to, dangerous, or weak. What a patient may experience is very different from what they thought schizophrenia actually is. Common myths of schizophrenia include the erroneous idea that people with schizophrenia have multiple personalities, a split mind, or a low IQ.

Schizophrenia is completely different from multiple personality disorder, and it does not represent a flawed personality. Anyone, including highly intelligent persons (such as the mathematician and Nobel Prize winner John Nash featured in *A Beautiful Mind*) and people of any socioeconomic status or race can develop it. Like cancer, diabetes, autism, and other medical problems, it cannot be simply overcome by willpower.

People with schizophrenia who take their medications regularly and do not abuse drugs are NOT dangerous. In fact, statistically, people with schizophrenia are no more dangerous than the general population, and they are more likely to become victims than perpetrators of crimes. Antisocial personality disorder is a far more common disorder in criminals and is strongly associated with criminality, unlike schizophrenia.

It is also important to note that the suicide rate in schizophrenia is high and second only to the suicide rate in major depression. However, antidepressants can help reduce the suicide risk, as can clozapine, which is approved by the FDA for suicidality in schizophrenia.

THEORIES OF SCHIZOPHRENIA

There are numerous theories of the actual pathology in schizophrenia because there are probably hundreds of different biological subtypes of schizophrenia, which share similar clinical features. Broadly speaking, disrupted brain development during fetal life is the biological basis of this syndrome. Two brain neurotransmitters are thought to be central to the basis of schizophrenia. Underactivity of the glutamate NMDA receptor neurotransmitter pathway is a leading theory of schizophrenia based on many lines of evidence, and dopamine overactivity in schizophrenia may in fact be due to low activity of glutamate. Some of the strongest evidence that schizophrenia may be due to reduced activity of the glutamate

NMDA activity is that PCP, or Angel Dust, which is a drug of abuse, can transform a healthy person into someone with a psychiatric illness that is indistinguishable from schizophrenia, including positive, negative, and cognitive symptoms. PCP is a very potent blocker of the glutamate NMDA receptor.

RECOVERY

The psychotic symptoms of schizophrenia are quite treatable. However, there are still no known treatments for the negative symptoms and cognitive deficits of schizophrenia. There is no shame in having schizophrenia, or in taking a medication for it, or for any other medical illness. Schizophrenia is no one's fault, any more than asthma, an infection, hypertension, diabetes, arthritis, or cancer is anyone's fault.

By emphasizing that schizophrenia is an illness of the brain and comparing it to other neurological brain diseases, it is very likely that the stigma of schizophrenia can eventually fade away. Stigma towards schizophrenia is a harmful consequence of poor understanding and irrational fear, and it can have a very demoralizing effect on the individuals who are suffering from this serious neuropsychiatric disorder. The general public should show people with schizophrenia the same compassion, acceptance and understanding that is extended to people with all other medical conditions like heart disease or cancer.

Today, on medication, full recovery from schizophrenia is possible, especially with clozapine, a medication approved by the FDA for hallucinations and delusions that do not improve with any of the dozen other antipsychotic drugs available in the United States. Clozapine is also the only medication approved by the FDA for suicidal tendencies in schizophrenia, which are quite common.

2

TREATMENT CHECKLIST

LEARNING ABOUT SCHIZOPHRENIA

Schizophrenia is a treatable brain illness ranging from mild to severe forms. It is diverse in its causes, symptom severity, and outcome, similar to the different types of Parkinson's disease or cancer. Persons with schizophrenia may have some similar features, but they also have different experiences.

For persons with schizophrenia, understanding and learning about the illness itself is vital. Therefore, consider investing some time learning about the biology and clinical aspects of the disease and ask your psychiatrist and treatment team all the questions you can think of.

Over the past 50 years, the medical care of schizophrenia has shifted from an inpatient institutional setting to community-based care, except when a psychotic relapse occurs and hospitalization is necessary. Today, many, but not all, people with schizophrenia can achieve significant improvement in their illness and can return to vocational and social functioning, especially with the help of long-acting injectable antipsychotic medications, which protect against relapse better than pills. Sometimes, other medications — like antidepressants or anti-anxiety medications — may also be needed.

SETTING GOALS WITH YOUR TREATMENT TEAM

You should ask your psychiatrist to explain the illness and the various available treatments (including pills or intramuscular injections once every 1-6 months without having to take any pills) and he or she should assure you that all available treatments will be tried until you have achieved a return to your baseline. For about 30% of patients whose psychosis does not respond to the standard drug therapies, a medication called clozapine may be necessary. (See below: clozapine can eliminate hallucinations or delusions 50% of the time when other antipsychotics fail.) Once you start improving, your doctor and the mental health team should work with you to establish goals for the future, such as returning to school or work, spending more quality time with family and friends, and engaging in hobbies and other meaningful activities.

Recovery, not continued illness and disability, should be the goal for most patients who suffer from schizophrenia.

LONG-ACTING INJECTABLE ANTIPSYCHOTIC MEDICATIONS

Adherence to antipsychotic medications in schizophrenia is very erratic leading to recurrence of psychosis, which is known to cause brain tissue loss, with clinical and functional deterioration and disability. Anosognosia (lack of insight), memory dysfunction, negative symptoms and substance use combine to preclude daily intake of oral medications. Fortunately, several long-acting injectable antipsychotics are available, eliminating the need to take pills every day. These include monthly injections (Invega Sustenna, Abilify Maintena, Aristada, Relprevv, Uzedy, Perseris), every 2 months (Abilify Asimtufii, Aristada), every 3 months (Invega Trinza) and every 6 months (Invega Hafyera). Ask your psychiatrist or nurse practitioner about these injectable formulations (some are intramuscular and some subcutaneous). They ensure that the brain receives medications without interruption, and are excellent alternatives to inconsistent adherence to daily pills. Avoiding psychotic relapses is critical to avoid brain damage, treatment-resistance, incarceration and homelessness.

VITAMINS AND SUPPLEMENTS

Studies show that several supplements added to antipsychotic medications during the acute episodes of psychosis may help in schizophrenia. These include omega 3 fatty acids (which may counteract the brain inflammation during psychosis), N-acetyl cysteine (which may help neutralize the harmful free radicals during psychosis), and vitamin D (which is important for brain development and ongoing health).

Omega-3 Fatty Acids (The Anti-Inflammatory Supplement Fish Oil)

Fish oil may help when added to the antipsychotic medication in early phases of psychosis when brain inflammation can occur. Fish oil is relatively cheap and has few side effects. You can find it at any drug store.

Fish oil contains an omega-3 fatty acid called DHA (docosahexaenoic acid) which may promote brain health. Consider talking to your doctor about a prescription for the more expensive, purified form.

The Antioxidant Supplement N-Acetyl Cysteine (NAC)

N-acetyl cysteine is a strong antioxidant, and some studies suggest it may help neutralize the harmful effects of elevated levels of free radicals, which are known to occur during psychosis. People with schizophrenia have been found not to make enough antioxidant (such as glutathione) in their cells to fight free radicals, and NAC helps increase glutathione levels. More research is being done on this supplement.

Vitamin D3

Exposure to sunlight prompts the body to manufacture vitamin D, which is important for brain health in schizophrenia, depression, and even multiple sclerosis. It is especially important for pregnant women to a have normal blood level of vitamin D3 to ensure normal brain development in their babies. Very low levels of vitamin D3 during pregnancy have been reported to increase the risk of developing schizophrenia in adolescence or early adulthood.

COGNITIVE BEHAVIORAL THERAPY (CBT) AS ADJUNCTIVE THERAPY

Since the 1990s, research has proven the effectiveness of CBT in depression, anxiety, and some symptoms of schizophrenia. It is considered one of the most effective psychotherapy methods.

CLOZAPINE CAN WORK IF OTHER ANTIPSYCHOTICS FAIL

Clozapine can work when other antipsychotic medications fail to reduce persistent hallucinations or delusions. (These cases are called "treatment-resistant" or "refractory" cases.)

Clozapine is associated with some side effects. It can cause a reduction in white blood cell count in very rare cases (less than 1%). That's why weekly white blood cell counts have to be measured with a quick blood test. Clozapine also may cause increased appetite and weight gain, sleepiness, constipation, and increased salivation. In high doses, it may cause other problems, such as diabetes or seizures, but most people do not need high doses.

Because patients on clozapine must be monitored for side effects, some psychiatrists avoid using clozapine or use it rarely. In the United States, while 25-30% of patients may benefit from a trial of clozapine, less than 5% actually receive it from their psychiatrist and may need to be referred to a clozapine expert.

All patients who have not achieved full remission — which means they are asymptomatic or nearly free of delusions or hallucinations after trying one or two different antipsychotic drugs — deserve a trial of clozapine.

DIET AND EXERCISE

Several studies show the benefit of exercise (walking 30 minutes a day) to help lose weight, improve cardiac health, and stimulate the production of new brain cells. Studies also show the benefit of a healthy diet (low calorie and low fat, with fiber from fruits, vegetables, and nuts) to avoid weight gain and reduce the risk of diabetes and high blood pressure, which are very common in schizophrenia.

CAUTION! DISCONTINUING PSYCHIATRIC MEDICATIONS CAN LEAD TO PSYCHOTIC RELAPSES

When your doctor prescribes a medication, ask what you should do if an intolerable side effect occurs. If you are experiencing side effects from your medication, do not stop the medication abruptly; get in touch with your doctor right away. Discontinuing medications can lead to psychotic relapses, and in some cases, it can cause withdrawal symptoms like insomnia, agitation, or muscle twitching. Additionally, psychiatric medications become less effective after each recurrence.

There are 12 new-generation antipsychotic medications available today. If you are experiencing side effects, know that there may be another medication that may suit you better. Every person's experience with medication is different because our bodies are biologically different.

TARDIVE DYSKINESIA AS A SIDE EFFECT OF ANTIPSYCHOTICS

Tardive dyskinesia (TD) is an involuntary movement disorder which is a serious neurological side effect of all antipsychotic medication, but especially on older (and harsher) antipsychotic drugs like haloperidol. TD's movements are often seen in the face, including the tongue, lips, jaw, and eyes (blinking/grimacing) but can also affect the neck, trunk, arms, fingers, legs, toes, and diaphragm.

Fortunately, two effective medications for TD were recently approved by the FDA. Valbenazine was approved by the FDA in April 2017, and deutetrabenazine was subsequently approved in August 2017. These medications can significantly reduce or eliminate TD movements.

Because the older antipsychotics like haloperidol are much more likely to cause acute muscle stiffness, tremor, rigidity, or restlessness (in the first few hours, days, or weeks), and a high rate of TD (usually after many years of use), they generally should not be used to treat schizophrenia or bipolar disorder. The newer antipsychotics have a much lower rate of TD.

CUTTING-EDGE AND UNDERUTILIZED MEDICATIONS

3

SCHIZOPHRENIA AND CLOZAPINE

Clozapine is the only FDA-approved medication that can treat hallucinations and delusions that persist despite treatment with other antipsychotic drugs. Clozapine is also the only FDA-approved medication for suicidal thoughts or tendencies in persons with schizophrenia.

A total of 70% of patients with schizophrenia respond to standard antipsychotic medications, are not treatment-resistant, and do not require a trial of clozapine. In 25-30% of cases, the voices or the paranoid feelings do not go away despite using several antipsychotic drugs. Clozapine has been proven to work when other antipsychotic medications don't.

When clozapine is used, blood is drawn weekly to check for any changes in white blood cells, which may occur in 1% of people. Measurement of the blood level of clozapine is also done.

To make it easier for patients to try clozapine, the CURESZ foundation has assembled a group of psychiatric clinicians who are experts in clozapine, so that patients around the country can connect with clinicians close to where they live.[1]

CURESZ does not have any financial interest in promoting clozapine use. It has been available in generic form for over 15 years. Our goal is to make this inexpensive but extremely effective medication available to more patients worldwide.

REMOVING BARRIERS TO CLOZAPINE USE
by Jonathan Meyer, MD

Clozapine is the only effective medication for treatment-resistant schizophrenia, with response rates ≥ 40% compared to < 5% for other antipsychotics.[2] Despite this, clozapine is significantly underutilized with up to 8-fold variation in rates of clozapine use between states in the United States.[3] The main barriers to clozap-

---

[1] https://curesz.org/clozapine-expert-panel/.
[2] Meyer. J.M. & Stahl, S.M. (2019). The Clozapine Handbook. Cambridge University Press.
[3] Stroup, T. S., Gerhard, T., Crystal, S., Huang, C., & Olfson, M. (2014). Geographic and clinical variation in clozapine use in the United States. Psychiatric Services, 65, 186-192.

ine use in the United States rest on two issues: the burdens of monitoring and prescriber fear.[4]

These two issues are intertwined and relate to the association between clozapine use and serious decreases in infection-fighting cells (i.e., neutrophils) in 1% of patients. Clozapine's U.S. approval (1989) came with mandatory monitoring to track neutrophil (white blood cell) counts: weekly for 6 months, every 2 weeks for the next 6 months, and monthly thereafter. While this monitoring has nearly eliminated infection-related fatalities from clozapine-related neutropenia (a low white blood cell count), the fear which this and other unusual adverse effects created dissuades many clinicians from using clozapine or learning how to use it.

Although data indicate that clozapine use lowers mortality,[5] many clinicians overestimate the risks of treatment and, sadly, subject patients to multiple trials of other agents with little chance of therapeutic benefit. Mandatory monitoring has vastly improved safety, yet it poses a number of difficulties for patients: travel costs, time, possible need for assistance to travel, discomfort from the blood draw, concerns among some about uses of their specimen, and delays in receiving the next prescription. Clozapine dispensing is tightly tied to pharmacy notification of blood results, and the quantity dispensed matches the interval to the next blood draw. For those on weekly testing, a delay of 24 hours in going to the lab or transmitting lab results places the patient in jeopardy of running out of clozapine.

Yet, there is hope. In the state hospital system I consult with, a regular lecture series on clozapine increased prescribing more than two-fold. Moreover, healthcare systems in New York and the Netherlands showed that supporting prescribers facilitates greater clozapine use. Knowledge is indeed power, and clinicians in the United States have two new resources to facilitate clozapine prescribing. One is a handbook that I co-authored inspired by the lack of clinically oriented published resources on clozapine;[6] the other is a web-based educational site that (importantly) also provides clinical consultations to registered users (www.smiadviser.org). This initiative is free and is sponsored by the American Psychiatric Association and the Substance Abuse and Mental Health Services Administration.

For patients, monitoring burdens may be lessened by a newly approved point-of-care (POC) device that uses a small drop of blood from a finger stick. The first of these devices (www.athelas.com) not only provides results within minutes, the results are automatically transmitted to the monitoring system, and the device is now FDA approved for home use. The discomfort is less, there is no risk of delay between obtaining the results and medication dispensing, and the patient sees

---

[4] Cohen, D. (2014). Prescribers fear as a major side-effect of clozapine. Acta Psychiatrica Scandinavica, 130,154-155.
[5] Vermeulen, J.M., van Rooijen, G., van de Kerkhof, M. P. J., Sutterland, A.L., Correll, C.U., de Haan, L. (2019). Clozapine and long-term mortality risk in patients with schizophrenia: A systematic review and meta-analysis of studies lasting 1.1-12.5 years. Schizophrenia Bulletin, 45, 315-329.
[6] Meyer. J.M. & Stahl, S.M. (2019). The Clozapine Handbook. Cambridge University Press.

exactly how their blood specimen is used. The lack of delay means that a patient can have the test done anytime, and in almost any setting with trained personnel.

The clozapine renaissance has begun.

CLOZAPINE QUESTION AND ANSWER
by Erik Messamore, MD, PhD

Q: Part of your work involves helping doctors use clozapine. What makes you so interested in this cause?

Clozapine saves lives and improves life quality in ways that other medications just can't. Clozapine is the best medication for about 20% of people with schizophrenia, yet in the United States, it's used in just 4%. This means that about 16% of people with schizophrenia (almost half a million individuals) are denied the quality of life that can be realized with this unparalleled medication.

I was once working at a state hospital and became the doctor for a lady with schizophrenia. Let's call her "Anna." She had been continuously ill for about 20 years, bouncing between the hospital, the street, and sometimes jail. As a homeless person with severe mental illness, she had experienced a number of really horrible traumas. Anna had never tried clozapine because: 1) doctors assumed that she would not take the medication regularly, or that her "lifestyle" was too chaotic to be able to show up for the weekly blood tests, and 2) she was very afraid of needles so would refuse the offer of clozapine anyway.

To address her fear of needles, I prescribed an anesthetic cream that we would rub into the spot where we would draw blood. The anesthetic cream numbed the skin and helped Anna feel comfortable with blood testing so she agreed to try clozapine.

Within two months, we saw the real Anna. She was a delightful lady with a sense of humor. She was able, for the first time since becoming ill, to actively participate in her discharge planning.

She took her medication regularly because she felt that it really helped her. (The reason she would stop taking her prior medications is because they were not really helping in ways that mattered to her.) She went on to get her own apartment and began to create the kind of life she wanted. Clozapine helped her break the cycle of illness and homelessness and allowed Anna to reclaim a life in which she was in charge.

For a variety of reasons, many doctors in the United States don't offer clozapine to their patients with schizophrenia. Part of my work these days is to assist doctors or psychiatric nurse practitioners to use clozapine so that they can see for themselves that success stories like Anna's are actually very common with this uniquely effective medication.

Q: Clozapine is sometimes called a "wonder drug." Do you agree with this?
I'm not a fan of labels like "wonder drug" for medications. The most successful outcomes are usually the result of treatment that combines multiple approaches like psychotherapy, environmental modification, bolstering social support, and helping people to reconnect to the things in life that give them meaning, purpose, and joy. Labeling a particular medication "miraculous" creates a risk of over-focusing on one approach even when others are also valuable. On the other hand, clozapine does appear to have a higher level of treatment effectiveness than any other medication for schizophrenia and can be uniquely effective in cases where other medications have failed. The average patient will have spent several years dealing with inadequately effective medications before she or he is offered clozapine. To someone who has struggled with symptoms for so long, finally being on a truly effective medication certainly can feel miraculous.

Q: Why do some doctors and psychiatric nurse practitioners not have much experience in prescribing clozapine?
Generic forms of clozapine became available in the late 1990s. When a drug becomes available as a generic, it is no longer actively publicized by a drug company. There is no more advertising in professional journals, no promotion at conferences, and no one coming to your office to help answer questions.

Around the same time, several other new "second-generation" or "atypical" antipsychotic medications were coming onto the market, and these newer medications were extensively promoted by their manufacturers. Corporate promotion of clozapine vanished while publicity for less effective newer drugs flourished. You would think that medical schools and the programs that train psychiatrists would pick up the slack. But this did not happen across the board. The national organization that dictates the training curriculum for the country's residency programs does not specifically address clozapine instruction.

Whether a particular training program offers clozapine-specific training is up to the individual program. It's not a national standard. So it is entirely possible for a new psychiatrist to enter practice with no firsthand experience to prescribe clozapine and to observe its often-remarkable benefits. Absent from this experience, a newly-minted psychiatrist may enter practice unprepared to use this medication. The situation is the same for psychiatric nurse practitioners. These gaps in training have created what I call a lost generation of clinicians who are hesitant to use clozapine.

Q: What do you think makes clozapine effective in situations where other medications have not been?

Not all schizophrenias are alike. Understanding that there are different kinds of schizophrenia helps to explain why clozapine appears uniquely effective. Most schizophrenias should probably be renamed "dopamine psychosis." Scientists have shown that many people with schizophrenia have unusually high dopamine signals in key brain circuits. These findings explain why antipsychotic medications are effective. Most of them are designed to adjust the elevated dopamine signals.

About two thirds of people with schizophrenia will have one of these high-dopamine forms of illness and will find relief from dopamine-adjusting medications. But there are other forms of schizophrenia where the dopamine signal appears entirely normal. A variety of neurochemical studies, including some recent PET scan work, has shown that people with these normal-dopamine schizophrenias don't get much symptom relief from the first-line, dopamine-adjusting schizophrenia medications.

This makes sense. Why would we expect that dopamine-focused medications would benefit someone without a high-dopamine brain? "Treatment-resistant schizophrenia" is the name that the field has sort of settled on to refer to the forms of schizophrenia that don't respond to non-clozapine medications. This label is unfortunate, in my opinion, because it is both discouraging and misleading. The majority of so-called treatment-resistant cases actually respond beautifully to clozapine. It's not that these illnesses were resistant to treatment. It's that these folks have a normal-dopamine form of schizophrenia that won't be served by dopamine-adjusting meds. Clozapine works in the majority of these schizophrenias because clozapine is not a dopamine-adjusting medication. Clozapine is the only thing we know of that works well for normal-dopamine schizophrenia.

Q: How does someone know if they have a high-dopamine or a normal-dopamine form of schizophrenia?
It's possible to measure dopamine signaling in humans, but the techniques are not available outside of research studies. On the other hand, medication response patterns can be useful guides. If symptoms respond to dopamine signal-adjusting medications, it's quite likely that the psychosis was of the high-dopamine type. On the other hand, if symptoms have not much improved despite adequately dosed dopamine signal-adjusting medications, then a normal-dopamine psychosis is likely. Paying attention to medication response is an indirect method of finding out if someone has a high-dopamine schizophrenia or a normal-dopamine schizophrenia.

Q: What severe side effects have you seen in patients who take clozapine?
Most people fear the possibility of suppressing the white blood cell count with clozapine. Because white blood cells are a first line of defense against infection, a drastic reduction in their numbers can lead to very serious infections. Though hav-

ing small dips in white blood cell count is relatively common, most are temporary and insignificant. Having a medically serious white blood cell suppression from clozapine is actually rare (less than 1%). Getting an infection from such suppression is even more rare because the white blood cell count is measured frequently.

The most common medically serious complication from clozapine is related to constipation. In its more severe forms, constipation can lead to a medical emergency. It's important to pay attention to the frequency of bowel movements and to take medications if necessary to ensure regular bowel movements. I have worked as a consulting psychiatrist for most of my career. The patients I see have only partially benefited from many prior treatment attempts. I have probably seen every possible side effect from clozapine during my career, but this is because I have worked primarily with patients with the most complex forms of illness.

Many of clozapine's side effects can be prevented by not using high doses, and by taking care to de-prescribe medications that won't be needed once clozapine reaches therapeutic levels. Weight gain is a risk with clozapine, but can be minimized or prevented by diet and exercise, possibly combined with medications like metformin or liraglutide that promote weight loss. There are similar work-arounds for several other of clozapine's possible side effects. Knowing what to look for allows early detection of potentially serious side effects and early intervention to prevent harm.

Q: What is the most important thing you share with doctors who are learning to use clozapine?
Don't delay. The research is clear: the longer someone experiences psychosis, the lower their prospects for long-term recovery. So, getting someone into remission as soon as possible is one of the most important goals in the care of individuals suffering from acute psychosis. Patients with recent-onset schizophrenia should go into remission (or be well on their way to remission) within no more than 8 months of treatment with antipsychotic medication (up to four months with medication #1, and up to four months with medication #2 if medication #1 failed to work). If delusions or hallucinations are not controlled by two different antipsychotic medications, the likelihood that the patient will respond to a third medication is minuscule, unless that medication is clozapine — where the response rate is more than 50%. Delaying the initiation of clozapine is equivalent to prolonging the duration of psychosis. And prolonged duration of psychosis has been shown to reduce quality of life in both the short-term and long-term.

Q: What advice would you like to offer to other doctors who prescribe clozapine?
A lot of people hate having their blood drawn often and may refuse to consider

clozapine because of this. Topical anesthetic cream, to numb the skin at the blood draw site, can be really helpful to someone who might not consider clozapine because of the white blood cell testing requirements.

CLOZAPINE SIDE EFFECTS: WORTH THE RISKS
by Henry A. Nasrallah, MD and Richard Sanders, MD

Clozapine is a unique medication, with higher efficacy than all the other antipsychotic medicines for patients with treatment-resistant schizophrenia. However, it can be more difficult to manage, it can have serious physical side effects, and certain rare side effects can be life-threatening. Still, what's most important is that according to published longitudinal studies, patients with treatment-resistant schizophrenia receiving clozapine have a lower mortality from medical conditions or suicide than those treated with other antipsychotic medications. This isn't because clozapine has a better safety profile than the other antipsychotics. People taking clozapine live longer because it works better against psychosis.

Clozapine's serious side effects are uncommon. For example, the weekly blood test will tell you if you are in danger of developing neutropenia (a white blood cell drop) which happens in only 1% of patients, and the medication can be discontinued without any danger. Because of this, the risk of death from clozapine-induced neutropenia happens about 1 in 10,000 people worldwide, and even less in the United States due to better monitoring.

The risk of seizures is uncertain, but it is higher than the 1% risk of seizures with other antipsychotic medicines. Seizure risk is related to higher clozapine dose, but this is typically an easily managed adverse effect. Death due to clozapine-related seizures is very rare. Inflammation of the heart muscle (myocarditis) occurs in 1%-3% of people starting clozapine during the initial 6 weeks of treatment, but less often when the dose is increased slowly. Many doctors check serum troponin and CRP (a blood test that reflects inflammation), every week for the first 6 weeks of treatment, the same time the patient undergoes lab tests for neutropenia.

Pneumonia occurs in 2-3% of people in the first two months of starting clozapine and may be related to an unusual side effect, sialorrhea (i.e., drooling). Drooling usually happens during sleep (people find a wet pillow in the morning), but it can happen while awake. This is treated by reducing the dose and/or using one of several medications (oral atropine drops or Botox injections in the salivary glands) that slow down saliva production. Pneumonia does not require that clozapine be stopped, but the dose may need to be lowered temporarily until drooling problems are better managed.

Constipation can become a serious problem to the extent that the FDA issued an advisory in January 2020 warning about the use of clozapine with other anticholinergic medicines that slow gastrointestinal motility. Those combinations can cause a severe problem (ileus). When starting clozapine, doctors usually prescribe a stool softener (docusate) and then add other medications (e.g., polyethylene glycol-3350, bisacodyl, linaclotide, etc.) to prevent extreme constipation and ileus.

Weight gain and sedation are common side effects, but they are rarely dangerous. Metformin, a widely used diabetes pill, is often used to help prevent weight gain due to clozapine, and is started when clozapine is started. The new glucagon-like peptide-1 agonists (e.g., semaglutide) have FDA approval for obesity in nondiabetics and have been studied in clozapine-treated patients to help manage weight gain. Sedation can be short-lived or persistent, and it can be mild or a real hindrance. It can be addressed in a variety of ways, including the administration of a waking medication like modafinil. Doctors should regularly check weights as well as lab tests and should ask patients about side effects at every visit.

Clozapine is worth the risks, especially when managed carefully, as treatment-resistant patients have no viable effective medication alternatives. It is the only antipsychotic medication that can restore mental wellness in patients who otherwise would remain disabled for the rest of their lives with intractable hallucinations and delusions. It is more likely to prolong than to shorten lives. It is also more likely than other antipsychotic medications to enable patients with severe schizophrenia to function vocationally and socially and improve their quality of life.

4

LONG-ACTING INJECTABLES INTRODUCTION

Long-acting injectables (LAIs) are an intramuscular formulation of antipsychotic medications that are already available in pill form. These injections were first developed in the United States in the 1970s to ensure continuous delivery of the antipsychotic medication to the brain of a person with schizophrenia who often is unable to take oral medication regularly and ends up relapsing and getting re-hospitalized.

There are several reasons why nonadherence with medications is common in schizophrenia:

1. Over 80% of people are unaware that they are sick and refuse treatment because they believe they do not need it.
2. Memory is impaired in most individuals with schizophrenia, so they actually forget to take their tablets.
3. Paranoid thoughts make people with schizophrenia think they are being poisoned if they have a side effect.
4. Alcohol and drug abuse are very common among persons with schizophrenia living in the community and that interferes with taking prescription medications.

Relapse is serious because psychotic recurrence destroys hundreds of millions of brain cells, eventually leading to brain atrophy and permanent disability. In addition to being very useful in preventing relapse, LAIs are a convenient option because they eliminate the need to take pills every day. Today, several newer antipsychotic medications are available as LAIs that can be given by injection every 4, 6, 8, 12 weeks or even 6 months.

HOPE IN A NEEDLE
by Craig Chepke, MD

When the FDA authorized the first vaccines for COVID-19, they were called miracles of modern medicine and saviors of society. Pictures of people weeping tears of joy while receiving the vaccine flooded the Internet. What stood out to me was that these were not people who were already sick with COVID — they were completely healthy. But they saw the vaccine as a symbol of hope and the first step in overcoming the oppression of living in fear of an uncertain future. It made me wonder, why do we have such a hard time believing that people living with schizophrenia could find hope in a needle too?

LAIs offer numerous well-documented potential advantages for the treatment of adults with schizophrenia, but less than 15% receive them.[1] Perhaps one reason they are so underutilized is that clinicians have assumed that patients would not be interested in receiving an injection every two to four weeks, as LAIs historically required. However, I can attest that even if the COVID vaccine needed to be taken every month to stay safe, I would still want to be the first in line!

Furthermore, recent advances have allowed the interval between injections of certain LAIs to increase dramatically over the past decade. For instance, paliperidone palmitate was introduced as a once-a-month LAI in 2009, but a newer preparation given just every three months became available in 2015. Even more exciting, a version administered every six months was approved by the FDA later in 2021. If this pace continues, perhaps there could be a once-a-year version in 2027!

Considerable evidence suggests that schizophrenia is a neurodegenerative brain disorder similar to Parkinson's or Alzheimer's disease. With schizophrenia, however, psychotic relapses drive the progressive loss of brain tissue.[2] As such, clinicians must think about relapse prevention in schizophrenia with the same urgency that we currently attempt to prevent someone from having a second or third stroke.[3] Broader use of LAIs could go a long way towards minimizing the brain loss and the resulting decline in functionality and quality of life that each relapse brings. Research has shown LAIs may reduce relapse rates in schizophrenia by 20% and mortality risk by 33% compared to taking the same antipsychotic

---

[1] Offord, S., Wong, B., Mirski, D., Baker, R. A., & Lin, J. (2013). "Healthcare resource usage of schizophrenia patients initiating long-acting injectable antipsychotics vs oral." *Journal of Medical Economics*, 2, 231-239.

[2] Andreasen, N. C., Liu, D., Ziebell, S., Vora, A., & Ho, B. (2013). "Relapse duration, treatment intensity, and brain tissue loss in schizophrenia: A prospective longitudinal MRI study." *American Journal of Psychiatry*, 6, 609-615.

[3] Nasrallah, H.A. (2018). "FAST and RAPID: acronyms to prevent brain damage in stroke and psychosis." *Current Psychiatry*, 17(8), 6-8.

in oral form.[4,5]

Despite these substantial benefits, most clinicians seem to reserve LAIs solely for patients who are more severely or chronically ill.[6] In contrast, clinicians typically prescribe medications that slow the decline of Alzheimer's disease early in the illness to protect the person's mental functioning at a higher level rather than waiting until there's less quality of life left to preserve. Given the evidence that each relapse accelerates the cognitive and functional decline for people with schizophrenia, LAIs should be considered as an early option, not a last resort intervention. There is no grace period for the destructive effects that schizophrenia has on the brain.

Some clinical practice guidelines have begun to recommend using LAIs in first-episode psychosis, and I have adopted this approach in my practice.[7] I explain it to patients with the analogy that if I jumped out of an airplane, I'd prefer to open my parachute at 50,000 feet above the ground, not 50 feet. In the fight to achieve a richer, fuller, and longer life, LAIs are too powerful of a tool to be as underutilized as they are. Earlier aggressive treatment of first-episode psychosis and subsequent relapses with LAIs can dramatically improve long-term outcomes.

I have found that LAIs can be a remarkable source of positivity in the lives of people with schizophrenia. With the confidence that the medication's consistency is optimal and the improved stability that LAIs often bring, both the clinician and the patient can focus on other issues such as deepening their therapeutic alliance or working on coping skills. The next step could be to foster the engagement needed to successfully pursue even higher goals, like going back to school, getting a job, or finding a relationship. LAIs can be life-saving interventions, but only if clinicians do their part by offering and educating about them. We need to do everything we can to make a person's first episode of schizophrenia their last episode — and for some, we can start by helping them find hope in a needle.

---

[4] Kishimoto, T., Hagi, K., Kurokawa, S., Kane, J. M., & Correll, C. U. (2021). "Long-acting injectable versus oral antipsychotics for the maintenance treatment of schizophrenia: A systematic review and comparative meta-analysis of randomised, cohort, and pre-post studies." *Lancet Psychiatry*, 8(5), 387-404.

[5] Taipale, H., Mittendorfer-Rutz, E., Alexanderson, K., Majak, M., Mehtälä, J., Hoti, F., Jedenius, E., Enkusson, D., Leval, A., Sermon, J., Tanskanen, A., & Tiihonen, J. (2018). "Antipsychotics and mortality in a nationwide cohort of 29,823 patients with schizophrenia." *Schizophrenia Research*, 197, 274-280.

[6] Kishimoto, T., Hagi, K., Nitta, M., Leucht, S., Olfson, M., Kane, J. M., & Correll, C. U. (2018). "Effectiveness of long-acting injectable vs. oral antipsychotics in patients with schizophrenia: A meta-analysis of prospective and retrospective cohort studies." *Schizophrenia Bulletin*, 44(3), 603-619.

[7] Florida Medicaid Drug Therapy Management Program. (2020. "2019–2020 Florida Best Practice Psychotherapeutic Medication Guidelines for Adults." Florida Medicaid Drug Therapy Management Program. https://floridabhcenter.org/wp-content/uploads/2021/04/2019-Psychotherapeutic-Medication-Guidelines-for-Adults-with-References_06-04-20.pdf.

EMPOWER YOURSELF
by Craig Chepke, MD

A mentor once offered me the advice that "if you never ask, you rarely get." But someone can't ask for something they don't know exists. The American Psychiatric Association guidelines for the treatment of schizophrenia support the use of LAIs "if a patient prefers such treatment or if they have a history of poor or uncertain adherence."[1] However, the unfortunate truth is that most people with schizophrenia are not even aware that LAIs exist. How would a clinician know if a person living with schizophrenia would prefer treatment with an LAI if they never offered the person that option? Knowledge is power — but only if you are empowered to benefit from it.

The guidelines may be correct that LAIs are a mainstay for those with a history of poor adherence, but they are so much more than that. LAIs can liberate people from the burden of daily pill regimens and ensure 24-hour guaranteed medication levels in the body. Published studies also show they may reduce the risk of relapse, hospitalization, and even death.[2] Furthermore, treatment of any chronic illness with daily medication is uncertain and riddled with poor adherence, regardless of diagnosis! The rate of nonadherence in schizophrenia is estimated to be 45%-80%, comparable to that of coronary heart disease and asthma.[3] The availability of LAI options for other areas, such as osteoporosis and contraception, are considered revolutions in convenience and effectiveness. Rather than associating LAI antipsychotics with the stigma of the "last resort," we should celebrate that schizophrenia is one of the select few conditions for which we are fortunate to have LAI options!

All too often in life, people make snap judgments based on incomplete information or fickle emotions. Sometimes these decisions send us down a path that makes it harder to get back on track with each passing day. Schizophrenia is an insidious illness, directly impairing a person's insight — the awareness and understanding of the seriousness of the psychosis and need for treatment. Antipsychotics help maintain this insight. The body eliminates most oral antipsychotics

---

[1] Keepers, G. A., Fochtmann, L. J., Anzia, J. M., Benjamin, S., Lyness, J. M., Mojtabai, R., Servis, M., Walaszek, A., Buckley, P., Lenzenweger, M. F., Young, A. S., Degenhardt, A., & Hong, S. (2020). "The American Psychiatric Association practice guideline for the treatment of patients with schizophrenia." *American Journal of Psychiatry*, 177(9), 868-872.

[2] Kishimoto, T., Hagi, K., Kurokawa, S., Kane, J. M., & Correll, C. U. (2021). "Long-acting injectable versus oral antipsychotics for the maintenance treatment of schizophrenia: A systematic review and comparative meta-analysis of randomised, cohort, and pre-post studies." *Lancet Psychiatry*, 8(5), 387-404.

[3] Buckley, P. F., Foster, A. E., Patel, N. C., & Wermert, A. (2009). "Adherence to mental health treatment." *Oxford University Press*.

from their system so quickly that if someone has a bad couple of days and forgets or doesn't want to take their medication for just a short time, the amount in the system could fall below an adequate level. In turn, one's ability to decide to get back on medication could be impaired. Straying from a consistent medication regimen essentially takes the power to make decisions about treatment away from the person and gives it to the disease.

Daily oral medication requires one to fight this battle 365 days a year. While potentially exhausting to the person, brain disorders like schizophrenia persist. Metaphorically speaking, psychotic disorders are relentless in seeking a crack in the person's resolve. Each successive missed day of oral medication can make it seem more enticing not to start retaking it. However, LAIs keep the medication levels consistent for a month or longer. The number of times someone must fight to stay on medication can be reduced to as few as 12, 6, 4, or just 2 times a year. Even if a scheduled injection is missed, LAIs can offer a longer protection period than oral meds before the therapeutic effect is lost.[4] LAIs are like insurance for your commitment to pursue treatment, giving you a second chance to remain well and avoid rehospitalization.

All psychiatric clinicians have room to expand their usage of LAIs in their practice — even strong advocates like me. I vividly recall a time several years ago when I put a stack of brochures for an LAI in the waiting room of my office. One day, I saw a patient I've worked with for a long time who had done quite well on an oral antipsychotic. When it was time for her appointment, she stormed into my office, clutching the brochure. She waved it animatedly towards me and asked, "I didn't know I could just get my medication once a month — why didn't you ever offer this to me before?" I was speechless because I had no excuse — there's no reason I shouldn't have at least offered it to her. If your clinician has not discussed LAIs with you, empower yourself to start that discussion. Take back the choice about your treatment from your illness!

---

[4] Correll, C. U., Kim, E., Kern Sliwa, J. Hamm, W., Gopal, S., Mathews, M., Venkatasubramanian, R., & Saklad, S. R. (2021). "Pharmacokinetic characteristics of long-acting injectable antipsychotics for schizophrenia: an overview." *CNS Drugs*, 35(1) 39-59.

5

TARDIVE DYSKINESIA
INTRODUCTION

Tardive dyskinesia (TD) is always a potential neurological adverse effect of dopamine receptor blocking agents, which includes all antipsychotic medications (though it is rare on clozapine). TD presents as involuntary movements often seen in the face, including the tongue, lips, jaw, and eyes but can also affect the neck, arms, fingers, legs, trunk, or diaphragm (sometimes causing grunting or barking sounds). The abnormal movements can be disfiguring and embarrassing to patients (for a concise overview of tardive dyskinesia, see our treatment checklist, page 184).

TD is different from the acute abnormal muscle movements or rigidity including drug-induced Parkinson's (DIP). It also differs from drug-induced restlessness (referred to as akathisia) and dystonia (a neurological movement disorder characterized by involuntary muscle contractions).

With the newer antipsychotic medications, TD occurs much less often than with the older antipsychotic medications.

TD often appears after months, but more typically years, of antipsychotic therapy. There are several risk factors for TD including high dose and long duration of antipsychotic treatment, older age, female gender, diagnosis of a mood disorder, drug and alcohol use, and diabetes. It is estimated that 500,000 persons in the United States currently suffer from TD.

For 50 years, TD had been untreatable and irreversible. However, research finally paid off and efficacious treatment for TD has been discovered. Valbenazine was approved by the FDA in April 2017, and deutetrabenazine was subsequently approved in August 2017. These medications have to be taken permanently because if stopped, the involuntary movements of TD will return. These medications are highly effective and can significantly improve the quality of life of individuals afflicted by TD.

The CURESZ Foundation has assembled a Tardive Dyskinesia Expert Panel with 35 clinicians from around the country who prescribe medications for TD. See www.curesz.org/tardive-dyskinesia-expert-panel.

BE YOUR OWN ADVOCATE
by Craig Chepke, MD

I am honored to be a part of the CURESZ Tardive Dyskinesia Expert Panel, but I haven't always been adept at diagnosing tardive dyskinesia (TD). For years, no one in my current practice seemed to have "obvious" symptoms of TD, so I came to assume that it was more of a historical problem associated with the older first-generation antipsychotics that I rarely prescribe.

In 2016, however, I began working with a young man with schizophrenia whose TD was unmistakable. With no FDA-approved medications for TD at the time, the best I could offer was to remove or reduce one of the two antipsychotics he was taking. He and his father wouldn't consider any change, because that combination was the only thing that had ever worked for him. When his father suddenly passed away months later, the patient's grief inspired me to learn as much as I could about treating TD. I couldn't give him his father back, but I could at least try to give him the dignity of control over his body.

I studied neurology journals and textbooks for months and realized that I had unconsciously set my bar for diagnosing TD at only the highest severity level. I had inadvertently become blind to detecting mild to moderate TD. Reading the numerous failed clinical trials of medications and supplements for treating TD, I gained an appreciation of the decades of powerlessness clinicians had felt in trying to treat it. It seemed that recognition of TD was gradually overshadowed by increased screening for other potential side effects of antipsychotics, such as blood sugar and cholesterol elevations — perhaps because the latter are problems for which we have long had good treatment options. In 2017, the FDA approved the first two medications for TD, and treating my patient with one of them benefitted him in profound ways I didn't expect.

Every psychiatric provider trained in an era in which there was little or nothing we could do to address TD, so many didn't have enough urgency looking for it. Our diagnostic skills withered, and many newer clinicians never established proficiency in the first place. Now that approved treatments exist, the mental health field will eventually enhance its recognition of TD, but if I didn't have this unique experience when I did, it might have been years before I stepped up my screening. Until every provider makes a thorough examination for TD a standard part of their appointments, I urge everyone taking an antipsychotic, especially anyone experiencing unusual or unexpected movement problems, to be your own advocate and take the lead in discussing tardive dyskinesia treatment with your provide.

---

[1] Carbon, M., Hsieh, C. H., Kane, J. M., & Correll, C. U. (2017). "Tardive dyskinesia prevalence in the period of second-generation antipsychotic use: a meta-analysis." *The Journal of Clinical Psychiatry*, 78(3), e264–e278.

MORE THAN A SIDE EFFECT
by *Craig Chepke, MD*

TD was first described in the early 1960s, but despite nearly 60 years of research, we don't have a clear understanding of why it happens. TD does seem to have a clear relationship with dopamine, which regulates a vast number of functions in our bodies, including attention, pleasure-seeking, and motor function. Some psychiatric disorders, including disturbances of mood, sensory perception, and thought processes are believed to be associated with an excess of dopamine stimulation in certain pathways or "circuits" of the brain.

We often use antipsychotic medications for these symptoms because they are dopamine receptor blockers (DRBs), and thus prevent dopamine from completing the circuit. In hyperactive dopamine circuits, this normalizes function, but DRBs are unable to discriminate between overactive and normal dopamine pathways. Sometimes blocking dopamine can reduce function in pathways it should not and cause unintended consequences.

The basal ganglia is the part of the brain that is responsible for controlling movements and is also dependent on dopamine to conduct its signaling. Prolonged use of DRBs can stimulate the basal ganglia to produce too many highly sensitive dopamine receptors. In an attempt to rebalance its diminished dopamine signals, the process may overcompensate for some. The motor system becomes hypersensitive, and dopamine now overstimulates it, which results in the involuntary movements, or "dyskinesia" that give TD its name. "Tardive" comes from the French word for "late" because it generally takes months or years of exposure to a DRB before the symptoms develop.

Imagine you're listening to music with a friend, and you think the volume level is normal, but it's too loud for him. He gets out ear plugs, but puts them in your ears as well as his. Now you can't hear the music at all, and you find the ear plugs won't come out, so you turn the volume way up to compensate. Eventually the ear plugs may malfunction and fall out, and the music sounds unbearably loud. Unfortunately, you find that the volume button is broken, and you can't turn it down. TD is like this.

The real problem with TD isn't that it can develop long after the start of a DRB, it's that it's generally irreversible. Not everyone taking a DRB gets TD, but those who do can't get rid of it by stopping the medication, and sometimes the TD severity spikes after medication discontinuation. While some risk factors for TD are known, we don't yet have a very good way of predicting who is going to get it before it happens. Or in the terms of the analogy above, we don't know whose earplugs are going to malfunction.

Therefore, we shouldn't consider TD a "side effect" of DRBs because side effects go away if you remove the medication that causes them. Rather, we should think of TD as its own syndrome that is caused by exposure to DRBs in vulnerable people. Just like cigarette smoking causes lung cancer in some people, those who get cancer don't go into remission just because they stop smoking. Improving TD at that point requires its own additional treatment.

DAWN OF HOPE
by Craig Chepke, MD

The previous section discussed that the removal of the medication that causes tardive dyskinesia rarely results in remission, and, therefore, TD requires its own specific treatment. However, there were no FDA-approved treatments prior to 2017. The few options for which the American Academy of Neurology (AAN) made even a moderate recommendation had significant problems: clonazepam has a serious risk of physical dependency, and certain over-the-counter supplements like ginkgo biloba have been found by the U.S. Government Accountability Office to contain much less than the amount advertised, or even none.[1]

Worse yet, the medication that seems to have become the de facto standard-of-care in the United States for nearly all drug-induced movement disorders is benztropine (Cogentin). Not only does it carry a heavy side-effect burden, its use in TD has been categorized as "unsubstantiated" by the AAN because there have been no controlled clinical trials. Even the manufacturer's official prescribing information says benztropine does not help TD and can aggravate its symptoms.[2]

Tetrabenazine, a medication from the 1950s, was not originally intended to treat TD but was found to have some benefit in other hyperkinetic movement disorders. Tetrabenazine inhibits a protein called VMAT2, which collects dopamine for release. People with TD have hypersensitive motor circuits, so inhibiting VMAT2 reduces the amount of dopamine released into those areas, alleviating some of the symptoms. Unfortunately, the active components of tetrabenazine are eliminated from the body so quickly that it must be taken three times a day, and this leads to other side effects, which limited its use.

In 2017, the FDA brought new hope to those with TD by approving two highly effective medications to treat it. Both valbenazine and deutetrabenazine were derived from the tetrabenazine prototype but delivered improvements in side effects and convenience by slowing its metabolism — each with a different twist.

---

[1] Benztropine Mesylate [package insert]. Lake Forest, IL: Akorn, Inc.; 2016.
[2] U.S. Government Accountability Office (GAO). (2018). "Memory Supplements: Results of Testing for Selected Supplements." U.S. Government Accountability Office (GAO). https://www.gao.gov/assets/700/696047.pdf.

Valbenazine slows elimination by elegantly attaching the amino acid valine to the component of tetrabenazine that is the most potent and selective. Deutetrabenazine slows its elimination by cleverly swapping eight of tetrabenazine's hydrogen atoms for those of a close variant of hydrogen called deuterium.

Valbenazine and deutetrabenazine are both usually well tolerated and have roughly similar benefits on average. Depending on the person, one may be more favorable than the other, and each has a different trade-off. Valbenazine has three once-a-day dosing options, each of which can be therapeutic. Deutetrabenazine has more potential dosing options, but requires titration over several weeks to an effective dose. VMAT2 inhibitors only treat the symptoms of TD and are not curative. If treatment with any of them is stopped, the symptoms return to their pre-treatment levels. Still, an increasing focus of psychiatric research involves circuits in the brain that use the neurotransmitter glutamate, which facilitates "synaptic plasticity," essentially the brain's ability to rewire itself. It will take much more investigation, but it is theoretically possible that future medications that modulate glutamate signaling could be found to help the brain remodel itself from the damage of TD.

Perhaps the dawn of hope for TD has only begun!

MORE THAN SKIN DEEP
by Craig Chepke, MD

Despite the recent availability of safe and effective treatments for tardive dyskinesia, many healthcare providers remain hesitant to use them. They may believe that TD does not bother those who suffer from it or feel that the impact of TD pales in comparison to the primary symptoms they are treating, such as psychosis or mania. My experience is that some clinicians just don't realize that the involuntary movements can cause physical, emotional, and interpersonal problems.

A specific case from my practice is a 61-year-old woman who was seeking treatment for depression, but I also noticed TD. Through our discussion, I found that she had loved to sing at church until her lip movements made the choir director think she was singing at the wrong times, so she quit. She stopped attending services when her hand movements caused her to rustle the church bulletin she was holding, drawing complaints from the congregation. She lives with her daughter and young grandchildren and was devastated when they called her a "monster" because of the facial contortions the dyskinesia caused. She refused to come out of her room, even for meals, and lost 40 pounds over 6 months.

She thought she needed an antidepressant, but a little over a month after I prescribed her a VMAT2 inhibitor, she was back to playing with her grandkids, attending church, and singing in the choir again!

Have you ever told someone they had food visibly stuck in their teeth? Almost everyone has done this, but stop and consider why we do so. The person generally has no idea that it's present, but we thought about how much it would embarrass us if the roles were reversed, and we'd hope someone would intervene for us. When such a minor cosmetic issue is universally recognized as problematic, how can it be denied that the irreversible movements of TD cause stigma?

Other disorders in medicine that don't have noticeable symptoms aren't written off so cavalierly. High cholesterol is a finding a clinician can make only when screening for it. Even though it "doesn't bother anyone," we still encourage treatment because it is a modifiable risk factor for cardiovascular disease. Similarly, healthcare providers should view TD as a potential source of other negative outcomes. People with TD can face social stigma and prejudice. However, dyskinesia in the trunk or legs can cause falls, and when it occurs in the muscles of swallowing, it can cause aspiration pneumonia. Just as knowingly not treating asymptomatic illnesses such as high cholesterol would be considered medical malpractice, so should failure to offer treatment for TD because it is a disfiguring and disabling neurological disease that must be treated, and the earlier the better.

There are so many tragic things that clinicians cannot easily change about their patients' lives, like being homeless, unemployed, or the effects of growing up in an abusive family. However, when the movements of TD cause people to face discrimination or withdraw from family or society, there is now something that we can do. With the new VMAT2 inhibitors, this is now an unnecessary burden and a treatable illness. It is up to us to identify TD and educate the people with it on how it can affect them.

TD is more than skin deep–we can and must give people with TD their functioning and dignity back.

IMPACT ON PATIENTS' LIVES
by Craig Chepke, MD

I was teaching a psychiatric physician assistant about tardive dyskinesia (TD) recently, and he told me his clinical supervisor, a seasoned psychiatrist near retirement, had expressed the sentiment, "I don't know why everyone gets so worked up over TD — it's nowhere near as bad as I used to see it in the state hospital. You young people just have too much of an emotional reaction to things." America has recently struggled with a long-overdue reckoning with social injustice, and I hope that the medical field can also change how it responds to the people suffering with TD as well.

There are profound social and occupational consequences that people with TD face. One of my patients is a smart, hardworking 49-year-old woman who works in an office setting. She'd long felt she was hitting "the glass ceiling" trying to climb the corporate ladder as a woman in a male-dominated profession. When she developed TD, she was terrified it would be yet another barrier to her superiors and coworkers taking her seriously. She was so self-conscious that she might be having involuntary facial movements without her noticing it, she set up her smartphone at her desk to record her face all day long. She would scrub through the video at lunch or after work and at any sign of movement, she'd begin crying and despair that she'd never achieve her career goals.

She remarked that she felt lucky that she had a good job when she developed TD because she didn't think anyone would hire her for even an entry-level position with TD. I have had other patients with TD feel discriminated against when applying for both blue- and white-collar jobs, and a recent clinical trial studied this situation.[1] Actors were filmed participating in a scripted interview that had two versions: one in which the actor imitated facial movements consistent with mild to moderate TD and another in which he did not. The 800 people were evenly randomized to watch either the imitated TD or the non-TD version, and all participants were asked questions about their impressions of the interviewee in regards to employment, friendship, or dating.

The study's results were disheartening, if not surprising. While about 65% of people shown the non-TD version felt the interviewee would be suitable for a client-facing job, just 25% of people who watched the same actor say the same words in the same way — but with apparent mild to moderate involuntary facial movements — thought he would be appropriate for the same job. The study also showed the participants perceived the actors mimicking TD as significantly less interesting, less friendly, and less favorable dating partners.

The 65 years that preceded the approval of VMAT2 inhibitors were filled with futility in treating TD, until minimizing or ignoring it became a habit. As with any suffering we turn a blind eye to, there are consequences we don't perceive until a light is shined on them. Healthcare providers cannot give our patients with TD a job. Still, with safe and effective treatments now available, there is at least one form of social injustice we can remedy far more easily than most of those our society currently faces.

---

[1] Ayyagari, R., Goldschmidt, D., Mu, F., Caroff, S. N., & Carroll, B. (2020). 115 "An experimental study to assess the professional and social consequences of mild-to-moderate tardive dyskinesia." *CNS Spectrums* 25(2), 275-275.

ESSAYS ON SCHIZOPHRENIA

6

ON RENAMING SCHIZOPHRENIA
by Carol S. North, MD

The psychiatric illness currently known as schizophrenia was originally named dementia praecox. This term, literally meaning "precocious madness" and first used by the French physician Bénédict Morel in 1853, was later popularized by the German psychiatrist Emil Kraepelin in 1896 to represent a chronic, incurable psychotic disorder with rapid cognitive disintegration that typically strikes in the late teens to early adulthood. In 1908, the Swiss psychiatrist Eugen Bleuler renamed it schizophrenia, to refer to splitting of mental functions including personality, thinking, memory, and perception.[1] Unlike Kraepelin's vision, Bleuler's view of the condition was that its prognosis was not uniformly poor and that it actually consisted of a group of disorders which he referred to as "the schizophrenias." Over the next century, a precise definition was established with formal diagnostic criteria and scientific validation.

In the last 25 years, a new movement to rename the disorder has emerged. This movement is motivated by concerns that the term "schizophrenia" is confusing and misleading, generating negative stigma surrounding the illness and those who suffer with it. This term has led to widespread misunderstanding of the disorder as a problem of "split personalities," which is an entirely different and unrelated disorder. The public is further confused by the media which has unfortunately perpetuated incorrect characterizations of schizophrenia as representing any incoherent, contradictory, or deviant behavior, depicting individuals with this disorder as criminal, violent, and dangerous. An alternative common usage of the word "schizophrenia" has found its way into secondary dictionary definitions referring to contradictory or antagonistic qualities or attitudes (e.g., "schizophrenic weather patterns"). Therefore, some experts have called for a new name, aiming to increase understanding, improve the public image of the disorder, reduce stigma, and lead to better care for the disorder.[1]

---

[1] Gaebel, W & Kerst, A. (2019). "The debate about renaming schizophrenia: A new name would not resolve the stigma." *Epidemiology and Psychiatric Sciences*, 28(3), 258-261.

Many alternative names for schizophrenia have been suggested.[2,3,4] Candidates include Bleuler's syndrome, Kraepelin-Bleuler disease, Schneider's syndrome, dopamine dysregulation disorder, salience dysregulation syndrome, neuro-emotional integration disorder, psychotic spectrum disorder, psychosis susceptibility syndrome, dysfunctional perception syndrome, and Youth Onset Conative, Cognitive and Reality Distortion (CONCORD). In 2002, Japan became the first country to rename schizophrenia, formally calling it integration disorder. In the same decade, Taiwan and Hong Kong officially renamed it dysfunction of thought and perception; next, South Korea adopted the name attunement disorder.

To date, the scientific community has not come to agree on any alternative name and it remains conflicted about whether renaming the disorder is advisable at all. Some experts do not think that a name change would necessarily affect the stigma surrounding the disorder because it is the negative public perception of the disorder based on ignorance and fear rather than the name itself that is the root cause of the stigma.[2] Further, concerns have been raised that changing the disorder's name might simply transfer existing stigma from the old name to a new name. Yet others think that the scientific definition of the disorder needs to be changed along with its name, and that agreement on a new name will require discovery of the underlying causes of the disorder — a scientific achievement not expected in the near future.

Experts advocating for a new name for schizophrenia have recommended adoption of an eponym that names a person.[3] For example, Down's syndrome is an eponym for the condition known as trisomy 21 (formerly "mongolism"), and Alzheimer's disease is an eponym for what was previously called "senile dementia." A recent example of an individual who lived a brilliant life with schizophrenia is the late John Nash; the motion picture *A Beautiful Mind* dramatizes the story of this acclaimed mathematician who won a Nobel Prize in 1994. An eponym based on his life with schizophrenia could transform the disorder's name to **John Nash disorder**, a term without negative connotations, reflecting a positive image.

Experts have cautioned that to achieve the desired ends, a new name must be accompanied by professional and public education, legislation, and availability and acceptability of effective mental health services. These efforts should involve patients and their families as well as psychiatric clinicians and researchers.[3] Finally, it will be important to study the medical, economic, legal, and social ramifications of a new name.[4] Renaming schizophrenia can be expected to be a long process, and an even longer process will be needed to achieve the expected ben-

---

[2] Gaebel, W & Kerst, A. (2019). "The debate about renaming schizophrenia: A new name would not resolve the stigma." *Epidemiology and Psychiatric Sciences*, 28(3), 258-261.
[3] Lasalvia, A., Penta, E., Sartorius, N., & Henderson, S. (2015). "Should the label 'schizophrenia' be abandoned?" *Schizophrenia Research*, 162(1-3), 276-284.
[4] Yamaguchi, S., Mizuno, M., Ojio, Y., Sawada, U., Matsumara, A., Ando, S., & Koike, S. (2017). "Associations between renaming schizophrenia and stigma-related outcomes: A systematic review." *Psychiatry and Clinical Neurosciences*, 71(6), 347-362.

efits of changing public understanding and improving life for the people who live with this illness.

7

NEGATIVE SYMPTOMS OF SCHIZOPHRENIA
by Henry A. Nasrallah, MD

Schizophrenia is a complex neuropsychiatric syndrome with multiple symptom domains. The most recognizable symptom cluster is the positive symptoms (i.e., psychotic symptoms like delusions, hallucinations and bizarre behavior), which is the reason patients are initially hospitalized. However, most patients with schizophrenia also suffer from three other symptom clusters including negative symptoms, cognitive impairments, and mood symptoms. In fact, the negative and cognitive symptoms are what lead to functional disability, even after the psychotic symptoms are eliminated with antipsychotic medications.

Negative symptoms were not widely recognized until the 1980s. Prior to that, the focus in schizophrenia was on the psychotic symptoms. The persistence of negative symptoms after psychosis is treated with antipsychotic medications led to many studies that focused on the various negative symptoms, which can lead to long-term social and vocational disability.

The following are the negative symptoms of schizophrenia, which are usually observed by the family or the psychiatrist, rather than being described by the patients themselves:

1. **Affect Pathology.** This refers to a flat, blunted, or restricted facial expression. In addition, there is poor eye contact, decreased spontaneous movements, monotone speech (referred to as aprosody), and failure to recognize the facial expression of other people (such as neutral, angry, sad, disgusted, or anxious).
2. **Alogia.** This is a reduction in the quantity and complexity of thought and poverty of speech, including speaking in monosyllables rather than sentences. Sometimes, patients may suddenly stop speaking in mid-sentence (called "blocking") which is an interruption of thought. There is often a prolonged pause before responding to a question.
3. **Associality.** This is absence or reduction of interest in having social

relationships or interacting with others. Patients also are unable to feel intimacy or closeness with others.

4. **Avolition and Apathy.** These are the loss of the ability to initiate or persist in a goal-directed activity. This includes not bathing, poor grooming, and not doing anything all day, often misconstrued as "laziness." Patients may become malodorous due to neglecting their personal hygiene.
5. **Anhedonia.** This is the loss or reduction in the capacity to experience pleasure, manifested by lack of interest in enjoyable activities. This is also a decrease in sexual activity, interest, or enjoyment. Unlike the anhedonia of depression, which is reversible, it is persistent in most patients with schizophrenia.
6. **Inattentiveness.** This is the inability to maintain a task or involvement/engagement for a reasonable period of time. The patient appears engrossed in an internal world to the exclusion of external tasks.
7. **Anosognosia.** This is also referred to as non-awareness of illness. The patient lacks insight into their illness or disability. It can also be regarded as a cognitive deficit. This lack of insight prevents patients from seeking treatment or help to alleviate symptoms or to solve personal problems. Anosognosia can be reversible with continuous adherence to antipsychotic therapy.

Researchers sometimes classify the above negative symptoms into two major categories:

1. **Diminished Expression**, which includes affective flattening and alogia.
2. **Apathy/Avolition**, which includes lack of motivation and lack of socialization.

In contrast to psychotic symptoms for which dozens of medications are available, there are no treatments yet for negative symptoms. It is a major unmet need in the field of schizophrenia. So far, many attempts have been unsuccessful in developing a pharmacological treatment for negative symptoms. Clozapine was thought to improve negative symptoms but further studies showed that to be not true. Thus, cognitive behavioral psychotherapy is currently the main approach to help patients recognize and overcome their negative symptoms. Occupational and recreational therapies can also be helpful. There are a couple of promising medications on the horizon, including a drug called pimavanserin, another drug called roluperidone, and a class of drugs called muscarinic agonists. However, the FDA has not approved any of these yet, but one of those promising drugs may be launched in 2025.

8

A DECADE OF DRUG DISCOVERY FOR SCHIZOPHRENIA: TAAR1 AND MUSCARINIC AGONISTS

by Elizabeth Beam, MD, PhD and Jacob Ballon, MD

Just over a decade ago, several major pharmaceutical companies decided to abandon research and development in schizophrenia medications. The move was disheartening to patients and researchers alike who had repeatedly heard promises of controlling more symptoms with fewer side effects. So why did big pharma make its departure? The data had come in from a massive trial comparing "typical" antipsychotics, discovered serendipitously in the 1950s, to "atypical" ones released in the 1990s after years of benchwork and trials. Little to no improvement with the "atypicals" could be confirmed. The investment in drugs for schizophrenia had been costly and did not pay off — that is, not yet.

In retrospect, it's not too surprising the first two classes of antipsychotics had similar efficacy. They both worked by blocking dopamine receptors. Pharmaceutical companies seemed to have run with dopamine as their target for schizophrenia the same way they ran with serotonin for depression and acetylcholine for Alzheimer's disease. Each chase for the cure was stalling. Just because a drug reduced symptoms did not mean it treated the underlying pathophysiology of disease. Imagine symptoms were a fire in the brain — a drug acting like water could douse the flames, but it wouldn't cool the hot air or stop the initial spark from reigniting.

However, the past decade has generated several promising directions for treating schizophrenia by turning to a fresh set of drug targets. Two new classes have no direct dopamine activity at all, acting instead on trace amine and muscarinic receptors. In early trials, the drugs have shown potential to address a broader range of symptoms, including the negative and cognitive symptoms that have eluded dopamine receptor blocking agents for decades.

Trace Amine Receptor 1 (TAAR1) Agonists

In early 2020, amid the pandemic headlines, news broke of a new pharmacologic approach to treat schizophrenia. TAAR1 agonists had been singled out in a search for non-dopamine blocking drugs that reduced schizophrenia symptoms in animal models. In mice, TAAR1 agonists have also shown that they may help better regulate blood glucose levels — possibly avoiding one of the major side effects of the atypical antipsychotics.

Ulotaront is a TAAR1 agonist thought to work by preventing neurons from firing in the ventral tegmental area, which serves as a starting point for dopamine along the pathway implicated in schizophrenia. While the mechanism of this new drug remains somewhat mysterious, the idea behind it is something like putting out the spark that ignites symptoms. In addition to its trace amine activity, ulotaront acts as an agonist at the 5-HT1A receptors for the neurotransmitter serotonin.

When analyzing the initial results of a randomized controlled clinical trial in patients, researchers found that ulotaront had outperformed placebo in reducing the total PANSS score, a global measure of schizophrenia symptoms. The drug also reduced the difficult-to-treat negative symptoms of schizophrenia (a preliminary result that was not adjusted statistically for the number of tests they ran, limiting our ability to draw firm conclusions). Unfortunately, as research progressed, two phase III trials of ulotaront both conceded that patients treated with ulotaront did not respond significantly better on the PANSS compared to patients taking placebo pills. Investigators suspected that this finding may be related to the high placebo response rates in these studies.

Another TAAR1 agent, a partial-agonist called ralmitaront, is also in development, but it is at an earlier stage in the process. Two phase II trials of ralmitaront studying its efficacy in treating positive and negative symptoms, respectively, were both ended early as the medication did not significantly reduce symptoms relative to placebo. It is an open question whether pharmaceutical companies will continue developing TAAR1 agents or take these mixed results as an indication to desist.

Muscarinic (M1/M4) Agonists

If you've ever taken diphenhydramine (Benadryl) and felt foggy afterward, you've discovered for yourself that blocking acetylcholine in the brain can have adverse cognitive effects. On the flip side, could drugs that stimulate acetylcholine receptors improve memory? This is the idea behind using agonists of muscarinic receptors, which mediate cholinergic activity to treat the cognitive symptoms of schizophrenia.

Because muscarinic agonists can have unwanted side effects outside the brain (muscarinic receptors are located throughout the body and act on most organ systems), one strategy has been to pair the muscarinic agonist xanomeline (which acts throughout the body and in the brain) with the muscarinic antagonist trospium, which does not act in the brain because it cannot cross the blood-brain barrier. By laying a trospium tarp from the neck down, the combination also helps ensure more xanomeline flows into the brain. The balance between the two remains a work in progress — common side effects include a mix of those related to increased cholinergic activity (nausea and vomiting) and those related to anticholinergic effects (constipation, dry mouth, blurry vision, and memory loss). Another drug in the pipeline, emraclidine, acts predominantly at only one of the five muscarinic receptors (M4) to help minimize the risk of the full-body side effects while improving psychotic symptoms.

Up-to-date information on ongoing trials for TAAR1 and muscarinic drugs can be obtained by searching the clinicaltrials.gov site managed by the National Institutes of Health. It will be important to remain cautious in our optimism, remembering how the early excitement for atypical antipsychotics in the 1990s was tempered by less exuberant results of a larger trial that compared the drugs directly. For now, it is worth celebrating the shift in momentum toward innovative new mechanisms of action and drug discovery advances for schizophrenia.

---

[1] Abbott, A. (2010). "Schizophrenia: The drug deadlock." *Nature* 468, 158-159.
[2] Brannan, S. K., Sawchak, S., Miller, A. C., Lieberman, J. A., Paul, S. M., & Breier, A. (2021). "Muscarinic cholinergic receptor agonist and peripheral antagonist for schizophrenia." *New England Journal of Medicine*, 384, 717-726.
[3] Goodwin, Kate. (2023). "Roche terminates second phase II trial." *BioSpace*.
[4] Koblan, K. S., Kent, J., Hopkins, S. C., Krystal, J. H., Cheng, H., Goldman, R., & Loebel, A. (2020). "A Non-D2-receptor-binding drug for the treatment of schizophrenia." *New England Journal of Medicine*, 382, 1497-1506.
[5] Lieberman, J. A., Stroub, T. S., McEvoy, J. P., Swartz, M. S., Rosenheck, R. A., Perkins, D. O., Keefe, R. S. E., Davis, S. M., Davis, C. E., Lebowitz, B. D., Severe, J., Hsiao, J. K., & the Clinical Antipsychotic Trials of Intervention Effectiveness (CATIE) Investigators. (2005). "Effectiveness of antipsychotic drugs in patients with chronic schizophrenia." *New England Journal of Medicine*, 353(12), 1209-1223.
[6] Pahwa, M., Sleem, A., Elsayed, O. H., Good, M. E., & El-Mallakh, R. S. (2021). "New antipsychotic medications in the last decade." *Current Psychiatry Reports*, 23,1-35.
[7] Sumitomo Pharma Co. & Otsuko Pharma Co. (2023). "Sumitomo Pharma and Otsuka announce topline results from phase 3 DIAMOND 1 and DIAMOND 2 clinical studies evaluating ulotaront in schizophrenia." *Sumitomo Pharma News Room*.

9

THE SEVEN CATASTROPHIC CONSEQUENCES OF PSYCHOTIC RECURRENCES
by Henry A. Nasrallah, MD

It is very unfortunate when individuals with schizophrenia relapse repeatedly. The number one cause for the recurrence of psychosis is either inconsistent adherence to antipsychotic (AP) medications or total non-adherence.[1] The reasons for poor adherence in schizophrenia are related to the illness itself, and patients should not be blamed.

The symptoms of schizophrenia that lead to non-adherence[2] include:

1. **Anosognosia,** or the lack of insight that one is very sick with delusions and hallucinations, leading to patient rejection of medication.
2. **Cognitive Difficulties** including serious memory impairment, which lead to forgetting to take the AP.
3. **Negative Symptoms,** including apathy, lack of motivation (avolition), and loss of the ability to do many things including taking medications every day.
4. **Suspiciousness** that the common side effects of AP medication is evidence of being poisoned.
5. **Alcohol and Drug Use,** which are very common in persons with schizophrenia living in the community, and preclude taking prescription medication. The combination of all those factors inevitably leads to a high rate of medication non-adherence after discharge from the first hospitalization.

Just like type 1 diabetes or hypertension, where medications must be taken every day or risk relapse, persons with schizophrenia must take their oral pills every day without interruption. A published study showed that a drop of only 25% in the AP blood level (which means missing a dose once every 4 days) is enough

---
[1] Velligan DI et al: *Patients Prefer Adherence* 11:449-468, 2018.
[2] Nasrallah HA: *Current Psychiatry* 16:4-7, 2017.

to cause a relapse in schizophrenia.[3]

Long-acting injectable (LAI) APs were developed in the 1970s, precisely to solve the problem of non-adherence with oral medication. However, due to the delay in scientific advances about the brain-damaging effects of psychosis (which appeared three decades later), clinicians were completely unaware that psychosis is associated with the dangers of recurring psychosis and resultant brain damage. They also believed that patients should "make their own decisions," despite the well-known fact that the decision-making region of the brain (frontal lobe) is impaired in schizophrenia. Patients were even led to regard LAI treatment as "stigmatizing" and as a "punishment" for multiple relapses, so they resisted the LAIs. Now LAIs are regarded as a most compassionate and effective therapeutic approach to save patients with schizophrenia from psychosis-induced brain damage.

Around the year 2000, psychiatric neuroscience research revealed that psychosis destroys brain tissue and causes brain atrophy[4] due to neuroinflammation and free radicals,[5] both of which damage gray and white matter. Brain structure and function deteriorate with every psychotic relapse. This prevents persons who develop schizophrenia from ever returning to their baseline preceding the first-episode psychosis (FEP), which is very tragic for young individuals in late adolescence or early 20s.

The following are seven catastrophic consequences of recurrent psychotic episodes[6] which are due to poor adherence:

1. Brain tissue loss and brain atrophy and disintegration of the extensive network of myelinated fibers (about 137,000 miles) is affected. These connect all brain regions and create a unity of self.
2. Treatment-resistant patients respond to low doses of AP in the first episode of psychosis (FEP) but need a higher and higher dose with each psychotic relapse until eventually they become completely treatment-resistant (and will need clozapine, which most patients never have access to). The brain structure deteriorates successively with each episode and that's why APs that previously worked no longer do so.
3. Non-adherence causes functional disability, and inability to return to school or college or to work, whatever patients were doing before the FEP. Thus, with repeated relapses, those young people become totally disabled instead of being productive members of society.
4. When individuals with schizophrenia become psychotic and behave

---

[3] Subotnik KL et al: *Am J Psychiatry* 168:286-292, 2011.
[4] Cahn W et al: *Arch Gen Psychiatry* 59:1002-1010, 2002.
[5] Kohler-Torsberg O et al: *Frontiers in Psychiatry* 11:1-3, 2020.
[6] Nasrallah HA: *Current Psychiatry* 20:9-12, 2021.

erratically, sometimes they are killed by police, and many more are arrested and jailed, often sentenced to prison. They no longer get admitted to state hospitals (because they have all been shuttered), and so are surrounded by armed guards instead of doctors, nurses, and social workers who compassionately provide them with medical care instead of being thrown into a prison with murderers and rapists.

5. Many people are not aware of the incredibly high rate of suicide among young people with schizophrenia when they relapse. Some studies report over 10,000% higher[7] death rates from suicide compared to young persons of the same age in the general population.
6. Non-adherence can lead to drug abuse, chaotic lifestyle, and living on the sidewalks of large cities, with risk of becoming victims of crime.
7. Psychosis can cause unusual behavior and poor dress and grooming, which intensify the public's negative bias against serious mental illness.

Yet, against this dismal outcome, there is hope and good news for persons with schizophrenia. The use of LAI very early (i.e., immediately after the first hospitalization) can make a huge difference in preventing deterioration. There are published studies that relapses in the first year after the FEP if LAIs are started is 650% lower than the rate of relapses in patients receiving oral AP.[8] I have personally had patients who did not relapse for five continuous years after switching them to injectable AP. Preventing relapses is vital because recent research demonstrates that disability actually begins after the second, not the first, episode of psychosis.[9] Preventing the second episode is the key to remission and recovery in schizophrenia. Thus, the deterioration and downhill course of schizophrenia can be prevented in most patients by using LAI AP right after the first hospitalization for schizophrenia.[10]

There are other important advantages to using second-generation LAI formulations. Twenty-four published studies report that they are neuroprotective (i.e., help preserve the brain tissue integrity).[11] Also, a seven-year follow-up study in Sweden reported that a second-generation LAI antipsychotic was associated with the lowest mortality rate from all causes.[12] This is very important given the high premature mortality in schizophrenia.

In summary, until a cure for schizophrenia is discovered, the best way to give patients a chance to return to their baseline and avoid the tragic, life-altering con-

---

[7] Zaheer J et al: *Schizophrenia Research* 222:282-38, 2020.
[8] Subotnik KL et al: *JAMA Psychiatry* 72:822-829, 2015.
[9] Taipale H et al: *Lancet Psychiatry* 9:271-279, 2022.
[10] Nasrallah HA: *Current Psychiatry* 21:6-9, 2022.
[11] Chen AT et al: *Schizophrenia Research* 208:1-7, 2019.
[12] Taipale H et al: *Schizophrenia Research* 197:274-280, 2018.

sequences, is to use second-generation LAIs immediately after discharge from the first hospitalization. Yet, inexplicably, this is rarely done, and 99% of clinicians in the country prescribe pills and do not use LAI APs for several years until patients have already relapsed several times. By that time, the patients have already lost substantial amounts of brain tissue and have become disabled and criminalized and incarcerated. Imagine how much different the landscape of schizophrenia would be if clinicians prevented any further episode of psychosis after the first one. Many young people with schizophrenia may be able to return to their baseline, further their education, get a job, get married, raise a family, and exercise their constitutional right to pursue happiness.[13]

---

[13] Nasrallah HA et al: *Current Psychiatry* 20:14-16, 202.

10

TELEMEDICINE AND SCHIZOPHRENIA: A BRAVE NEW WORLD
by Craig Chepke, MD

March 2021 marks a year since the United States declared the COVID-19 pandemic a national emergency, and the healthcare world is still trying to sort out the details in 2023. In an instant, telemedicine went from being a niche service to a baseline expectation for healthcare providers in every setting, from large healthcare systems to private practices.

Unlike many other specialists, most psychiatrists don't require a significant amount of equipment to do our jobs, so one would think that the field would be ideal for transitioning smoothly to telemedicine. However, many psychiatrists did so very begrudgingly — myself included. In almost every facet of my life, I am an avid user of every piece of technology I can get my hands on. However, in my clinical practice, I insisted on face-to-face appointments and handwriting my notes to keep eye contact as much as possible. But desperate times called for desperate measures, so I became a temporary telepsychiatrist overnight. Early on, there were two common concerns I heard from colleagues that:

1. People with schizophrenia would have difficulty using the technology required for telemedicine.

OR

2. Delusions or hallucinations would be too disruptive to appointments.

My experience, however, has been different. On the whole, I've found people with schizophrenia to be very comfortable with navigating technology. More troubling has been the so-called "digital divide," which refers to the fact that not everyone in the country has equal access to fast, stable Internet connections and adequate hardware to take advantage of it. I have also not seen psychosis present a source of problems that would not have been equally challenging if the person was in the same room. However, it can be more difficult for a clinician to assess the scope and severity of psychosis virtually, so I'd recommend patients try to be more proactive with voicing the symptoms they're experiencing. Many people also find it helpful to make a list of topics they want to discuss ahead of time. Of course, schizophrenia is so much more than just the positive symptoms. I have noticed that some people who have more prominent cognitive symptoms of schizophrenia have been somewhat more distracted. On the other hand, many people with more prominent negative symptoms seem more at ease in our virtual interactions than face-to-face.

Telemedicine has also shown usefulness as a supplement to in-person care rather than a replacement. A dilemma for people who are prescribed long-acting injectable antipsychotics (LAIs) in the pandemic has been that they absolutely require in-person administration. I believe that LAIs are life-saving interventions, so I had to figure out how to continue offering injections while doing my part to keep everyone healthy. Early on, I transitioned people to LAIs that can be injected in the shoulder to allow people to drive up and receive the injection while remaining in their car. As we gained confidence in our ability to use masks and distancing to reduce infection risk, I started to bring people who need LAIs administered in the hip muscle back in the office to do so. After I administered the injection, we conducted the remainder of the visit virtually to reduce the chance for transmission of the virus.

There have also been clear positives to the widespread usage of telemedicine. The elimination of travel time has made it easier for people to schedule appointments around other obligations. As a result, I've been able to work people in more quickly when they need an appointment urgently, people who live far from the office have been able to schedule more frequent meetings, and the number of missed appointments has decreased. Telemedicine has also empowered people to reach out beyond their local geography to seek out specialist care. It's easier than ever for people who live in rural areas to access treatment or a second opinion from a specialist in schizophrenia across the state or beyond.

They say that necessity is the mother of invention. While the transition's urgency caused us to get some things wrong, both clinicians and patients adapted quickly. The result has transformed healthcare in a way I don't see us abandoning. Whatever telepsychiatry ends up looking like, one thing is clear: it is the future of medicine in some form or another.

11

SUICIDE AND SCHIZOPHRENIA
by Stephen Rush, MD

According to the National Institutes of Mental Health (NIMH), in 2017, 10.6 million adults in the United States had serious thoughts of committing suicide, 2.8 million made suicide plans, 1.3 million attempted suicide, and 47,173 died by suicide. The World Health Organization estimates that 1 million people across the world die by suicide each year at a rate of 3 people every 2 minutes.

Death by suicide in those with schizophrenia occurs at a rate much higher than that of the general population, sometimes reported as high as 13,000 per 100,000 people with this disorder compared to 13 per 100,000 in the general population. It is the largest cause of premature death in this population. The risk of death by suicide is highest in the first 2 years after the onset of schizophrenia and occurs more often in males, those with co-occurring depression and substance use disorders, and those with a history of suicide attempts. Often, the focus of treatment in schizophrenia is reduction in hallucinations and delusions, but clearly, an important part of any treatment plan involves suicide prevention strategies.

Prevention of suicide in schizophrenia requires breaking down barriers around the stigma of mental illness and bringing discussions of this topic into the light, whether with clinicians, family members, or support groups. This is a challenging task given the stigma that already exists, even among those affected by this brain disorder. It has been reported that most people who commit suicide give definite warnings about their intentions and often do so in ample time before an attempt. Additionally, a majority of people who are suicidal are ambivalent about death. This contradicts stigma that suicide occurs in people who never discuss it, without warning, and who are intent on ending their lives. The high risk of suicide in persons with schizophrenia mandates that we must discuss this topic openly, without bias, and without fear of negative consequences. Increased awareness of suicidal thinking is, in fact, associated with decreasing the risk of completed suicide.

Universal prevention strategies must include dissemination of accurate information through media outlets and dispelling inaccurate and biased information that marginalizes individuals with a predilection toward suicide. Restricted access to highly lethal means of suicide (such as guns) has been shown to reduce the incidence of suicide and requires that, as a society, we advocate for laws and regulations that protect our vulnerable citizens, even in the face of sharp criticism from opposition.

Selective strategies must target those at risk for suicide and require broad screening of these populations and having frank and open discussions about suicide. We must educate and train all members of society to manage issues of suicide in the same vein as interventions such as cardiopulmonary resuscitation (CPR), a widely known treatment for cardiac arrest with education provided in many sectors of society not limited to healthcare professionals. Imagine if raising suicide awareness is established as a requirement in the same way various occupations and activities require CPR training and what this could do to reduce completed suicide.

Individual strategies involving patients with schizophrenia must include family, community, and physician involvement. Psychiatrists must be educated about the clear benefits of clozapine in reducing suicide risk in those with schizophrenia[1] because as studies demonstrate, this treatment is widely under-used. Community collaboration, in which multidisciplinary teams are available to provide a range of supports for those with schizophrenia, such as Assertive Community Treatment (ACT), should be standard of care and more easily accessible to all segments of society. Family education, social skills training, and cognitive behavioral treatments, were they easily accessible to all patients regardless of insurance and ability to pay, would similarly have a significant impact on suicide prevention.

In summary, we must, as a society, recognize the high risk of suicide among those in our communities living with schizophrenia as a first step toward prevention. We must reduce stigma surrounding this brain disorder and suicide and be aware of risk factors. We must advocate for legislation and healthcare reform. Perhaps most of all, we must act as a community to surround this sect of our population with support and increase access to effective care.

---

[1] Meltzer, H. Y., Alphs, L., Green, A. I., Altamura, A. C., Anand, R., Bertoldi, A. Bourgeois, M., Chouinard, G., Islam, M. Z., Kane, J., Krishnan, R. Lindenmayer, J. P., Potkin, S. & International Suicide Prevention Trial Study Group. (2003). Clozapine treatment for suicidality in schizophrenia: International Suicide Prevention Trial (InterSePT). Archives of General Psychiatry, 60(1), 82-91.

[2] Bourgeois, M., Swendsen, J., Young, F., Amador, X., Pini, S., Cassano, G. B., Lindenmayer, J. Hsu, C., Alphs, L., Meltzer, H. Y., & The InterSePT Study Group (2004). Awareness of disorder and suicide risk in the treatment of schizophrenia: Results of the International Suicide Prevention Trial. American Journal of Psychiatry, 161, 1494-1496.

[3] Fontanella, C. A., Warner, L. A., Steelesmith, D. L., Brock, G., Bridge, J. A., & Campso, J. V. (2020). Association of timely outpatient mental health services for youths after psychiatric hospitalization with risk of death by suicide. JAMA Network Open, 3(8), e2012887.

[4] Kasckow, J., Felmet, K., & Zisook, S. (2011). Managing suicide risk in patients with schizophrenia. CNS Drugs, 25(2), 129-143.

[5] National Institute of Mental Health (2020). Suicide. National Institute of Mental Health. (https://www.nimh.nih.gov/health/statistics/suicide.shtml#part_154969.

[6] Sher, L. (2004). Preventing suicide. QJM, 97(10), 677-680.

[7] Zaheer, J., Olfson, M., Mallia, E., Lam, J. S. H., de Oliveira, C., Rudoler, D., Carvalho, A. F., Jacob, B. J., Juda, A. Kurdyak, P. (2020). Predictors of suicide at time of diagnosis in schizophrenia spectrum disorder: A 20-year total population study in Ontario, Canada." Schizophrenia Research, 222, 382-388.

12

COMORBIDITIES IN SCHIZOPHRENIA: A HIDDEN MEDICAL EMERGENCY
by Craig Chepke, MD

Why try to improve someone's life psychiatrically if we let them die from cardiovascular disease 10-20 years earlier than people without serious mental illness? My psychiatry training program maintained that one is "a physician first, and a psychiatrist second." Therefore, I have increasingly asked myself this question over the past several years.

In addition to being a severe brain disease, schizophrenia is also associated with a greater risk of many other physical disorders, referred to as comorbidities. Common comorbidities include obesity, cardiovascular and metabolic disease (e.g., diabetes or high cholesterol), respiratory illnesses, infectious diseases, and many other disorders.

People with schizophrenia have more than double the mortality rate, and the lifespan is reduced by 10-25 years compared to the general population (WHO, 2023). While part of this difference could be due to the much higher risk of suicide (12 to 170 times higher than the general population), the number of excess deaths from cardiovascular disease alone outnumber those resulting from suicide for people with schizophrenia.[1,2]

Perhaps it's time to start thinking of comorbidities as an emergency the way we do suicide!

We should also consider that many people with schizophrenia are socioeconomically disadvantaged. This increases the likelihood of having lifestyle risks such as smoking, lack of exercise, and unhealthy diets. They may also lack access to regular preventative medical care due to an overwhelmed medical system, insurance problems, or transportation issues.

This is a powder keg of risk factors, and on top of that, most antipsychotic

---

[1] Ösby, U. Correia, N., Brandt, L., Ekbom, A. & Sparén, P. (2000). "Mortality and causes of death in schizophrenia in Stockholm county, Sweden." *Schizophrenia Research,* 45(1-2), 21-28.
[2] Zaheer, J., Olfson, M., Mallia, E., Lam, J. S. H., de Oliveira, C., Rudoler, D., Carvalho, A. F., Jacob, B. J., Juda, A. Kurdyak, P. (2020). Predictors of suicide at time of diagnosis in schizophrenia spectrum disorder: A 20-year total population study in Ontario, Canada. Schizophrenia Research, 222, 382-388.

medications have some degree of weight gain or other metabolic problems as potential side effects.

People with schizophrenia deserve a life with both mental stability and good physical health.

Psychiatrists have a significant challenge in figuring out how to proceed when these complications develop. A common strategy is to switch the person to an antipsychotic medication with a lower risk, such as ziprasidone, lurasidone, cariprazine, or lumateperone. However, the antipsychotic medications that carry the highest risk for these obstacles also have some of the best reputations for efficacy, including clozapine and olanzapine. Antipsychotic medications are usually not interchangeable when it comes to maintaining treatment response, which puts the person at risk of relapse.

Finding the balance between benefits and side effects can be like walking the razor's edge at times. Both are important, but which one should we prioritize? The National Institute of Mental Health performed a large clinical trial to answer questions like this. The CATIE study took a more "real-world" approach by comparing the length of time people with schizophrenia continued to take the antipsychotic medications they were on. This approach is based on the theory that if someone keeps taking a medication over the long run, the benefits must exceed the drawbacks. People stayed on olanzapine longer than the other antipsychotic medications tested despite having the highest amount of weight and metabolic side effects, presumably because of its superior efficacy.[3] CATIE also highlighted the unfortunate lack of medical care for people with schizophrenia. Participants in clinical trials generally get a higher level of care than in the general community, but in the CATIE study, 30% of participants with diabetes, 62% with high blood pressure, and 88% with high cholesterol were not receiving any treatment for these conditions.[4]

The saying that "an ounce of prevention is worth a pound of cure" is common for a reason. It's much harder to lose weight than it is to prevent weight gain from happening, so waiting to react until after weight gain occurs isn't usually a good strategy. As such, it's becoming increasingly common for psychiatrists to prescribe metformin (also used in type 2 diabetes) at the start of treatment with an antipsychotic medication to reduce the risk of weight gain proactively. Similarly, a medication was approved by the FDA in 2021 containing the highly effective antipsychotic medication olanzapine with a medication that reduces weight gain

---

[3] Lieberman, J. A., Stroub, T. S., McEvoy, J. P., Swartz, M. S., Rosenheck, R. A., Perkins, D. O., Keefe, R. S. E., Davis, S. M., Davis, C. E., Lebowitz, B. D., Severe, J., Hsiao, J. K., & the Clinical Antipsychotic Trials of Intervention Effectiveness (CATIE) Investigators. (2005). "Effectiveness of antipsychotic drugs in patients with chronic schizophrenia." *New England Journal of Medicine*, 353(12), 1209-1223.

[4] Nasrallah, H. A., Meyer, J. M., Goff, D. C., McEvoy, J. P., Davis, S. M., Stroup, T. S., & Lieberman, J. A. (2006). "Low rates of treatment for hypertension, dyslipidemia and diabetes in schizophrenia: Data from the CATIE schizophrenia trial sample at baseline." *Schizophrenia Research*, 86(1-3), 15-22.

potential, samidorphan, in a single pill.

It may not be obvious to think of physical health as part of the psychiatric treatment plan, but it's essential to do so. Getting started may seem overwhelming, so here are some action items to help people with schizophrenia fight back against the physical toll it can take on their body:

1. Talk to your psychiatrist about your physical health and ways to help you support it.
2. Keep track of changes in your weight and size of your pants, as the waist size is a useful predictor of metabolic syndrome.
3. Be sure to have regular checkups with a primary care provider.

People living with schizophrenia deserve a life with both mental stability and good physical health. Let's make fighting for the best of both worlds your New Year's Resolution!

---

[5] World Health Organization (WHO). (2023). "Mental disorders information sheet." World Health Organization. https://www.who.int/news-room/fact-sheets/detail/mental-disorders.

13

SECONDARY PSYCHOSIS
by Stephen Rush, MD

Psychotic experiences are common in those who are diagnosed with schizophrenia. In fact, the presence of psychotic symptoms can lead to the diagnosis of this brain disorder if both delusions and hallucinations are present for six months, including one month of persistent symptoms. In other medical specialties, a diagnosis is often made after a physical exam, imaging (X-Rays or CT Scans) and bloodwork that are crucial to determining a diagnosis and appropriate treatment. In psychiatry, however, this same diagnostic process does not often yield much useful information except in the case of secondary psychosis (caused by other medical disorders).

Secondary psychosis is a term more frequently used in recent decades as there is a growing realization that it is vital to understand when symptoms such as delusions and hallucinations are due to a known medical illness or substance. Previously referred to as "functional" when having a psychological origin and "organic" when there was an identifiable biological origin, the shift to "primary" and "secondary" reflects an understanding that every psychiatric condition and symptom has a biological component. This understanding first appeared in the revised version of the fourth edition of the Diagnostic and Statistical Manual of Mental Disorders (DSM-IV-TR) in 2000. Any substance, prescribed drug, or medical condition that affects the central nervous system can result in psychiatric symptoms including psychosis, and, unfortunately, we continue to see cases where a presumptive diagnosis of schizophrenia is made before a thorough medical evaluation confirms the absence of a source of secondary psychosis.

In a 2016 article published in The Primary Care Companion to CNS Disorders, Dr. João Gama Marques studied how often patients initially diagnosed with schizophrenia had an underlying source of secondary psychosis that was not recognized. This retrospective analysis of 250 patients in Portugal demonstrated that 25% of patients diagnosed with schizophrenia actually had an underlying medical condition causing psychotic symptoms. And, further, the average delay in correct diagnosis was 12 years. The consequences of such a delay in diagnosis can have devastating consequences to patients and their loved ones.

Through the research of scientists done over decades and centuries we can now say that secondary psychosis can result from 13 main groups of disorders identified in the following graphic.

Causes of Secondary Psychosis

DISORDERS THAT LEAD TO SECONDARY PSYCHOSIS	
Trauma	Traumatic Brain Injury
Autoimmune	SLE, AE (N-methyl-D-Aspartate receptor Encephalitis)
Congenital Disorders	Velocardialfacial syndrome, agenesis of corpus collosum
Toxic/Substance Induced	PCP, cocaine, cannabis, lead, arsenic, mercury
Iatrogenic	Steroids, antimalarials, isoniazid
Cerebrovascular	Stroke, subdural hematoma
Space-Occupying Disorders	Tumors
Metabolic Disorders	Wilson's Disease, Pheochromocytoma
Dietary Disorders	Pellagra, B12 deficiency, Vit D deficiency
Infection	HIV, Syphillis, toxoplasmosis
Degenerative Disease	Parkinson's, Huntington's, MS, Lewy Body Dementia
Seizure Disorders	Temporal Lobe Epilepsy
Endocrine Disorders	Thyroid, parathyroid disease

SLE = Systemic Lupus Erythematosus   HIV = Human Immunodeficiency Virus   MS = Multiple Sclerosis
AE = Auto-immune Encephalitis   PCP = phencyclidine

Adapted from Keshavan M and Kaneko Y. Secondary Psychosis: An Update. World Psychiatry. 2013;12:4-15

How do clinicians determine if a psychotic disorder is "primary" or "secondary?" First, the causative substance or medical condition must be identified. Then, the relationship between a medical condition or substance used and the psychotic symptoms should be identified. In doing so, clinicians should consider three key aspects of the patient's symptoms: 1) atypicality, 2) temporality, and 3) explicability.

An underlying medical cause of psychosis should be suspected if the presentation is atypical in regard to the age of onset and the type of symptoms observed. For example, the presence of multiple types of hallucinations (auditory, visual, tactile, and olfactory) is not typical in schizophrenia and increases the likelihood of a secondary psychotic disorder such as those seen in dementia or some types of epilepsy.

The temporality of symptoms, or when they occur, should be considered when the psychotic symptoms follow the start of a medical illness or ingestion of a substance and resolve when the medical condition improves or the substance is eliminated from the body. Finally, because comorbid medical illnesses are very common in people who have schizophrenia, it is important to ask if the symptoms present are best explained by a primary or a secondary psychotic disorder. For example, in a patient with a strong family history of schizophrenia in their parents and siblings, longstanding psychotic symptoms, even in the context of a co-occurring medical illness, may be most accurately explained by schizophrenia given the genetic predisposition present.

In April of 2018, the University of Cincinnati Medical Center instituted the First Episode Evaluation and Services (FEELS) program. This program includes a multidisciplinary team of physicians, nurses, social workers, pharmacists, psychologists, and occupational and recreational therapists who work together to rule out secondary causes of psychosis in patients within the first two years of symptom onset while on a psychiatry inpatient unit. This work-up includes thorough bloodwork, imaging, review of any medications and substances taken, and psychological testing. This evaluation helps the treatment team to identify the most likely cause of psychosis in any given patient and guide treatment. If a medical condition is identified, clinicians who specialize in the treatment of that condition then become involved in treatment. This protocol was inspired by working with patients whose secondary psychotic disorders were not identified early in their illness, leading to long-term negative consequences. While many academic medical centers have similar procedures, there is still a lack of awareness about the identifiable causes of secondary psychosis in many places around the world. Physicians, patients, and family members alike must be educated about these issues and advocate for standard assessment of secondary causes of psychosis to further our common goal of healing through correct diagnosis and treatment.

---

[1] Gama Marques, J. (2020). "Organic psychosis causing secondary schizophrenia in one fourth of a cohort of 200 patients previously diagnosed with primary schizophrenia." *Primary Care Companion for CNS Disorders*, 22(2).19m02549.

[2] Keshavan, M. S. & Kaneko, Y. (2013). "Secondary psychoses: an update." *World Psychiatry*, 12(1), 4-15

14

ENOUGH IS ENOUGH: THE CASE FOR ASSISTED OUTPATIENT TREATMENT

by Ashoke Rampuria, MS (Co-Founder of AOTNOW),
Vinita Rampuria, MSW (Co-Founder of AOTNOW),
and Ann Corcoran, RN, MSN

Any parent can attest that it is heartbreakingly difficult to watch your child suffer. This is particularly true when your child suffers from a chronic illness, such as a serious mental illness (SMI).

For us parents, our anguish is compounded by the fact that our adult children continue to be harmed by the failures of our mental healthcare system here in Massachusetts — a system we believe fails to help those most in need. Specifically, in adults suffering from SMI, a history of treatment avoidance too often leads to frequent involuntary hospitalizations or incarceration.

Often, these individuals also suffer from anosognosia, a condition that prevents them from acknowledging their mental illness and adhering to treatment.

In these extreme cases, families witness their loved ones stuck in an endless cycle of repeat hospitalizations, homelessness, joblessness, and despair. These conditions not only can seriously impair one's quality of life but are often fraught with danger, leading to interactions with law enforcement and potential incarceration — or even worse outcomes including death by suicide or homicide.

Assisted Outpatient Treatment (AOT), also referred to as Community Based Healthcare Services, provides community-based behavioral health services under court order to people suffering with SMI who have demonstrated an inability to adhere to treatment and have difficulty living safely in the community without close monitoring.

A true AOT program is not voluntary — it provides person-centered, compassionate services for those who meet very specific criteria usually because of anosognosia. It provides involuntary treatment in the community rather than waiting until someone deteriorates to meet inpatient involuntary commitment standards.

By providing continuity of care under court supervision, these programs treat people suffering from SMI on an outpatient basis within their community. Also, an AOT order is limited to one year and can be extended if needed. For most patients, one year of continued care and supervision can provide the stabilization needed to live independently.

Unfortunately, Massachusetts is one of just three states without an AOT law on the books. Despite years of attempts to bring AOT to the Commonwealth, the initiative has been routinely blocked by patient rights advocates and defenders of the status quo system. This opposition appears to be rooted in a grave misunderstanding of what AOT is and what it is not.

To begin with the latter, AOT is not forced medication nor is it institutionalized care. The sole goal of AOT is to provide treatment and care in a community setting — not in a hospital or locked facility.

In addition to treatment, this type of community-based healthcare can also include housing and other services that are crucial in improving the overall quality of life for those suffering from SMI. This coordinated approach ensures continuity of care, which can break the endless cycle of our current failed mental health system.

We are also aware that some of those opposed to this approach do so out of the belief in individual freedom. They believe that court-supervised care is "coerced" care and, therefore, a violation of personal rights.

We believe strongly in personal rights. Our children have a right to live free of the debilitating effects of their SMI. They have a right to live freely in their community without being imprisoned by a treatable disease or disorder.

As a society, we are failing the most vulnerable among us. As parents, we have witnessed the failings of the system firsthand. Enough is enough! The system must change.

While there is no magic cure for SMI or a one-size-fits-all approach to treatment, AOT or community-based healthcare services are proven to be effective. Under court supervision, people suffering from the most acute cases of SMI can get the help they deserve.

Our loved ones deserve better than they have received from our failed mental health system. They need our help in speaking up and getting them the help that they truly deserve.

As parents, we refuse to sit idle and watch our children suffer within a failed system.

CURESZ
PROGRAMS AND RESOURCES

15

INTRODUCTION TO CURESZ FRIENDSZ CAREGIVER'S MENTORING: THE FAMILY BURDEN OF SCHIZOPHRENIA

by Mary Beth De Bord, JD

Providing care for one of the estimated two million people in the United States who suffers from schizophrenia can be overwhelming. Caregivers report experiencing stress related to caring for a loved one, including hurt feelings from stigma associated with the illness, financial concerns, and anxiety about the future care and welfare of a loved one. Caregivers may have decided to quit work for some time or find another form of employment more suitable to providing necessary support. Their ability to spend time doing things they love such as social and leisure activities may be curtailed. Other family members may feel neglected by the time spent caring for an ill family member because caregivers (often parents) may not be able to spend as much time with the other family members as in the past.

These are just a few of the ways that caregivers report the changes disrupting their lives from looking after a family member afflicted with schizophrenia. The impact of these changes is commonly referred to as family burden. This article seeks to offer some helpful insight and advice to assist caregivers in their role of helping a family member with schizophrenia.

First, avoid the blame game. It is natural to question the nature and causes of the illness. Schizophrenia is a neurobiological brain syndrome that is likely caused by a disruption of brain development during fetal life and is not the fault of the person with the illness or of parents' interactions.

Second, educate yourself on the nature and symptoms of schizophrenia. A helpful resource is *Surviving Schizophrenia* by Dr. E. Fuller Torrey. Knowledge is power, and knowing what to expect in terms of symptoms and treatment is crucial to a loved one's recovery. Patients are often unable to process information about the nature of their illness and recommended treatment during the initial onset of the disorder. Therefore, it is critical that a caregiver be informed and be able to advocate on a patient's behalf. Thorough knowledge of schizophrenia can empower you to care for your loved one and to educate others about the nature of the illness and eliminate the unjust stigma associated with the disorder.

Third, take care of yourself. Although it may seem implausible and difficult, it is critically necessary that you get proper sleep, sustenance, and support. Getting between seven and nine hours of sleep a night will help recharge your body and allow you to be better prepared to help your family member. Eating a healthy diet will keep you strong and resilient and give you the necessary energy to get through your day. Exercise can help you feel stronger and take your mind off the difficulties of living with this illness. And finally, ask for support from family, friends, coworkers, and others. You may wish to attend programs that connect you with other caregivers or seek help from a licensed therapist. Whatever support you choose, be kind to yourself and give yourself the time you need to adjust and thrive.

The good news is that there is hope for those struggling with schizophrenia. Although it has a chronic course, schizophrenia is a treatable disorder. Those afflicted with it may recover and live fulfilling lives with proper treatment. The role of caregivers is instrumental in the recovery process, and caregivers can feel a great sense of gratitude and accomplishment by assisting a family member in their journey of recovery. Focusing positively on the recovery process is critical not only to the recovery of a family member suffering with schizophrenia but also to the health of caregivers and other family members.

To better support caregivers, in 2020, CURESZ Board Member Mary Beth De Bord developed an idea for a caregivers' mentoring program, "FriendSZ." The program now has 34 active mentors and has served over 160 mentees.

16

CURESZ ON CAMPUS: EDUCATION IN THE AGE OF RISK
by Bethany Yeiser, BS

The onset of psychiatric brain disorders, such as schizophrenia, depression, bipolar disorder, anxiety disorders, eating disorders, and alcohol and drug abuse, is more prevalent during the teens and twenties than at any other phase of life. To help educate students about brain disorders, the CURESZ Foundation (which has education as one of its major missions) organized its initial event for students, Mental Health on Campus, in February 2020 at the University of Cincinnati. In the fall of 2020, CURESZ founded its first CURESZ on Campus Club at the University of Cincinnati. Through our clubs, we hope to educate students and encourage them to seek professional help, as well as inspire them to support their friends who are struggling. We aim to equip students to recognize the early warning signs of psychiatric disorders and know what actions to take.

As a Schizophrenia Survivor and President of the CURESZ Foundation, I have become aware of many people like myself who have developed psychotic symptoms, dropped out of school or work, and became homeless. Their parents contact me, at a loss to know how to proceed. Recently, a mom called me about her son who is a physics PhD candidate in his last year of school. Months before he was supposed to graduate, he fled the university, began living in his car, and refused all contact with his family members.

I wonder, could this physics student's life have been different if he, or his friends and family members, had been educated about the early warning signs of mental illness (i.e., psychiatric brain disorders) and known what to do?

I am passionate about educating students because I had my first psychotic episode while a senior in college. After I lost my scholarship because of my illness, I dropped out and became homeless for the next four years, suffering from delusions and hallucinations.

Looking back, there are so many things I wish I had known prior to my initial psychotic break. I wish I had been educated to recognize the early signs of schizophrenia and see it as a treatable brain disorder. Upon my initial diagnosis of schizophrenia, I wish I had been told that if the usual antipsychotic medications didn't eliminate the symptoms, clozapine was an effective option. I also wish my doctors had explained to me that if I discontinued my medication when I improved, I might develop treatment-resistance to the same medication that had worked for me and would need higher and higher doses, which also means more side effects.

I wonder, if I had been educated about brain disorders while I was in high school or college, would I have been better prepared when schizophrenia disrupted my life?

When a student demonstrates behavior which appears to be out of character for him or her, it is important to pay attention to the warning signs and to take action. Out-of-character behavior could present as a sudden decrease in academic achievement in a once successful student, or social withdrawal in a person who typically enjoys social activities. Not eating or overeating and neglecting personal hygiene such as showering may also be warning signs.

In addition to learning about the early warning signs that may start in high school or college, I wish I had been told that there should be no hesitation to seek help for a brain disorder and that the earlier one receives treatment, the better the response and outcome. I wish my teachers and professors had encouraged students to be compassionate observers as friends to their peers who suffer from psychosis, depression, anxiety, or any other type of mental illness.

We encourage you to support the CURESZ Foundation in 2024 as we aspire to reach this vulnerable population of students with much-needed educational information and hope. Even for young people who fall the farthest, as I did over my four years homeless, there can still be hope and a future for those who consent to and actively engage in treatment, just like persons suffering from diabetes, asthma, or epilepsy.

17

CURESZ PROGRAMS
by Catherine Engle, LPCC-S

At least 8.4 million people in the United States provide care to an adult with a psychiatric disorder. Caregivers of adults with severe and persistent mental illness spend an average of 32 hours per week providing care. Families who have a loved one with schizophrenia often find themselves frantically searching the Internet for resources that will improve the situation of the one they care for. Sometimes, caregivers can become exhausted and can feel depleted of options and of hope. The following are CURESZ Foundation resources for you and your family.

CURESZ FRIENDSZ
This mentoring program partners caregivers with extensive experience caring for a loved one with schizophrenia (mentors) with newer caregivers (mentees) who may have less experience or who are seeking support at any stage of their caregiving journey. Mentors offer support and encouragement by "walking" alongside the mentee, offering their own personal experiences. They do not provide medical or legal advice, and they are not licensed professionals, but they are loyal and dependable friends. Enduring friendships have been forged through this program. Our goal is to ease the burden of caregiving through compassionate one-on-one support. To date, the CURESZ Foundation has paired over 160 mentees with mentors. CURESZ FriendSZ is directed by CURESZ Board Member Catherine Engle, LPCC-S.

Finding a Mentor Through CURESZ
If you are interested in becoming a mentor or mentee through FriendSZ, we ask you to complete a questionnaire with your contact information, age of your loved one with schizophrenia, age of onset, religious preference, and other information. Whenever possible, we like to pair mentees with mentors based on geographic location and/or based on situation. For example, the mentee's loved one may be struggling with treatment non-adherence, substance use, lack of insight, or may be experiencing psychosis. In each of these situations, a specific mentor's experience may be invaluable to the mentee.

We are also always looking for new mentors. If you would like to be considered to become a mentor, we ask for a 15-minute interview over Zoom, a background check, and if accepted, watching an hour-long training video. We hope you will share CURESZ FriendSZ with those you know who have loved ones with schizophrenia, as well as any caregivers in your support groups or community.

From Catherine Engle, LPCC-S, CURESZ Board Member and Director of CURESZ FriendSZ:
"I have been working in the mental health field for the past 13 years and completed my master's degree at Xavier University in clinical mental health counseling. During my undergraduate studies, I had an encounter that became the catalyst for my career in the mental health field. I met a woman who expressed that her son had recently been diagnosed with schizophrenia. She was a single mother and said she felt completely overwhelmed and unsure of how to help him or get the support for herself that she greatly needed. The CURESZ Foundation impressed me so much as I learned more about it. To me, it's about offering others information, empathetic connection, and support so they can feel empowered and navigate a successful future and the best quality of life for themselves and the loved ones they are caring for."

A Comment About FriendSZ
"I wanted to send you a huge THANK YOU. You connected me with a mentor [named] Georgia. I wanted you to know that this has been one of the most positive experiences. As I have navigated through my son's recent episode, three hospitalizations, and medication change Georgia has been there like a rock for me to lean on. She helped me find hope and new perspective when I felt at my lowest point. Thank you for setting up this program and connecting us. I am forever grateful."

In addition to the FriendSZ program, the CURESZ Foundation provides many other important resources.

CURESZ.ORG AND CURESZ YOUTUBE CHANNEL
These websites offer extensive educational and clinical information about schizophrenia, comorbidities, and related disorders. This information includes our Clozapine in Schizophrenia Expert Panel web page where families looking for a doctor who prescribes clozapine can find one or locate a physician for a second opinion or possibly ongoing care. The website also offers an extensive archive with newsletters focusing on many topics.

CURESZ ON-CAMPUS CLUBS

The typical onset of schizophrenia commonly occurs between the ages of 18 and 25 years old. Unfortunately, this time frame coincides with college years when so much is already at play in a young person's life. CURESZ Clubs educate students about potential early signs and symptoms as well as treatment options for brain disorders including schizophrenia, bipolar disorder, anxiety, and depression. CURESZ sponsors campus clubs at the University of Cincinnati and Babson College in Boston and supports a student-led group in London, the United Kingdom. We have members who attend our virtual events from all around the country.

During the school year, we usually hold one in-person event per month plus one virtual event per month. Most club members are undergraduate students studying nursing, counseling, or planning to become a doctor or researcher, as well as students from all majors who have an interest in mental health. Many members have siblings or family members struggling with brain disorders. We are actively searching for new club student leaders.

SUPPORT GROUP

Families faced with the challenges of a loved one's illness can find encouragement and support from families whose loved one has achieved recovery in groups, currently meeting twice monthly. Visit CURESZ.org to register.

ASK THE DOCTOR

These monthly events provide 6 families with 90 minutes to ask a CURESZ psychiatrist anything about brain disorders. Although this is not a forum where individual cases are discussed, it is a valuable opportunity to receive expert medical information.

18

THE COGNITION SELF-ASSESSMENT RATING SCALE FOR PATIENTS WITH SCHIZOPHRENIA

by Henry A. Nasrallah, MD

This new instrument facilitates routine cognitive assessment of patients with psychotic disorders.

Cognition represents the most important function of the human brain and the essence of the mind. Cognitive functions such as memory, learning, comprehension, processing speed, attention, planning, and problem-solving are the best indicators of the status of brain health.

Many psychiatric brain disorders are associated with cognitive impairments. Decades of extensive research have documented that the most severe cognitive deficits occur in schizophrenia. No wonder Emil Kraepelin coined the term "dementia praecox," which means premature dementia (in youth)[1] for this neuropsychiatric brain disorder. This condition was later renamed schizophrenia by Eugen Bleuler,[2] who regarded it primarily as a thought disorder, with splitting of associations (not split personality, as misinterpreted by many in the public). Interestingly, a century ago both of those early masters of psychiatry de-emphasized psychotic symptoms (delusions and hallucinations), regarding them as "supplemental symptoms."[3] Yet for the next 100 years, clinicians overemphasized psychotic symptoms in schizophrenia and overlooked the more disabling cognitive impairment and negative symptoms, referred to as Bleuler's 4 A's — Associations disruption, Ambivalence, Affect pathology, and Avolition — symptoms that persist even after the psychotic symptoms are successfully treated.[3]

Most contemporary researchers regard cognitive impairment as the "core" feature of schizophrenia.[4] The justification of this view is that cognitive deficits

---

[1] Kraepelin E. Dementia Praecox and Paraphrenia. Barth; 1904.
[2] Bleuler E. *Dementia Praecox or the Group of Schizophrenias*. International Universities Press; 1950.
[3] Nasrallah HA, Smeltzer DJ. *Contemporary Diagnosis and Management of the Patient with Schizophrenia.*" Handbooks in Health Care Company; 2011.
[4] Kahn RS, Keefe RSE. "Schizophrenia is a cognitive illness: time for a change in focus." *JAMA Psychiatry.* 2013;70(10):1107-1112.

are detected in childhood and early adolescence (by age 13),[5] long before the appearance of psychotic symptoms, and many studies have confirmed that cognitive deficits are the primary cause of functional disability and unemployment of patients with schizophrenia. Cognitive dysfunction is also found in milder forms in the parents and siblings of patients with schizophrenia,[6] and is thus considered an "endophenotype" of the illness.

Because of its centrality, cognition has emerged as a major focus of schizophrenia research over the past 20 years. Multiple stakeholders (academic investigators, the National Institute of Mental Health, and the FDA) have collaborated to develop a standard measurement for cognition in schizophrenia. The project culminated in what was labeled MATRICS (Measurement and Treatment Research to Improve Cognition in Schizophrenia).[7] The MATRICS settled on a battery of 7 major cognitive functions that are often impaired in individuals with schizophrenia. Most contemporary researchers have adopted MATRICS in their studies, which facilitates replication to confirm research findings.

Measuring cognition in patients with schizophrenia is extremely important, as critical as measuring fasting glucose in patients with diabetes or blood pressure in patients with hypertension. Measuring the extent of impairment or nonimpairment across various cognitive tests can help with vocational rehabilitation, to place a patient in a job consistent with their level of cognitive functioning. In addition, once medications are developed and approved for cognitive impairments in schizophrenia, measuring cognition will be necessary to gauge the degree of improvement.

Currently, few psychiatric practitioners measure cognition in their patients. This is perplexing because cognitive measurement is important for confirming the diagnosis of schizophrenia in first-episode psychosis, or distinguishing it from other psychotic disorders (such as drug-induced psychosis, brief reactive psychosis, or delusional disorders) that do not have severe cognitive deficits.

The scores of various cognitive functions in individuals with schizophrenia range from .75 to 2.0 SD below the performance of the general population (matched for age and gender).[8] This translates to dismally low percentiles of 2% and 24%. It is essential that all clinicians measure cognition in every patient with psychotic symptoms. It can be argued that cognition should even be measured

---

[5] van Oel CJ, Sitskoorn MM, Cremer MPM, et al. "School performance as a premorbid marker for schizophrenia: a twin study." *Schizophr Bull.* 2002;28(3):401-414.

[6] Jameson KG, Nasrallah HA, Northern TG, et al. "Executive function in first-degree relatives of persons with schizophrenia: a meta-analysis of controlled studies." *Asian J Psychiatry* 2011;4(2):96-99.

[7] Marder SR, Fenton W. "Measurement and Treatment Research to Improve Cognition in Schizophrenia: NIMH MATRICS initiative to support the development of agents for improving cognition in schizophrenia." *Schizophr Res.* 2004;72(1):5-9.

[8] Heinrich RW, Zakzanis KK. "Neurocognitive deficit in schizophrenia: a quantitative review of the evidence." *Neuropsychology.* 1998;12(3):426-445.

in other psychiatric patients because cognitive deficits have been well documented in bipolar disorder, major depressive disorder, attention-deficit/hyperactivity disorder, and other disorders, albeit not as severe as in schizophrenia, and these deficits usually correlate with the patient's vocational and social functioning.

So how is cognition measured, and can clinicians incorporate cognitive batteries in their practices? The most logical answer is to refer the patient to a board-certified neuropsychologist. These specialists are well-trained in assessing cognitive functions, and their evaluations generally are covered by health insurance. They use various validated cognitive batteries. Psychiatrists can have nurses or medical assistants administer a brief cognitive test.

C-SARS: A Self-Rated Cognition Scale

Patient self-rating can provide psychiatric clinicians with valuable information, and is a time-saver. The widely used Patient Health Questionaire-9 (PHQ-9)[9] is an excellent example of a self-rating scale for depression that enables patients to recognize and rate their depressive symptoms. It immediately informs the clinician how depressed their patient is and whether the severity of the depression has improved from the previous visit, which can indicate whether the prescribed medication is working. Based on the PHQ-9, which I regularly use — and recognizing that there is no cognition counterpart and that almost all clinicians could use a practical method of measuring their patients' cognitive function — I developed an instrument called the Cognition Self Assessment Rating Scale (C-SARS). The C-SARS can be completed online at https://curesz.org/csars/ and patients will be emailed the results within a minute. The C-SARS can be completed by the patient (with the help of their family or caregiver, if necessary, who observe the patient's daily functioning, which corresponds to their cognition). The main purpose of the C-SARS is to inform the clinician about serious cognitive dysfunction in their patients, which should instigate a referral for formal neurocognitive assessment by a neuropsychology expert.

The items on the C-SARS reflect how well the patient is performing routine daily functions, each of which correlates with one of the cognitive domains of the MATRICS battery. In the future, when the FDA approves medications for addressing cognitive impairment (and several molecules are currently undergoing clinical trials), clinicians will be able to gauge a patient's response to such treatments using the C-SARS and formal testing as needed. It may take several weeks to detect a significant reversal of cognitive deficits, but doing so would address a major unmet need in schizophrenia and may speed up vocational rehabilitation. The C-SARS also contains 2 items related to social cognition (items 11 and 12),

---

[9] Kroenke K, Spitzer RL, Williams JB. "The PHQ-9: validity of a brief depression severity measure." *J. Gen Intern Med.* 2001;16(9):606-613.

which is also impaired in schizophrenia.[10] Future medications that improve social cognition in addition to neurocognition may also lead to improved social functioning among patients with schizophrenia.

In conclusion, the C-SARS, which needs to be validated in controlled studies, is the first cognition self-rating scale for schizophrenia and may be useful for other major psychiatric disorders. It will be a substantial time-saver for clinicians and will facilitate the routine incorporation of the cognitive assessment of patients with psychotic symptoms to help with the differential diagnosis of schizophrenia vs other psychotic disorders. Measuring cognitive functions is a vital step towards the valid diagnosis and treatment of this major clinical challenge in schizophrenia and improving patient outcomes in this serious psychiatric brain syndrome, in which up to 98% of patients have cognitive impairment across several domains.[11]

---

[10] Green MF, Horan WP, Lee J. "Nonsocial and social cognition in schizophrenia: current evidence and future directions." *World Psychiatry.* 2019;18(2):146-161.

[11] Keefe RS, Eesley CE, Poe MP. "Defining a cognitive function decrement in schizophrenia." *Biol Psychiatry.* 2005;57(6): 688-691.

[12] Neuchterlein KH, Barch DM, Gold JM, et al. "Identification of separable cognitive factors in schizophrenia." *Schizophr Res.* 2004;72(1):29-39.

ACKNOWLEDGEMENTS

The authors and the CURESZ Foundation are grateful for the many exceptional colleagues who contributed to the publication of *Awakenings*, over several months and multiple drafts.

- We thank **Carol North, MD** for providing a thoughtful and comprehensive edit of the entire document and appreciate her encouragement and patience throughout this project.

- We appreciate **Karen Yeiser, RN**, for helpful edits on Part One.

- We would also like to thank **Lora Anderson, PhD** for her general edits of the manuscript.

- We appreciate the artistic excellence of **Matcheri Keshavan, MD** who designed the cover art of this book.

- We also thank **Eric Oehler, BS** for formatting the text of *Awakenings* and helping to format the cover.

Made in the USA
Columbia, SC
20 October 2024

44767043R00150